Happy trails?
Art Latham

Lost in the
Land of Enchantment

Art Latham

With Love,
PAT Titus

ARROYO PRESS
Las Cruces • New Mexico

Published by
Arroyo Press
P.O. Box 4333
Las Cruces, NM 88003
(505) 522-2348

ISBN 0-9623682-8-8
Printed in the United States.

Library of Congress Cataloging-in-Publication Data

Latham, Art, 1944–
     Lost in the Land of Enchantment / by Art Latham.
          p. cm.
Includes bibliographical references (p.) and index.
ISBN 0-9623682-8-8
1. New Mexico—Description and travel. 2. New Mexico—Tours.
3. Landscape—New Mexico. 4. Latham, Art, 1944– —Journeys—
New Mexico. I. Title.
F801.2.L38   1995
917.8904'53—dc20
                                                           95-30909
                                                           CIP

Photographs by Art Latham.

Contents

Preface

T he following chapters aren't Transcendentalist Thoreauvian essays on Walden-like environs, but verbal snapshots of a few of New Mexico's distinctive destinations, recorded in the mid-1990s, before they're lost to the changing millennium.

I have assumed the reader sets out with at least a modicum of New Mexico knowledge, aware of such subtleties as always carrying water and a spare fan belt, and checking on weather and road conditions in advance.

All roads included in this book are in William Burdett's *The Roads of New Mexico* (1990, Shearer Publishing), available at local bookstores. The exceptions are Forest Roads and Indian Reservation roads, which are posted as such but are listed on maps specific only to those lands.

Thanks to Rob Dean, managing editor of *The Santa Fe New Mexican,* who commissioned me to write the "Get Lost" travel columns from which this book evolved.

Also thanks to my wife Benita Budd and my daughters Kelly and Shannon for their patience during my time on the road.

Art Latham
1995, Las Vegas, N.M.

The River Road

L ate autumn in the Sangre de Cristo Mountains of New Mexico, and a swirling gray-white vapor, source unseen, ascends the steep canyon walls. The wisp, dissipating as it clears tall conifers, vanishes at Gallinas Canyon's snowy, glittering upper rim.

Like souls returning home, other puffs follow, again, again, drifting lazily into endless sky.

I have witnessed this canyon winter wonder elsewhere in three decades of New Mexican peregrinations, journeys that eventually merged in my mind into a single pilgrimage. I caught a similar cloud most recently attempting to spiral quietly off Rowe Mesa, 30 miles southeast of Santa Fe. As now, I puzzled over the mesa-top wraith's origins, unable to rationalize the eerie phenomenon.

New Mexico is like that. Discrete, unlikely incidents loom for no logical reason, often forcing me to invoke protective Santa Fe Pyschobabble, switching brain sides to consider various distracting mist clouds through other angles of reality's prism. Contemplating the cosmic is easier here, where awesome geographic proportions distort perspectives. In New Mexico of the mind, logic should reign; in New Mexico of the heart, truth lies beyond logic, intellect. It lies in intuition, vision. Visibly massive as the landscape is, it shelters elusive secrets capable of reducing to a state of calm what Buddhists call "monkey mind," an unfocused awareness. The scenery grabs that monkey by the throat and suspends it in mid-anxiety.

I need to scurry back across a mountain range to pack for a series of upcoming photo sorties, but the canyon holds me. A couple of acres of aspen clumps have blazed to yellow, accenting the golden wildflowers among the canyon floor thickets. It rained last night and will again tonight. Elk tracks trot through the riverside mud, but no elk appear. Any day now my breath will turn white as those vapors.

I decide either the vapors are spirit communications with the world above, or the visual echo of ancient campfires.

I glance around for corroborating witnesses, somebody to interview, but only quivering aspen and whispering ponderosa gather here today.

Looking for witnesses is an occupational tic, a sort of repeated paranoid eye twitch sometimes suffered by those who purport to report truth.

My peripatetic photojournalistic career, such as it is, has revolved around witnessing and sometimes recording historic events of various degrees of societal import, those electronically impaled instants that molded my generation. While surfing the leading edge of the Baby Boom Wave by a couple of years, I've reported both trivial and significant, frivolous and tragic, as would any other journalist of the period.

Such professional experience should mean my cautious perspective is relatively balanced, my decisions intelligently informed.

And they are, to a degree, with an intuitive slant supplied by a little extra information thrown in courtesy of my American Indian friends.

Let me explain.

I'm a scout. That's my dominant romantic self-image, my sustaining fantasy.

I'm a philosophical half-breed, prowling *La Frontera:* both the U.S.-Mexico border and the frontiers between people, places, things. I often visit the unfamiliar. And wandering about as I do, I've been lost many times: physically, spiritually, mentally.

Front-loaded with such inclinations, I'm always struggling to keep my psychic and mental balance. But since the late Sixties, when I returned home from the Pacific, my take on reality has been skewed by a series of visions. The visions and related incidents hadn't crossed my mind much until I started travel writing. My New Mexico jaunts invited deep on-the-road contemplations to fill the voids between waterholes. But I somehow sense the visions changed my direction more than once.

Consider these episodes: Three decades ago, the spirit of an old native woman rose from her lagoon-side Pacific island grave to straddle my back like the untamed monkey rides an addict; a band of long-departed American Indians appeared like these mountain mists from a hilly, red-clay North Carolina kudzu bed to challenge my return stateside. For years after my first visit to Taos, any expanse of white flipped me out to Taos Ski Valley. Those transporting blank patches ranged from the pizza dough I rolled while working a part-time job to a photo proportion wheel I twirled a few years later as an editor.

By the standards of American Indian mysticism, those visions are pedestrian. Still, whether they sprang from overly yeasty pizza dough or the collective subconscious, they and others have illuminated and directed my life.

Since New Mexico is rich in psychic possibilities, a scout's job here is exciting and sympathetic, but the scout fantasy is stalked by a darker version. It historically emerged as a *kokoman* character, one of the legendary Aztecan *pochteca,* informers who visited target villages posing as traders, reporting back to the bloodthirsty Aztec leadership.

I prefer to recount information with less deadly results to readers in the safety of their homes back in the settlements, but I sometimes visualize pochteca on the back trails, especially around *kokopelli* petroglyphs.

Since I first photographed Taos in 1971, New Mexico's elemental and often inexplicable contrasts have fascinated me: they're koans, unanswerable.

I arrived in New Mexico right on New Age schedule in 1971, home from helping expand the fringes of the Pacific Empire and eager to assume my English teaching post at Taos High School. Here, in wannabe heaven, I attended American Indian dances and read voraciously about Indian tribes, flaying the scars of my white man's guilt. I don't do that any more. Guilt is a nonproductive emotion.

But often I do leave corn meal offerings to the sacred directions and the holy spark imbuing every spot with what New Mexico authors for years have called "a sense of place," a quality of uniqueness. Sometimes, following the teachings of several medicine people I've been lucky enough to have known, I'll build a small rock shrine to the spirit of a place, sprinkling it with cornmeal, my way of expressing appreciation of the elemental situation. The stones represent Father Sky and Earth Mother and sacred directions; the cornmeal represents and evokes the life force that surges through all existence. Ask any medicine man.

To that heady intercultural mix I add a developing interest in ancient Celtic mysticism, spurred, I suppose, by an American Indian criticism of Anglos who attempt to learn Indian spiritual ways. Why, say my Indian friends, can't you pursue your own path? Why imitate us?

3

Good questions. I answered them by researching my own Celtic tribal ancestors, discovering a common thread of shamanic practice in both Indian and Celtic religion. And a common heritage of repression by an invading culture.

Nevertheless, my take on New Mexico seeps through an eclectic belief system much influenced by American Indian pantheism, animism and reverence for place.

I see the state as circumscribed by a great waterwheel, spun by its life-sustaining rivers. It's the valleys of these rivers I intend soon to investigate again, traveling from northeast to southeast, southwest to northwest to central, hunting for a definitive icon. Not to mention a good hot tub and a decent cup of coffee.

I chose rivers rather than highways as a construct for organizing my photographic odyssey for several reasons. In this parched country, I'm drawn to water like my ancestral Celtic priests to mistletoe. Obviously snowmelt, male and female rains as the Navajo classify them, waterfalls, rivers, lakes, have been and are the keystone of Southwestern American civilization.

Rivers also defined the entry routes of New Mexico's first human entradas. Eons before the Spanish even knew how to spell Tenochtitlán, how did wandering bands of Paleo-Indians—Clovis and Folsom—enter this area? Did our first tourists drift in from the northeast on stiff prairie breezes, or bend into fierce southern sandstorms, lugging cultivated corn seed from Mesoamerica? Whatever their courses, they followed dinner tracks along the arroyos and waterways.

If they entered from the northeast, they probably best enjoyed autumn, the season of plenty, when stifling heat lessens slightly in the Llano Estacado, raspberries ripen in pollen-dusted upland valleys and the wildflower-dappled northeastern plains and foothills wait for the waning year's most perfect, flaxen day.

Whoever our earliest inhabitants, they left enough evidence of their river passings for archaeologists to approximate some aspects of their lives.

Later occupants also left marks along rivers: Memories of Spanish, Mexicans, French, North Americans, Brits, Scots, Poles, Jews, Lebanese, Chinese, Japanese, clutter our New Mexican physical, cultural and historical landscape.

Now I happily bushwhack for my predecessors' dim, abandoned trails. I wander among empty mesas, plains, arroyos, river valleys and mountains from my redoubt east of the old castle near the hot springs in a canyon named for a long-dead Aztec. I avoid humans, meeting eagle and bear, hawk, deer and elk. I'm looking, always scanning for sign, for ghostly evidence of spectral apparitions, for the perfect image skulking there in the darkening hollows and refracting stones, for the salient clue revealing to where vanished cultures dispersed.

To set the scene for evoking the consummate New Mexico image involves following centuries-spanning traces in the appropriate season: Paleo-Indians in autumn, Mogollón in early winter, Anasazi in late spring, Pueblos in summer. On the trail, I lose myself in contemplating the Zen of travel, the dance of the elementals, the roll of the centuries.

There's another benefit.

As I write, I'm refreshed by the waterfall language tumbling from unseen springs to splatter the page, filtered through years of clinging to low-paying jobs out here the Indian-Spanish-Mexican-American borderlands.

Like the ascending white clouds transfixing me in Gallinas Canyon, the words I write, the photographs I frame, may airily disperse, their eventual fates simply lost.

On the other hand, like the "lost" civilizations I shadow, my images may outlive the originals. Like an Ansel Adams photo of moonrise over a small, now-changed New Mexican village or an Eric Sloan water-color of a forever-vanished skyscape, they may endure.

With an effort, I tear myself from the peaceful Gallinas. Tomorrow, I seek another river, the wild Canadian.

The Canadian

To get lost, I start in nowhere's middle: early autumn on a barren, windy Great Plains cliff high above the Canadian River in northeastern New Mexico.

Canadian River

Here, if ever the weather would clear, I could see much of the mighty Canadian's watershed in an 80-mile radius I already had visited in the past two years.

Meanwhile, there's little to do but review notes from previous ramblings and plan a series of journeys to retrace earlier routes, seeking better photos and more profound insights.

Fat chance of much progress today, however. Massive dark, cumulus clouds swoosh in from the north, hurling themselves onto the Sangre de Cristo Mountains to my west, dumping sheets of snow that obscure the higher peaks.

I glance nervously at ponderosa tops whipping and pitching at eye level in the canyon below. If I don't decide something soon about the last two jarring miles down the narrow dirt road to the Canadian River bottoms, I might not be able to get in later. And once in, maybe not out.

The red sandstone canyon I contemplate verges on the spectacular. As far as I can tell, there are no other humans for miles, but after earlier hanging over a ledge and peering down into one the Canadian's narrow feeder canyons to sniff the wind, I strongly suspect that might not be true for big cats.

The road dipping into Mills Canyon near Roy runs along this rugged side canyon above the Canadian River.

Parking my imported station wagon on a flat rock outcropping, I listen to the banshee winds howl disaster and think it over while the stinging blasts shake my metal shelter. I glance at the nearby dirt road's slightly ascending angle again to assure myself I can drive out if snows blow in while I'm preoccupied. Then I pull out notes to review my past tours of the Canadian's drainage, from Ratón in the north to the eastern Sangre de Cristo's mountain valleys.

As they do all across New Mexico, ghosts walk these byways. On earlier wanderings, I often had come across visible remnants of the historic trails of three cultures as they pass very near each other in this section of New Mexico's northeast, where square miles outnumber people. The Jicarilla Apaches followed game trails to the buffalo plains, and later the Goodnight-Loving cattle drive trail from Texas to Colorado stretched across otherwise trackless country about 20 miles east of this canyon. Comancheros—Hispanic and Indian New Mexicans who traded with Comanche Indians from 1786 to 1874—followed nearby trails down to the Canadian Basin. And the last 100 miles or so of the Santa Fe Trail ran parallel to today's I-25, about 30 miles west of the canyon.

Earlier today I had checked out treeless Chicosa Lake State Park at the southern edge of the Kiowa National Grasslands, east of the small ranching community of Roy. My advice: forget it. I saw a badger near the park, and picnic shelters, a playground, an old chuck wagon and a poster exhibit that recalls longhorns watering at this tiny, muddy pond during the drives of yore. But in autumn, rest rooms are closed, the lake shrivels into an alkali-crusted bowl, and the wind sure does blow cold way out there, as Ian Tyson once sang about another Canadian plain far to the north.

Mills Canyon

Disappointed by the homogeneous plains, I had doubled back across a dirt ranch road and onto State Road 39, which runs north from Roy to Mills, then turned east to dirt Forest Road 600 towards precipitous Mills Canyon on the Canadian.

Mills itself consists of a few scattered ranch houses and the ruins of a few rock home foundations that easily could have been named for the three nearby windmills. Actually, its namesake, Melvin Mills, was a partner to the Santa Fe Ring's Thomas B. Catron, and district attorney for northcentral and northeastern New Mexico.

I checked my notes: Mills, a controversial politician and businessman, built a 32-room, Victorian mansion in Springer, on bluffs of the Cimarrón, which empties into the Canadian a few miles downstream.

Springer, northeast of Mills Canyon, didn't exist during the Santa Fe Trail's glory days. Sheltered from the prairie winds in the Cimarrón's lower valley, it's near I-25, the trail's contemporary version.

To satisfy the exacting appetites of the railway's Harvey House patrons, Mills also planted a ten-mile-long, 14,000-tree fruit orchard in Mills Canyon, the declivity now yawning below me. Twenty-five miles downstream from Springer, but upstream from my vantage point, the canyon was scoured out in the 1904 flood. Upstream dams, dikes and ditches should make such a catastrophe less likely now, but who knows?

Melvin Mills also was washed away, but by the tides of history. He opposed New Mexico statehood, favoring a separate nation with a capital in Ratón, free of "Mexican domination." He died a pauper in 1925, his schemes buried with him, his mansion foreclosed on by Catron. As our state song notes: *Asi es nuevo méxico.* Strictly translated that's "Thus is New Mexico." More simply, "That's how it goes here, *compadres.*"

Today, Mills' manse slumps in moldy disrepair at the end of a Springer street, inhabited only by birds and rodents. A local group is working to restore the house, now owned by Nathan Smith. Smith's father, Jerry, owns "The Brown," a renovated, upscale Springer restaurant.

Cattle ranching and farming made Springer, and the town hasn't forgotten. The rodeo and fair grounds are obvious to visitors pulling off the interstate from the south.

Named for the influential Springer brothers—Charles, who ranched near Cimarrón and Frank, a lawyer for the Maxwell Land Grant—the town slipped in one century from a thriving ranching center to a sleepy backwater. Today Springer shows signs of a gentrifying revival, despite the presence a few miles northwest of town of the New Mexico School for Boys, from which the incarcerated make regular breaks.

I'll get to the revival; first, a little more history.

The all-powerful railroad rolled into Springer in 1879, a decade earlier than it crossed the Texas panhandle and the eastern Plains, so for a while the town's streets rumbled as cattle were driven here from distant ranches.

By 1883, Springer was the activity center in a region criss-crossed by huge irrigation projects. Water from the east face of the Sangre de Cristos sprouted ranches and farms from the arid high plains desert. The area grew so fast the Territorial Legislature ordered all Colfax County records moved to Springer. The proud townsfolk built a courthouse in 1879, spending $9,800. But as coal mining dug in at Ratón, just to the north, Ratón's aggressive citizens lobbied the legislature to make their town the county seat.

A nasty political fight ensued. M. M. Salazar, Colfax County clerk, vowed never to release his county records to the upstarts from the north. After two years of rabid intra-borough squabbling, the state Supreme Court ruled in favor of a law moving the courthouse to Ratón. That didn't impress Salazar, who resisted so vigorously officials had to remove the county's records by force.

But remove them they did. The courthouse slipped through the cracks of history, later serving as a town hall and jail, and from 1910-1917 as the predecessor for the New Mexico Boys' School.

On a similar, but more violent note, several men were killed here during the Colfax County War, which ignited when foreign investors who bought the huge Maxwell Land Grant from Lucien Maxwell tried to evict area settlers. The conflict raged until Gov. Lew Wallace managed to smother it.

Today, the old courthouse is preserved as the Santa Fe Trail Museum, which unfortunately opens only from June to Labor Day. The museum, I'm told, displays memorabilia attesting to the difficulty of traveling in years gone by. In the future, if gasoline prices and energy taxes continue to rise, as they will, maybe the museum will feature a tire or a cylinder from a 1992 Japanese import.

As for gentrification: along Maxwell Avenue, the main street, a half-dozen antique stores offer Western ranching bric-a-brac. The Brown boasts the only yuppified breakfast and lunch menu in an otherwise beans-and-tortillas town.

Capulín Volcano National Monument

Springer, despite its village-like charm, wasn't my type of photo destination, so I headed up I-25 and northeast to a more obvious candidate: Capulín Volcano National Monument 30 miles east of Ratón, near Folsom in Union County.

Several pronghorn antelope herds grazed on the east slopes of the Sangre de Cristo's snow-capped peaks and on the Plains near Capulín. Hawks held down telephone posts, but the American eagles who fly reconnaissance over this part of the state must have been busy plucking ducks from one of the wildlife refuge lakes around Maxwell or Las Vegas.

Capulín's conic cinder remains tower 1,000 feet above the surrounding Plains, about as high as cinder cones grow. The cone, one of state's youngest, has retained its symmetry, partially protected by its vegetation.

The gray, cindery earth and various lava rocks and boulders around the national monument are solid reminders that active volcanos sprayed the state with all manner of red-hot detritus as recently as from 8,000 to 2,500 B.C.

Not so recent?

Maybe not, but geologists classify any volcano active in the past 25,000 years as young and potentially rambunctious. There's no telling what influence New Mexico's occasional earthquakes might have on dormant magma beds.

Hunters from the Clovis and Folsom civilizations, hanging out under these dark cindered mesas from 9500 to 8500 B.C., probably quaked in their tracks when the volcano or neighboring cones first spewed steam and smoke, then hurled ashes and cinder. Standing like rabbits mesmerized by a hunter's whistle, these early plainsmen watched red-hot lava snake to the horizons, then finally broke and ran for cover.

The charred remnants of those flows are visible today at the park, where the visitor center includes a small museum, interpretive video and gift shop.

The short nature trail outside displays several lichen-covered basalt formations that remind me of dyed toothpaste. Called lava squeeze-ups, they were formed when the top layer of Capulín's flowing lava solidified and cracked, letting later lava squish to the surface. The trail's flora, from the chokecherry—capulín in Spanish—to the gambel oak are forage for the plentiful mule deer, emphasizing how rapidly life adapts in seemingly inhospitable environs.

I climbed the slippery, guardrail-challenged road that winds around the cone like a string around an old-fashioned wooden toy top. Except for the Sangre de Cristos to the west, every mountain and mesa I saw from the windy crater's top share a volcanic origin.

Near the summit on the cone's west side is a trailhead parking lot from which I ventured along a loop trail on the cone rim, then down into the crater to stand at the exact spot where fire belched forth eons ago.

In autumn and winter, it's the closest to a thermal vent this side of my car heater, but I really didn't want it to heat up.

The weather held, so I eyeballed the valley near the foot of Johnson Mesa where in 1908, cowboy George McJunkin found the bone pit that pushed archaeologists' estimated date of humanity's first North American wanderings back to 8500 B.C. Evidence since then has shoved it back even earlier, to at least 26,000 B.C. and Apache and Pueblo friends of mine claim American Indians originated on the North American continent.

Regardless, McJunkin's discovery came after a flood that devastated the small town of Folsom also deepened an arroyo that drains to the Cimarrón Seco northwest of town. The scouring exposed grooved arrow points wedged in bleached bison bones. It took McJunkin years to convince anyone about the seriousness of his discovery, but archaeologists finally flocked to the site.

The protected Folsom site is on private range and closed to the public, but I caught an overview of the area off State Road 72, which tops Johnson Mesa west of town. And I learned more about it and Folsom's past in the Folsom Museum (open off-season by appointment only).

For example, the 1908 Folsom flood produced a local heroine. Telephone operator Sarah Rooke stayed at her switchboard warning town residents of the approaching deluge until she was swept away and drowned. She saved many lives, but the town was leveled.

Since State Road 72 was dry, I approached Ratón over Johnson Mesa, an extensive ancient lava flow as bare as Arctic tundra. Across its top streams feed several ponds, which breaks up the otherwise monotonous topography.

I needed coffee, good coffee, but that possibility was miles away. Keeping one eye on the weather, I boosted the volume on Tom Petty's "Running Down a Dream" and indulged in another detour.

Sugarite Canyon State Park

Sugarite Canyon State Park lies a few miles east of Ratón.

The park's canyons once were mined for coal, but today the park is a diamond in the wilderness rough.

Combining my favorite New Mexican high-country staples of spectacular green scenery, ample recreation choices and an interesting history, the canyon is a cool, generously watered retreat just a bit more than two hours from Santa Fe, the City Difficult.

I considered the benefits: no gun-toting gangs, no graffiti, no snarling, territorial, antediluvian night-brawlers. Just me, Ma Nature and a few wandering bears without shaved heads,

Let me note that one of Sugarite's historical quirks is the long-standing (and non-violent) controversy over the origin of the name Sugarite, used for a creek, canyon and mesa, all in the park.

The appellation apparently is a corruption of the Spanish *achicoria,* a wild chicory that flourishes in the area. Some sources claim it's a corruption of an Indian word for the zone's numerous birds, citing the Comanche for hen, *cocora* (probably prairie hen or wild turkey), a name that shows up in several New Mexican locales as variants of *gallina,* Spanish for hen. But cocoro doesn't come anywhere close to Sugarite to my ear.

Oblivious to its evasive etymology, Sugarite Creek rises in Colorado, just across New Mexico's undulating northern border. Broad and marshy at first, the creek's flow soon picks up as it winds down to Lake Maloya through meadows and *cienegas* spread with pink and white valerians and blue field mint. The lake is one of the park's two fishing holes. Smaller Lake Alice is easy to reach lower down on State Road 526, which traverses the park. A third lake, Dorothy, is accessible from the park a quarter-mile north of Maloya in Colorado.

Gasoline-powered engines are banned on the lakes, adding to the canyon's wilderness ambience, as does the wildlife. I spotted a doe grazing unafraid in a green, blue and yellow meadow above Maloya in broad daylight.

More elusive but just as prevalent are wild turkey, turkey vultures, beaver, tassel-eared squirrels, elk, cougar, bobcat and bear.

As for bruins: the day I first visited the canyon, park rangers at Soda Pocket Campground were trying to corner a black bear that persisted in rousting Boy Scouts from their mountainside camps and rummaging through their garbage. They didn't catch her while I was there, and I left the Scout leaders grumbling about how many times they'd told those kids to keep food out of their tents.

To ensure solitude and increase my chances of bumping into wild critters, I hiked the half-mile Grande Vista Trail at dusk. The relatively easy trail starts near a picnic area at the edge of Bartlett Mesa, then winds past a spring and through deer country thickets. Groves of large gambel oaks, mountain mahogany and chokecherries provided cover, so I kept my eyes peeled, tough to do while watching montane panoramas unfold below.

Tiring of the wildlife search, and afraid I might actually meet a bear, I eased back down-canyon to the visitor center, a rock building in the old Sugarite Mining District. This canyon's population from 1910 to 1941 soared from 400 to 1,000 coal miners, mostly immigrants: Italians, Czechs, Yugoslavs, Irish, Japanese.

Today, a few old buildings and rock foundations laced with weeds mark the ruins of a community that once bustled about its mundane daily life. This mountain valley was miles from Ratón's amenities, but on an all-important connecting railroad spur.

The coal company's railroad no longer hooks the back canyon to the outside world, having retreated nine miles east over the mesa to Ratón when the coal ran out. But vestigial coal veins here still display carbonaceous drifts high on the canyon walls that bracket the visitor center. Inside the center, I compared today's view with site photos from the three mines' productive years.

The center attendant, a lively retiree transplanted from a Northeastern urban center, cheerfully shared Sugarite Canyon lore, including the story of the imposing, spooky gray ruins of a wooden Victorian mansion high on a knoll in the lower canyon.

Its owner, she said, was an English promoter who built a guest ranch at which he guaranteed—for a huge fee—360 days of sunlight a year. The house of rays never opened, ironic here where our state's early tourism promoters dubbed us "The Sunshine State" years before Florida snagged the slogan.

The house's dreadfully depressing demeanor is spookier than any I've seen in New Mexico. Roof sagging, shutters askew, paint a forgotten luxury; from its isolated knoll it repelled, yet called me. I couldn't yield to the invitation, forced instead to pull over to the berm to sit out a fiercely crackling thunderstorm laced with hail.

Like the storm, the Brit mysteriously disappeared at night, say local historians, who don't include whether or not he was spirited away, but who note he maybe owed somebody some money. Or some sunshine.

Ratón

Ratón's a cross between a company and a tourist town. And in its own way, Ratón is a border town, for centuries a setting for cross-cultural encounters.

As for tourism, just south of town, for instance, the internationally known National Rifle Association's Whittington Center's firing ranges sprawl across 33,000 acres of piñon-juniper hills. At La Mesa Park's racetrack, the ponies thunder on summer weekends.

Yet Ratón, conscious of its importance as a major railroad switching station and coal mining and storage site, bills itself as "the Pittsburgh of the West," never mind that it's short a couple of major rivers and a stadium. After ubiquitous state government, Ratón's second largest employer is the Pittsburgh & Midway Coal Mining Co.

Downtown Ratón hides its proud center away from I-25 traffic, embracing a five-by-three-block historic district adjacent to the Santa Fe Railway yard. Today's Amtrack station, which occupies the original Santa Fe Depot, reflects the town's varied past. Several buildings in the district, such as the sandstone Palace Hotel (1896), have stood since early railroad days and the Shuler Theater has staged entertainment since 1915.

For information, I tried the Ratón Museum on First Street, just across from the depot. It was closed, but vintage photos of the area decorated the walls of a nearby First Street ice cream shop near the garishly painted, boarded Territorial exterior of the old Marchiondo Building.

The harbingers and in many cases, providers of Ratón's Victorian glories was the Atchison, Topeka and Santa Fe which by 1878, had spiked down rights-of-way over Ratón Pass, New Mexico's northernmost point on the Santa Fe Trail.

The railroaders set up yards in 1879 at Willow Springs, eight miles south of the pass. They moved buildings from Otero, a small Hispanic railroad town a bit south, renaming the new 3,000-population consolidation Ratón after the pass.

Ratón, like Trinidád, Colo., north over Ratón Pass, lies along the historic fringe of 19th-century Mexico's northern expansion, as reflected in its 1990s population's mix: 7,372 people: 47 percent Hispanic, 51 percent Anglo.

Another factor contributes to Ratón's ambience: the southern Rockies. The central business district, except for the relatively flat historic area, slopes west to streets where homes dot the Sangre de Cristo's sandstone foothills. The wooded hills lend a Southern Colorado atmosphere, as do *Denver Post, Rocky Mountain News* and *Pueblo Chieftain* newspaper racks around town. Santa Fe? Where's that?

At 6,666 feet, Ratón certainly shouldn't be compared with Aspen, Sugarite Ski Area notwithstanding.

It's much more gritty; coal towns usually are, even when the coal mining jobs are slowly slipping away. It's a friendly cowboy paradise sporting a weathered exterior, where June's Professional Rodeo Cowboys Association rodeo is a big deal. And like a rodeo cowboy, the town's game; it's going to hang on for all eight.

Ratón seems to know itself: it's still the "Pittsburgh of the West," emphasis on both Pittsburgh and West.

Rendezvous on the Santa Fe Trail

A few summers ago, I enjoyed Ratón's bucolic hinterlands by attending an old-fashioned "mountain man" (and woman and child) rendezvous in Coal Canyon, staged by the Santa Fe Trail Rendezvous Association on NRA land southwest of town.

I was no mountain man. And the instant I topped the rise that blocks Coal Canyon's northeastern approach from Ratón and the rest of the world, I knew I wasn't dressed for the occasion.

In this pre-1840 microcosm, black powder weapons, tomahawks and knives, accoutrements of the Mountain Man Mystique, prevailed. My jeans and striped shirt would stand out among the authentic outfits like an albino skunk in a coal patch, marking me a pilgrim, outsider, tenderfoot. At least I was wearing sturdy moccasins.

After all, the Mountain Man Mystique conjures up awesome images: scraggly bearded, buckskin-clad behemoths festooned with leather and metal beaver traps.

The mystique briefly shimmered in the American Southwest from about 1820 to 1840, disintegrating when silk replaced beaver as the tophat material of choice.

Both fur-company employees and independent French-Canadian and American trappers and traders filtered into the wild New Mexico uplands early in the 19th century. Some deliberately sought isolation in the splendid but dangerous beauty of the whispering high mountain forests and lush meadows, sustaining themselves in winter on meager staples and jerked game.

Loners or extroverts, the mountain men loved to congregate annually in rendezvous, a sort of landlocked shore leave and trade fair, where they'd sell pelts, race and swap horses, chugalug the notorious local moonshine, chase women, shoot black powder rifles and pistols, throw knives and 'hawks and generally raise hell.

A mountain woman practices firing her black powder weapon at a rendezvous in Coal Canyon, near Ratón.

Actual rendezvous' were testosterone-charged events one historian describes as "... barbaric, colorful, maleness gone berserk."

Along the New Mexico-Colorado border, the old hosses did their congregating in choice high valleys and canyons, often where Pueblo Indians for centuries had hosted similar gatherings for Navajos, Apaches, Kiowas, Utes and Comanches.

Taos, for instance, was a favorite rendezvous site and home of the sometimes-blinding Taos Lightning, an alcoholic concoction also known as "Turley's skull varnish" for the miller who manufactured it.

The village, a $15,000-a-year market in 1822, became the area's trading center for beaver pelts, with 414 wagons wheeling in $1.7 million in fur in 1846, just before the outraged Mexican and Indian natives abruptly ended the career of one erstwhile fur trader, Gov. Charles Bent. Other former mountain men, such as Kit Carson and his friend, Cerain St. Vrain, not only survived the rebellion's storm clouds, they prospered after the gale blew over.

In communities like Don Fernando de Taos, Lo de Mora, Cimarrón and all across the former Beaubien-Miranda Grant east of the northern Sangres, the surviving wild ones eventually married native Indian or Mexican-American women and settled. Some of their names endure in remote northeastern New Mexico locations such as Sapelló (Shapellote), Charette Lakes and LeDoux.

Until this rendezvous, it was from raconteurs and movies that I'd formed my impression of mountain men.

This surely was no movie. Over the rise and under gathering afternoon thunderheads lay a few acres of parked cars and RVs, real-world transportation for rendezvous aficionados, who if so inclined, can attend more than a hundred U.S. black powder firing matches a year. Most such events also require participants to don dress authentic to the period.

I was about to enter another of those time warp portals I so love: this one into a reflection of a hopefully peaceful camp of gringos, Hispanics and Indians whose physical essences dissolved into earth at least a century-and-a-half ago.

I topped the rise and stood, taking in the spectacle below. The carefully nourished pre-1840s image worked.

A mile of white tepees and canvas military-style tents bordered the stream that split the green mountain valley floor, more tepees than I'd seen massed anywhere except sun dances and the Crow Trade Fair. Up-canyon a horse corral contined a dozen nervous ponies, switching at the biting flies. Although campground activity was brisk, there were no internal combustion engines within sight, sound, or scent.

A restless, brisk pre-storm breeze drove down bluish smoke from 50 campfires and snapped red, green and white pennants on the tepee-pole tops, stretching flags to reveal symbols boasting various allegiances: California Bear, Lone Star, *fleur-de-lis.*

Before walking any deeper into camp, I talked with Bob Kaiser, the booshway (camp director) and his segundo, Mel Campbell, both of Ratón. Both were decked out in leather britches and loose-flowing cotton overshirts, no synthetic cowboy shirts or faux-pearl buttons in this outfit.

Mel walked me through the mercantile buzz of bustling trader's row, a line of tents penetrating deep into the encampment.

The traders' shelters overflowed with all manner of handmade goods, no imports allowed, thanks. Most of the backwoods merchants specialized in items that might help a rendezvouser authenticate a costume, pushing anything from brightly colored trade beads and hand-worked silver jewelry to beaded leather clothing and all-purpose pouches called "possible" bags. Serious part-time traders did business away from the formal shopping area, usually from a blanket or fur spread in front of their tent. Kids, especially, seemed ready to trade at the drop of a bead.

Kids?

I looked around the valley, craning to see all 200 or so of the tepees and tents. A couple dozen young'uns, mostly pre-teens camping with their families, showed up when Booshway Bob set up a running and carrying game aimed at sharpening their survival trail skills.

Mel introduced me to an extended family, the Arana-Trujillo-Wheelers. They were so friendly I almost forgot to talk to anybody else.

The women—Diane, Debbie and grandma Janie—kidded each other about cooking in a dutch oven and about who would live through the women's survival trail. Their talk didn't interrupt their work, as they dished out *posole*, breakfast burritos with homemade *salsa picante*, biscuits and gravy and range coffee, all for a small fee.

Their men—Gary Wheeler of Belen and Randy Trujillo of Loveland, Colo.—cleaned their rifles and joked with the women about missing "labor-saving devices" and wondered how they'd all last through tonight's singalong.

Still concerned about my citified slouch look, I quizzed patriarch Greg Arana of Los Lunas about the cost of a basic rendezvous wardrobe.

While lightning flashed outside his open-flapped canvas tent, Arana recited: Deerskin pants, he told me, ran $190; leggings and breechcloth, $140; knife scabbard, $20; and low-cut moccasins, $30. A woman's fringed buckskin dress, he said, could run from $400 to $500.

To arm myself, Mountain Man style, I'd need about $300 for a used Thompson Center Hawken-style .50-caliber percussion rifle with scabbard; $150 for a used, .50-caliber, wood-handle, percussion pistol; and $25 for a powder horn, good for 50-60 loads. For shelter, I could spend up to $1,063 for an 18-foot diameter canvas tepee, but other shelters are available for less.

For pilgrim and non-pilgrims there are plenty of activities to help stiff new leathers acquire that spotted, used sheen, including the on-going best costume contest. From just after breakfast until 9 p.m., men, women and children slog in their outfits through mountain survival walks or compete at matches: pistol, percussion and flint rifle, knife and 'hawk, and bow and arrow.

That night, after the storm blew over, we bravely attacked "Blue Eyes Crying in the Rain," "Desperado" and "Goodnight Irene." Gary even sang the coming-of-age-on-the-rez "Navajo Candy Bar Song." Juice harps and banjos twanged faintly at distant campfires. We howled until midnight, youngsters snoozing safely in tepee or tent, older kids God knows where, while a billion suns danced overhead like they did over Rendezvous Taos, 1832.

Vermejo Park Ranch

While Mountain Man clothing and weapons might be expensive, I figured I'd pay less for a rendezvous habit than I would for a radically different contemporary version of roughing it offered 45 miles west up State Road 555 from Coal Canyon.

The site: the Vermejo Park Ranch, west of Ratón. The road, not even listed on the state map, is hard to find. I approached on I-25 north, and turned west at Ratón's race track south of town. But I didn't just drop in. I called first; this is a private resort.

After William Bartlett, a turn-of-the-century, cigar-smoking, Chicago grain speculator, first summered in Northeastern New Mexico's high country, he dreamed of someday moving here for good.

He finally did, in 1902 founding Vermejo Park Ranch on the Sangres' magnificently wild eastern slope.

Once established at his sumptuous new 30-bedroom stone ranch house, Casa Grande, Bartlett's first goal was to restore his tubercular son's failing health. His second was to restore the depleted native herd by importing elk from Yellowstone Park; his third to dig out or improve a series of upland trout lakes.

His son survived. How well he accomplished his latter two goals is obvious at upscale Vermejo Park Ranch, today a vast, pricey, private outdoor recreation resort and working cattle ranch.

At Vermejo Park Ranch, where altitudes vary from 7,000 to 13,000 feet, visitors can hunt, hike or ride horseback far from the population pressures from which our national forest areas increasingly suffer. Also available: photographing scenic wonders, with or without a guide, and with luck, even snapping a few elusive elk, agile antelope or bucolic buffalo.

Stalking the wily rainbow, German brown or cutthroat in pristine, rushing mountain streams or, as Bartlett did, angling through the 21 jewel-like lakes languishing among lofty blue peaks also is popular.

And on any given frosty morning, a visitor might encounter some of the rest of Vermejo Park's 160 wildlife species, including elk and mule deer by the thousands (yes, thousands), turkey, bear or mountain lion.

Since 1973, owner Pennzoil of Houston, Inc. has overseen Vermejo Park's 588,000 high-altitude acres under a philosophy they call "managed wilderness."

The area's wildlife has not always been managed.

Originally, in 1843, about the time most of the indigenous Jicarilla Apaches departed, the land was included in the Beaubien-Miranda land grant. Later, canny fur trapper Lucien Maxwell married Beaubien's daughter, clamping shut his claim like a steel beaver trap on 1.7 million acres later known as the Maxwell Land Grant. In 1886, Maxwell sold out to a group of English investors, which ignited the Colfax County War, a year-long series of battles between the investors and squatters.

The settlers lost.

After William Bartlett "discovered" the area, he bought 200,000 acres of the old Maxwell grant. Subsequent owners enlarged the holdings, imported wild game and established an exclusive hunting preserve.

In Bartlett's day, Vermejo Park cowboys roped bull elk to yank the animals' incisors, which they sold for $10 apiece in Ratón.

Hunts in the 1990s are a bit tamer and a good deal more expensive, ranging from about $6,000 to $15,000 for a combination deer-elk hunt. Non-hunters can accompany hunters for from $225 to $275 per day, depending on the hunt.

The ranch, which invites vacationers to "rough it in style," boasts an 80 percent elk hunt kill rate success. Buffalo, mule deer, antelope and turkey hunts also are available in season.

I can't afford this kind of fun, however, so I found an alternative.

Just northeast of Cimarrón, Forest Road 1950 ascends into Kit Carson National Forest. A few miles past the forest's west edge, I ran into paved State Road 196, which eventually drops to Costilla, an old Spanish colonial plaza about 45 minutes north of Taos on State Road 522.

The forest road cuts just south of Vermejo Park Ranch's locked gates. But if I were a browsing high-range elk, I wouldn't be able to tell the difference between the free side of the mountain range and the side that costs.

***

Interesting stuff I'm reading as wind fingers probe my car here on the Canadian. The small primitive campground at the canyon's bottom can wait. The channel catfish rumored to haunt the river pools below won't miss me. A thin snow mist pings against my windshield. I've reviewed as much Canadian culture as I can today. I'm gone.

Besides, I had already glimpsed the canyon when I crossed the Canadian on State Road 120 from Wagon Mound to Roy. Access there is denied by fences and "keep out" signs posted by the Canadian River Cattle Co. But that doesn't keep me from marveling at the twisting, 600-foot-deep gorge the river has gouged through sedimentary High Plains rock, nor from appreciating the salient and redeeming fact of life in this desolate quarter of New Mexico: a river runs through it.

I consider my logistics: gasoline and general store in tiny Roy, small restaurant in tiny Wagon Mound. No drinking water in the Kiowa National Grasslands nor the Canadian River Canyon.

The sky lowers, showering white: hail, sleet, snow in sequence.

Then, as if to prove my lack of judgement, sunlight dapples Wagon Mound mesa by the time I merge with I-25 north. I can chance the Moreno and Mora valleys for a couple of photos tomorrow if I overnight nearby. Given New Mexico's variable seasonal weather, I have a

50 percent chance of the squalls blowing through to the east to plague the Oklahoma and Texas panhandles. I'll stay in Cimarrón and set out early for some dramatic upcountry landscapes among the lofty peaks that water the Canadian via the Cimarrón River.

Cimarrón and the High Country

Springer, Maxwell, Rayado and several other Canadian River-dependent towns epitomized the Wild West and mountain men rendezvous' keep even earlier frontier memories alive.

But let's face it, unless you cut your teeth on cinch rings, your images of the Wide Open Spaces are warped. We all ingested, depending on our ages, large doses of The Lone Ranger, Gunsmoke, Maverick or Hang 'Em High and other such entertaining bologna with our white bread lunches.

But in New Mexico, the Real West has endured for the past century in the hard-riding cowboy and cattle culture of our north- and southeastern Plains. Some communities, still embracing the lariat and latigo lifestyle, have taken pains to preserve their heritage.

One of these is Cimarrón, into which I roll just as a shower washes its streets clean.

Nestled (a word to which the cowfolk might object) against the northern Sangres at the mouth of impressively deep Cimarrón Canyon, the town was a stop on the Mountain Branch of the Santa Fe Trail in the 1860s and '70s.

The mammoth Beaubien-Miranda Land Grant, of which Cimarrón once was part, was settled in 1841 when Taoseño Carlos Beaubien's son-in-law, mountain man Lucien Maxwell and his friend Kit Carson organized a ranch in Rayado, south of Cimarrón. Maxwell moved his headquarters north to the south bank of the Cimarrón River in 1857. The town soon hosted area ranchers and outlaws, who preyed on the gold miners who swarmed over the area after 1867 like plague fleas on a coyote carcass.

During their heyday, Maxwell and his wife inherited or bought more than two million acres, an empire three times the size of Rhode Island, in an area that included present-day Ratón, Springer, Maxwell, Vermejo Park, Ute Park and Elizabethtown. He kept himself in business through beef sales to the military and the Indian agency that supervised Utes and Jicarilla Apaches from 1862 to 1876.

Maxwell employed 400 people, and in 1864 built a block-long house where local gentry and rowdies danced, gambled and shot billiards and each other. In the early 1860s, he tried sheep and goat ranching with "Buffalo Bill" Cody, who staged Wild West shows in Cimarrón and helped with an annual children's Christmas program at the St. James Hotel, erected in 1873 near the town's original plaza. The builder was Henrí Lambert, a chef for Abraham Lincoln and U.S. Grant. Maxwell retired to Fort Sumner, where his family's now-dissolved, rambling Territorial-style adobe home was the site of Billy the Kid's alleged demise.

Cimarrón sleeps in the midst of its own violent history. Twenty-six men reportedly were shot to death in the old hotel, a carnage rate that once prompted the *Las Vegas Gazette* to report: "Everything is quiet in Cimarrón. Nobody has been killed for three days."

A now-ruined building on the old plaza housed the Indian agency, and later, the bilingual *Cimarrón News and Press,* founded in 1875. Clay Allison, a rancher-gunfighter and a populist Maxwell enemy, once threw the paper's type cases and office equipment into the Cimarrón River.

Another local baddie, Thomas "Black Jack" Ketchum, fared worse than the newspaper. He and his gang robbed a train in 1899 in nearby Turkey Creek Canyon, but soon were engaged in a bloody firefight by lawmen. Ketchum suffered a wound that separated him from his arm, but his lynching in Clayton soon afterwards separated him from his head. Literally.

A new town built by railroad interests in the early 1900s north of the Cimarrón River was mostly destroyed by a fire in the early 1930s. Today, the "new town" houses a modern municipal building and library, and its old square is edged by a few art galleries.

There's not much left of the original plaza to the south, but I dined at the restored, bullet-pocked St. James, where Frederick Remington once painted and Zane Grey wrote a novel.

While Maxwell's magnificent Cimarrón house is in ruins, the old mill he built in 1864 about a quarter-mile north houses a museum that opens May 1. The Kit Carson Museum at Rayado also is closed until late spring. Cimarrón's relatively quiet before the arrival of summer tourists and the thousands of Boy Scouts who seasonally inhabit Philmont Ranch a few miles south. There are several restaurants, motels and gas stations, and the town's too small to get lost, so I forge west up Cimarrón Canyon to some of the Canadian's high country.

Moreno Valley

The next morning, winding up past yellowing riverside aspen, I parallel the sometimes troublesome Cimarrón River past the formidably vertical Palisades cliffs, which I recall from a visit to the Moreno Valley I enjoyed last spring.

That spring was dusty down below, as usual. Topside it also had blown raw and rough, but in the valleys I visited above 8,000 feet, there was a compensating factor: the runoff.

I love autumn's cooler days and colder nights as much as the next pilgrim, but my memory of last spring's warming melt will sustain me through bleak, white winters to come.

Most years, the melt's a symphony of water coursing through swollen year-round streams, augmented by multi-toned choruses of trickles from millions of extemporaneous rivulets, branches, streams, arroyos. To an aquaphile like me, it's one of New Mexico's rarest and most enchanting sounds.

From late August to September, the Moreno Valley to which I climb echoes with other pleasant sounds: critically acclaimed Music from Angel Fire, featuring classical sounds so delicate hearing them lofts me back into the symphony of the melt.

I slipped on my earphones and cued J.S. Bach's "Brandenburg Concerti," but there's no better seat in Nature's house than a temporary island for absorbing outdoor liquid music, so I snapped off the tape. My eyes drank in the sky above, blue-white from the glare of recalcitrant snow. Soggy and tenuous at best, the earth beneath my feet was undercut by water, the life-blood of our people, splashing through the veins of the Blood of Christ Mountains.

And I found an orchestra seat on the relatively new Elliot Barker Trail in Carson National Forest, one of many locations in the Moreno Valley to bathe in that "blood."

Far below the trail, villages garland Eagle Nest Lake. Ranches and summer homes dot the valley floor, miles from their nearest neighbor.

Eagle Nest, a major village, is a former ranching center turned tourist headquarters. Angel Fire, out of sight beyond the lake to the south, includes a ski area, golf course and convention center among its chalet-style wooden condos and scattered year-round homes.

Topping the ridge from Ute Lake, I descend to Eagle Nest, at the State Road 38/U.S. 64 junction on the southern shores of five-mile-long Eagle Nest Lake. The settlement was built in 1920 as Therma. Settlers changed its name after noting golden eagles in the surrounding mountains, or so say the legends. Eagle Nest Lake, dominated by a ring of soaring peaks, looks natural in its alpine setting, but the 2,200-acre lake resulted from a dam built in 1919 by cattlemen, including the Springer brothers from the plains to the east.

Today, it's a good spot to trout fish (permits available in Eagle Nest) and view Mount Baldy and Touch Me Not peaks to the northeast and Wheeler Peak to the west.

Before tourism, mining and ranching drove area development.

Mining began in the valley's north end in 1866, when Ute Indians at Fort Union offered to trade copper they'd found on Baldy Mountain, a 12,441-foot peak that looms northeast of Eagle Nest. The military assessor sent to the area found gold.

The skeletal remains of one of the many resultant mining towns—a couple of ruined buildings—still stand at the site of what once was Elizabethtown, on private property north of State Road 38, about five miles north of Eagle Nest.

E'Town, as the miners called it, sheltered several thousand brawling people, a newspaper, two hotels, seven saloons and three dance halls. Fire destroyed most of the business district in 1903, a few years after the gold played out. Returning to Eagle Nest, I skirt seven miles south along the lake to Angel Fire, which draws heavily on the Texas and Oklahoma trade.

A local legend claims Angel Fire's name originated when Moache Ute Indians who hunted the area witnessed a fiery glow atop 11,086-foot Agua Fria Peak, southeast of the village. Another concoction has Kit Carson describing dawn sunlight on the frozen dew as "angel fire." Since neither of those alleged events was recounted until after land developers moved in, I'm wary.

A strange cold fire did descend on the Moreno Valley once, when it snowed blue here early in May, 1955. Valley residents thought the foot-deep blanket beautiful, but a few worried when their cattle developed inflamed udders. Kids who played in the snow developed water blisters on their faces and hands. Fallout from a southern Nevada bomb test was suspected, but not proven.

The Moreno Valley's tenuous link with the Atomic Age apparently doesn't deter tourists, although between ski and summer seasons, the valley's occupied mostly by year-round locals.

I stop off to shoot pool and browse the salad bar sequestered among the antique farm implements and other rural Americana hung about the rafters at Jebadiah's, one of the few Angel Fire restaurant/bars open all year. I chalk up a cue and rack up a little practice, but nobody challenges me. Enough young men and women lounge around for me to suspect the joint heats up at night, but I'm an old married man. What do I know?

⇒ Information
Canadian Canyon road conditions: 1-505-374-9652
Sugarite Canyon State Park, Ratón: Fee. 1-505-445-5607
Rendezvousing, Coal Canyon, Ratón: 1-505-445-9637
Vermejo Park: 1-505-445-3097
Angel Fire: 1-505-377-6661
Eagle Nest: 1-505-377-2420

The Mill Valleys

Near Black Lake, at the Moreno Valley's higher southeastern slopes, two routes offer access to the plains by way of Ocaté or Coyote. I take both as often as I can, since both traverse a forested paradise. When I choose Ocaté (from Nahuatl: pitch pine), I gas up in Angel Fire, because where I'm headed there's lotsa nada.

Ocaté

On a previous autumn trip, I'd taken my time between Black Lake and Ocaté, rewarded by the lovely but private landscape on the Old Taos Trail and the Santa Fe Trail's Mountain Branch. Enough pull-offs exist to enjoy the scenery, but they're often muddy.

As summer light fades, New Mexico's illumination is incomparable, as generations of artists, artisans and other adventurers can attest. But nowhere does autumn's latent nostalgia strike more suddenly than in the high meadows of the north, where wildflowers rage out of control, enjoying their last warm hours of waning sun before the killing frosts.

Years of good rainfall were evident last autumn in the size of the firs and scrub oak groves bordering County Road 120 as I rose to a high valley. On the road's descent a few miles east, thick-trunked oaks, in New Mexico usually pitiful shadows of their Eastern cousins, evoke Druidic mysteries in a land far removed from that tradition.

Topping the mesa, I had entered two caldera, one at least a mile in diameter, flower-appointed, with lushly grassed range fenced by thick forest, especially aspen groves just flashing a little color.

A few miles west of Ocaté, after dropping through Manuelez Canyon and past the secluded homes of a few Hollywood refugees, I had skirted Ocaté Creek, passing private pastures and wooded back country.

At Ocaté, the old stores and haciendas, some still occupied, snooze around the base of 7,788-foot Ocaté Peak. Built in the functional New Mexico vernacular style found all over Mora County, the thick-walled Territorial adobes are capped with steep tin roofs to protect against the severe winters. The village didn't have a post office until 1866, but a few of the homes must have seen Gen. Stephen Watts Kearny trot by in 1846 on his way to Las Vegas and the U.S. military occupation of New Mexico.

For a closer look at Santa Fe Trail history east of Wagon Mound, at milepost 25, at the Mora Ranch sign on State Road 120, I had turned north for 1.6 miles on a fairly good dirt road over private land to Ocaté Creek. It appeared a good idea to stay in the car here. On the road's east side, or on the creek's north, is a gentle dirt grade creaking wagons once descended after winding around Apache Mesa to the north. Known as Ocaté Crossing, it was the only place for miles where loaded Santa Fe Trail wagons could safely ford.

Coyote Creek

This trip, however, I choose the Coyote Creek downhill run from Black Lake, on paved State Road 434. The road narrows dramatically and bristles with signs threatening horrors on anyone who yields to the considerable temptation to trespass on the roadside private property.

Eventually, after many serious twists, the road passes the tan gates of Coyote Creek Campground, a fee-area state park. I can't miss it: the stuccoed fake adobe portals are emblazoned with pastel murals of coyotes howling at the moon and inlaid with a mountain valley trademark, stucco chipped by random gunfire.

I don't let that put me off.

Behind the wounded gates, the riverside campground, at 7,700 feet, offers clean air, fishing, hiking and beaver ponds. I don't see beaver, but I see tracks and toothy signs of recent aspen-cutting along the river.

The campground has flooded in the past, but the damage usually is repaired soon. The park offers a kids' play area, plenty of picnic tables, potable water and canyon views, most shaded by aspen and other poplars, scrub oak and a sprinkling of ponderosa.

Bullet holes decorate a coyote mural at the gates to Coyote Creek
State Park.

Less than a mile up-canyon is a small grocery next to rustic cabins for rent. Across the road a half-mile or so beyond is a fenced state Game and Fish area where I sometimes explore the willow-bordered Rio Coyote without paying a cent.

For all its beauty, something about Coyote Creek Valley haunts me. Maybe it's the sense of isolation and history pervading the old villages. Maybe it's something more primal. One of these villages, Guadalupita, once a logging and farming community, is sparsely populated today. But, as at Mora, I can trace its old plaza in front of the still-active post office.

Many memories cling to the valley's floor: rock foundations and adobe ruins scattered in yellowing fields and emerald fringing forests, skeletons of someone's former barn or home; Guadalupita cemetery, silently guarded by an elaborate wrought-iron gate; deserted storefronts.

It was a Guadalupita woman, Luisa Torres, who told folklorists in 1903 that one spring day, her grandmother had levitated.

"There were millions of orange and black butterflies around the corn plants," she said, in an account of the event in Marta Weigle and Peter White's *Lore of New Mexico.*

"My grandmother ran towards the butterflies and gathered so many of them in her apron that she flew up in the air, while she laughed contentedly," she recounted.

Given the spellbinding nature of this neck of the state, if somebody says their abuelita flew, *¡hijolé, hombré!* I'm inclined to believe she did.

But butterfly flights weren't enough to save Guadalupita. A few ridges west of town were balded by a forest fire that roared through years ago, but the flames couldn't do what the inexorably encroaching 20th-century economy did: force many valley people from their mountains to earn livings elsewhere.

Mora River

I follow the Rio Coyote until it peels away to the southeast. Continuing southwest on State Road 434, I transit a series of sparsely populated ranching valleys beneath the shadow of the Sangre's spur Rincón Range, which drains into Coyote Creek.

I cross the cottonwood-shaded Mora River into town at the abandoned St. Vrain mill.

Cerain St. Vrain, Kit Carson's wealthy friend, built Mora Valley's largest old mill about 1860. St. Vrain's is but one of four area mills surviving since the more-prosperous 19th century, when valley farmers grew so much wheat the area was known as the "Ukraine of the Southwest." Today it's boarded and deserted, although its proud stone shell a few hundred yards north of the Mora County Courthouse still guards the narrow, twisting route to Coyote Creek.

For centuries, the secluded valley provided American Indians, early fur trappers and Hispanic and Anglo settlers access to hunting grounds and passage through the Sangre de Cristo's high peaks, which loom at its western reaches.

Mora originally was called Santa Gertrudis, after the old adobe church which has now melted away on the plaza. Its partially stone-faced replacement is in use here today. The old plaza's remains lie behind the present post office.

From 1865 until the 1950s, most Mora Valley students attended school on this plaza at the old Santa Gertrudis convento, just southwest of the church. The valley's public and private schools were run by church personnel. These included the same fine folks who helped educate Territorial Santa Fe: the Christian Brothers, who founded St. Michael's College for boys in 1859; and the Sisters of Loretto, who opened Loretto Academy for girls in 1852.

Marin County, Calif., isn't the only place that boasts a verdant "Mill Valley." New Mexico's is just a bit less urban and a damn sight more removed from the ocean.

The Valley of the Mora, a spectacular setting with panoramic mountain views, is home to a traditional Northern New Mexico culture, its architecture distinctive even by this state's standards.

The valley also enjoys a lively history, considering which, it's a wonder much architecture survives here at all.

In 1843, an army of filibustering Texans invaded and won a pitched battle at Mora, retreating to a later defeat near Wagon Mound. In 1847, after the Mora Revolt (when former Mexican citizens violently reacted to becoming U.S. citizens) Americans attacked the fortified town in a snowstorm, but retreated after insurgents killed Capt. Israel Hendley, the U.S. commander. Shortly after, Missouri Volunteers burned almost every village building, destroying surrounding ranches and grain fields. Finally, in 1904, a disastrous flood dug Main Street into an arroyo and swept away bridges, forcing refugees to the old courthouse, since destroyed.

Colorful past and a few sporadic hippie-era incidents notwithstanding, the valley's been relatively peaceful for the past 90 years or so.

Many of the local folks concentrate now on matters such as restoring and reactivating old village churches, once the center of Northern New Mexico's Hispanic culture.

I had met one of these restorers when I was photographing the area earlier.

Michael Rivera fondly remembered his childhood in Llano del Coyote—today's Rainsville—a small, community in the rolling hills east of Mora. Llano's near its namesake, Coyote Creek, which joins the Mora River southeast of La Cueva.

After years away, first attending the University of New Mexico, then as a manager at Los Alamos National Labs, Rivera came home in the mid-1990s, bringing his wife Susie, a Nambé native, and their daughters to enjoy the same sort of rural life he had experienced. Here, in the Rio Coyote's rolling valley, he recalled many *funciónes* (activities)— weddings, confirmations, funerals—at Sagrado Corazón (Sacred Heart), the neighborhood's 1860s-era mission church, one of many in New Mexico now crumbling from decades of neglect.

But the Riveras believed in community involvement and soon were voted the church's mayordomos (managers).

That volunteer job landed them squarely in the middle of a project they loved: restoring Sagrado Corazón.

With mostly volunteer labor and with technical assistance, machinery and tools provided by the New Mexico Community Foundation, workers chipped away the church's Portland cement stucco exterior that builders once swore would last forever.

Durability didn't turn out to be the concrete's drawback. It did last several decades, but during that time, it didn't "breathe." Instead, it forced the adobe to suck groundwater up into the church's walls, dangerously weakening them.

Restoration projects not only extend the lives of the *placitas* (small villages) another 50 to 100 years, they also provide a skilled-labor force villagers can summon when the churches or homes need more work.

On a typical summer workday Sagrado Corazón's work crew consisted of neighborhood teenagers with names like Barela, Cortéz, Salcido, Vigíl and Fernandez.

Older men volunteer to help when they're not working their full-time jobs.

"The three or four guys in their 40s and 50s who work weekends really are committed," said mayordomo Rivera. "One of them told me

'Even if the next mass we have here is my funeral mass, it's worth it.'

"It's going to take quite a while," he said, "but we're working on it."

And to recapture a childhood memory, that's a small price to pay.

* * *

At the valley's southeast end, storerooms for La Cueva Mill, built in the 1860s, were converted a decade ago into Salman Ranch Store, a great place to gobble raspberries from late summer into early autumn and to find fresh local produce, plants and flowers until late autumn.

Today, La Cueva Mill's waterwheel spins mostly in summer and fall for tourists. La Cueva generated electricity until after World War II, as did the Cleveland Mill closer to Mora. But its original use was grinding the valley's copious grains for its first owner, Vicente Romero.

Romero came to the valley in the early 1800s and engineered the elaborate system of irrigation canals that crisscross Salman Ranch's fertile blueberry and corn fields.

During the mill's heyday, up to 60 horse- and ox-drawn wagons carted wheat, corn and beans in season daily to Fort Union and other area outposts. On a hill north of the store are ruins of a blacksmith shop, harness and tack rooms and stables. As summer approaches, the old rock corrals behind the store blossom with dazzling display of hand-sown wildflowers of every hue.

Northwest along State Road 518—from La Cueva to Holman—interspersed among a few stores, schools and gas stations, lies the real pride of the valley: its homes, built in intensely personal variations on traditional New Mexico adobe steadfastness and Victorian predictability. Combination hip-and-gable tin roofs, one of the valley's trademarks, evolved as efficient ways of enduring deep winter snows. Individual craftsmen added their wooden curlicues to doors, windows and arched porches.

At Cleveland, Dan Casssidy, descended from the pioneering Cassidys of Ireland, has restored the Cleveland Roller Mill his family has owned for decades. He stages annual Labor Day crafts fairs during which the mill's wheel and all its equipment turn again. He also maintains changing historic exhibits inside the mill and manages his landscaping business along the Mora's chokecherry bush-clogged banks.

A ridge or two south of Mora, the now-boarded-up Pendaries Mill stands near Pendaries, a pine-shaded golf course development. Jean

Pendaries' mill was as important to the area's mid-19th century economy as the better-known Mora mills. In the past, I've visualized the days when the mill's still-intact 18-foot wheel was turning by riding along the agricultural Manuelitas Valley down- and upstream from the mill.

The Rociadas, Upper and Lower, a few miles closer to the Sangre range than Pendaries, continue as ranching communities. The area's coves and meadows were home to José Baca, the state's lieutenant governor in 1924. His widow Marguerite was New Mexico's secretary of state (1930-1934).

Oliver LaFarge, who married Pendaries' great-granddaughter, Consuelo Baca, wrote about the Bacas and the Pendaries outfit, by then called the Baca Ranch, in his *Behind the Mountains,* now back in print after a decades-long absence. Since I once lived in one of his family's homes at Uppertown (San Antonio), north of Las Vegas, I appreciate the book. I'll return later to the "Baca Mansion."

Fort Union

My final stops in the Mora—a.k.a. Mill—Valley via I-25, are surrounded by vistas of the Great Plains, through which the Mora runs almost as soon as it sweeps around the Loma Parda curve and the ridge south of Fort Union, where I'm headed.

Given the few brick walls and earth mounds that remain today, it's easy to underestimate the importance of now-silent Fort Union to the remote communities of New Mexico's northeastern frontier.

Several towns that thrived off trade with the fort survived: Las Vegas, Mora, Wagon Mound (Santa Clara).

Some, such as Watrous (La Junta) and Ocaté, exist today as shadows of their former selves. Others, such as Loma Parda, are rodent palaces, nothing but crumbling stone edifices and sagging, rotten timbers.

More than 140 years ago, a U.S. Army general determined that New Mexico's capital city's major attribute was surfeit. The ruined results of his opinion of the City Difficult brave the endless prairie winds at today's Fort Union National Monument.

Lt. Col. Edwin Vose Sumner, for whom Fort Sumner on the Pecos River later was named, ordered the Army's New Mexico headquarters and principal supply depot moved from Santa Fe, "that sink of vice and extravagance," to a spot on the Territory's eastern frontier. In all fairness to the City Sinful, Sumner also had been commanded to move his troops nearer to Indian Country, closer to the Apaches, Utes and Comanches who favored the Plains for buffalo hunts.

The wind-blasted tract he chose in 1851 for Fort Union was at the base of a mesa near where the Santa Fe Trail's two forks joined, 100 miles from Santa Fe's immoral temptations. No stranger to the location, Sumner had camped near there when he was Gen. Stephen Watts Kearny's dragoon commander in 1846. But Sumner was no fool. In January, 1852, he found it "indispensably necessary" to move his head-

The snow emphasizes Santa Fe Trail ruts alongside Fort Union's ruined walls.

quarters to Albuquerque. To deal with Indian problems west of the Rio Grande, so he said.

The troopers left behind battled mostly bedbugs and boredom. The wooden fort they erected in the northernmost reaches of an area early Spanish settlers called *el gran despoblado* (the great unpopulated) eventually rotted into the ground. It was replaced in 1861 by a heaped-earth "star" fort, then still later by a sprawling Territorial-style adobe installation that took from 1863 to 1869 to build. That fort, the ruins of which stand today, included the Post of Fort Union, the Fort Union Quartermaster Depot and the Fort Union Ordinance Depot.

During the 1860s, the fort's headquarters store did a $3,000-per-day business and more than 1,000 carpenters, wagon builders, smiths, harnessmakers and laborers worked here.

The fort's troopers served during times in which they anxiously scoured the eternal horizons for signs of hostile Apaches and Utes, and through the Civil War and the Battle of Glorieta, for which the fort supplied Union soldiers and volunteers, many of them Hispanos. And they performed gallantly during the fort's days as protector of the Santa Fe Trail's final leg, as did the wives, mothers and sisters banished to this most distant of postings.

Some of what the troops saw and heard over those lonely years I see and hear: Startling commands from unseen bugles blare regularly across the deserted parade ground and over the rumpled, almost treeless valley to bounce off the now-ruined walls, where ghostly dragoons play endless card games in roofless rooms.

Loma Parda

Nearby, old Santa Fe Trail ruts deeply trench the fragile prairie land as they descend a gentle slope from the nearby Turkey Mountains and run by the fort. A less distinct abandoned trail wanders through the ridges to the south to Loma Parda (Gray Hill).

To get to Loma Parda, at I-25 immediately south of Watrous, I turn west on State Road 161 for seven miles, then right onto a rough, often muddy, dirt road at a white pipe fence. A small sign warns: "Overton Ranch and Wildlife Preserve. No Hunting." I believe it.

The road steeply descends 1.2 miles into the Mora River Canyon, ending at a gate, behind which I see the ruins across the river. I close the gate and drive 100 yards to the site of an old mill, where

Loma Parda, home away from home for lonely Fort Union troopers.

I clump across a swaying suspension bridge and like the long-dead Bluebellies, enter Loma Parda.

The dozen or so ruined buildings that remain are strung along a sunken dirt road on private land. A C de Baca family member lives just south of the ruins. I'm courteous and quiet.

Don't attempt the Loma Parda trip in a low-slung car, *mis batos,* my guys. And don't blame me if you get lost. Or worse. After all, even Fort Union's isolation couldn't insulate its men from the creeping rot of human temptation, so who knows what insidious moral havoc spirits may wreak? Loma Parda, a few miles downstream on the Mora's north bank, met the soldiers' physical needs with dance halls, saloons and gambling houses. The troops called it "the Lome," or more often, the "hog farm."

The town fell into ruin after it was invaded in 1872 by 60 Texas gunmen searching for cattle they claimed were stolen by Comanches, traded to Comancheros, and herded into New Mexico. Edward Seaman, the town's police chief and postmaster, was shot dead and the *alcalde* wounded in both legs in the ensuing fracas. Although the town had an official post office until 1900, it couldn't survive the combined onslaught of crazed gringos and the fort's 1891 closing.

Loma Parda was indeed a Comanchero stronghold, established in the 1830s, well before the fort. But the temptations of the fort's business must have been too much for the townsfolk.

Pvt. Frank Olsmith wrote in his diary about other temptations.

"Dancing pavilions," he said, "most of them with gambling places in connection, were plentiful and were for the most part well patronized from early eve to dewy morn.

"Every night parties were formed with consent and often the participation of our commanding officers, where we danced, smoked and indulged in flirtations with the native damsels over glasses of white Mexican wine."

The officers weren't always so accommodating.

Several incidents led to post commanders declaring the town off limits. Early in 1862, shortly before the Battle of Glorieta, troopers jailed two Loma Parda businessmen until they proved they weren't Confederate spies. In mid-1865, commander Col. James Carlton discovered someone was storing stolen army property in town, including 300 pounds of flour and several sacks of bacon.

Incidentally, speaking of lost communications, Carlton first read in the May 1, 1866 edition of *The New Mexican* that he'd been relieved of his commandant's duties.

His successor, Maj. John Thompson, immediately engaged in a fight with Loma Parda's *alcalde*, who had arrested, disarmed and held hostage several U.S. soldiers assigned the thankless duty of keeping their comrades out of town. The unlucky troopers, mostly New Mexico volunteers, were charged with being absent without leave when they were released.

By 1870, more than 100 buildings, including a church, and more than 400 inhabitants occupied Loma Parda's 17 acres. By 1872, official disapproval notwithstanding, Loma Parda was granted a post office, but it lasted only until 1900.

The town's most popular dance hall, a long, low, wooden-roofed field stone and mortar building, once sheltered tables where its owner, Julian C de Baca, dealt three-card monte.

Patterned paper once decorated the hall's walls, and plaster hid crude roof rafters. Back then, visitors were more interested in the low shed (or cribs) out back, where the willing women waited.

One historian noted in 1967 that "Loma Parda is so lost that there isn't even a road leading to it, nor does it rate notice on the maps of today."

As the expert on Lost, let me say that's not true.

⇒ Information
Fort Union: Fee. 1-505-425-8025

Return to the Canadian

After an overnight at home in Las Vegas, I set out the next morning for Roy and Trementina. I seek photographic variety in the static Great Plains scenery, an image to represent the Canadian's dominant icon.

The Canadian Escarpment

Perhaps, as I contemplated earlier near Mills, that icon is the canyon's edge, similar to the invisible border Castañeda's crazy old shaman, Don Juan Mateus, supposedly intuited when he called dawn and dusk "the cracks between the worlds." In the case of the canyon, that hairline would open between the point at which I could lean over the canyon's invisible border and defy gravity and the point at which gravity lured me down to certain death.

It's not easy to draw extended metaphors out here on the Lone Prairies, when my mind's already grappling to relate gargantuan chunks of uninhabited landscape to something humanly comprehensible. Maybe the icon's more subtle than obvious.

Plenty of canyons streak through Canadian country, some bordered by narrow secondary roads. These usually paved ribbons offer both a firsthand look at jumping-off points and a disconcertingly swift ride down. When I'm barreling along the Canadian River Escarpment, free-ranging bovines better beware the Canadian Cowcatcher.

The Great Plains, associated with Kansas and the endless Texas Panhandle, once touched the Sangre de Cristos. Over time, erosion pushed the Plains' alluvial cover east, abandoning isolated, caliche-toughened mesas like giant barges on a sand bar. The largest of these calcium carbonate prominences rises as the flat-topped Llano Estacado, or Caprock, south of I-40 near Tucumcari and San Jon.

Cowcatcher Country is a unique, devastated outpost of the much more extensive Caprock miles south. From the tortuous yellowish and pinkish walls of the Canadian Escarpment east of Watrous, Las Vegas and Trujillo, plains-like Caprock-remnant plateaus flank a broad, east-west, terraced Canadian finger valley known as the "Canadian Breaks."

Today I coast the northwestern and northern rim of that valley to consider the curving horizontal lines marking the Caprock's ancient northern boundary, the Canadian Escarpment. Photos are where you find them.

Earlier today, at Roy, I had headed south to just north of Mosquero, where I cut southwest on State Road 419 and entered the orange-and-pink sandstone world of the Upper Canadian Breaks.

Now, at Trujillo, I climb the escarpment on State Road 104, back up to the westernmost plains, over challenging Corazón Hill. Behind me lie the Breaks, before me the isolated chunk of High Plains that gently rolls 31 more treeless miles west from this hill to smash like weedy surf against the Sangre de Cristo Mountains.

The surf simile, certainly not original, helps me see something else, an almost too-subtle icon relating to this land.

The barbed wired, grassy, arroyo-delineated ridge north of me is more than the limit of two ranchers' ranges. On one side, the ridge drains to the Canadian, on my side, rain and snow melt drop eventually to the Pecos River. Water from the Canadian side flows to the Mississippi River, while the Pecos side ends up in the Rio Grande. Both rivers wind to the Gulf of Mexico. I pull over and on my map trace the ridge from the canyon's edge at least 40 miles west, where it ascends into the high canyons and to the Sangre de Cristos' ridgeline. Could subtle ionic charges from such ridges affect the weather? Radio transmissions? Anything?

If such a significantly delineating geological indicator remains invisible, what other unseen players linger in the shadows of these *barrancas,* these gorges among the back hills?

Whatever, I soon tire of observing the limitless view from my car window. I know where I can examine the microcosmic sheltered world of canyon and rim more closely. About 25 miles west of Trujillo, I turn left on State Road 281 to Las Vegas National Wildlife Refuge.

Box Canyon

I check in at the ranger station for the code for the locks to the metal gates barring the public from Box Canyon.

Due to seepage from McAllister Lake, once-dry Box Canyon has evolved into a delightful, lush, watered warm-weather jungle, with even a jungle-like insect population. I swat at gnats and watch for snakes. After I inspect the stone ruins of an old homestead, I descend from the plains along a relatively steep, rocky trail to the canyon's green floor to an obvious reward. An almost year-round water flow trickles into a reflecting pool beside a boulder: the contrasting effect is of a Japanese garden in the wilds. I photograph the pool and the stream that splashes down a gentle grade, then through a steep, sparsely wooded canyon to the wider Gallinas Canyon. The trail, however, doesn't lead to the Gallinas. It avoids even Box Canyon after a few hundred yards, looping up into surrounding hilltop piñon-juniper stands, re-entering Box Canyon near the reflecting pool.

A trailside pool reflects the peace of Box Canyon at Las Vegas National Wildlife Refuge.

Conchas and Ute Lakes

Since I've crossed the Canadian-Pecos divide, I'm ready to forge ahead to the Pecos, but there's always a little time for a bonus.

It is, after all, early autumn, a good season to pack kids and water toys and head east of Las Vegas to either of two state parks surrounded by human-made New Mexico lakes so large their ripple patterns even remind me of waves sloshing in an ocean estuary. I do enjoy a good imagination.

Both lakes—Conchas and Ute—are fed by the sometimes-mighty Canadian River, its precipitous cliffs much reduced from the dramatic canyons it gouged 50 miles upstream. In fact, as the Canadian flows from Conchas, the uppermost lake, down to Ute Reservoir, the natural, sheer-walled course to which it's confined surges like a large acequia.

That doesn't fool me.

Conchas, also fed by its namesake river, was created by the U.S. Army Corps of Engineers in 1939 for $15.8 million (that's pre-inflation bucks), providing irrigation water for downstream projects, bringing agriculture, ranching and scarcer-than-snake's-teeth shade trees to a large area of the otherwise semi-arid Canadian Valley.

At Conchas, the retaining wall south of the concrete dam itself is almost worth the trip. I pass under the towering dam to reach the north recreation areas, driving on a one-way road along the dam's base, with tons of red boulders perched over my head. On the return, I roll along the dam's rim, high over the lake. The aquatic panorama that spreads below, whitecaps sometimes chopping the otherwise turquoise and aquamarine waters, sea gulls squawking, is an absolute transport. Sure, the cool breeze is fresh, not salty, but who's complaining?

Of course, lofty vegetation is not the strong suit of New Mexico lakes at this altitude. That's why it's even more shocking when, after passing the wall and crossing the narrow drive across the concrete dam, I enter a thick cottonwood and grass oasis that hides the park's administration buildings and includes a picnic area out of all that water-in-the-desert glare.

The lake's north side is lined with a marina, lounge, cafe and small grocery, as well as a nature trail, amphitheater and campsites with sheltered picnic tables and grills, and a restroom. While it's obvious that speedboat maniacs and bobbing bassboat fisherfolk dominate both lakes some seasons, there are many sandy-bottomed

Ute Lake's refreshing waters attract sail-boaters.

coves where daring late-season visitors can hop right in, without life-guard supervision, of course. I don't indulge, wanting to see Ute Lake before lunch.

***

The banks of Ute Reservoir seem a bit starker than those at Conchas, but Ute hides more sheltered little coves and the sandy-bottomed, acres-wide swimming area near the state park's first entrance is absolutely perfect. My wagon's cab had heated uncomfortably in the waning autumn sun, so I gratefully slide into the cool water, floating, watching the wind blow lazy white puffs overhead, then tread water, noting whirring and chattering red-winged blackbirds hopping in the pesky but lacily lovely salt cedar and slender cattails.

A few families play in the chop, bobbing along the clean gentle sand bottom to at least a hundred yards offshore, where the deep water is demarcated by floating red balls. I crawl-stroke out to floats, determined to stay in the water until my skin prunes. A lone sailboat skims the whitecaps like a hungry gull, lofting my imagination to the Gulf of Mexico.

Grounded again by hunger, I dry off and hit Logan, a waterside community in the desert. I sit down in Logan's tiny Fireside Cafe, owned and operated by the Harris family, about the time the after-church crowds do. Since Logan is the only game on the Great Plains for miles around, the place is chock-full of healthy ranch families asserting their rights not to cook on Sundays. In the chaos, the waitress overlooks me for 15 minutes, so I'm chewing the menu by the time she sees me again.

But she more than makes up for it: my lunch is on the house.

The Canadian River's dominant icon, I decide, may well be unrecordable by photograph. It may be the free exercise of the compassionate virtues: kindness, consideration, hospitality.

⇒ Information
Conchas Lake: Fee. 1-505-868-2270
Ute Lake. Fee: 1-505-487-2284

The Upper Pecos

A short hometown break later and I'm on the road again, singing along with Waylon and Willie's "Pancho and Lefty," a road song if ever one were. I follow that with some Gypsy Kings and Los Lobos, feeling fine. I've always liked ranging the mountainous upper Pecos, especially in autumn, when photo ops pop almost anywhere.

The Pecos, the next major New Mexico river south of the Canadian, is festooned with limestone-ringed springs and lakes from its Santa Fe National Forest origins south some 300 miles to Carlsbad and beyond. At Carlsbad, the Pecos' width rivals that of the Rio Grande in some of The Great River's wetter moments.

Santa Rosa

Crossing the Pecos at Santa Rosa, I wonder how much of its water ever sees the Gulf of Mexico after joining the Rio Grande. The Big River empties into the ocean through sand banks that support the Southwestern extremes of a littoral maritime-cowboy subculture singer-writer Jimmy Buffett calls "Gulf and Western."

I know what he means. When the south wind sometimes captures enough Gulf moisture, I smell nostalgic traces of salt air, even up here in the high meadows, imagining strains of "Margaritaville" on the evening breezes. And I'm obsessed with trading my boots for flip-flops.

Oppose that evocative saline odor—estuary seaweed, salt-laden breeze on the incoming tide—with the misery of sinuses crammed with snootsful of juniper and grama grass pollen and I'm done in. Since I was a kid, for me there's been only one cure for the Pollen Blues: a Road Trip to the Ocean.

Of course, from my Northern New Mexico home, that's almost impossible without a bottom-blistering two-day drive, so I settle for the next best thing: large quantities of relatively clean fresh water. Ute Lake, pleasant as it may have been, hasn't done it for me, so I'll try again in Santa Rosa, that watery Pecos-side oasis.

Some know Santa Rosa as that huge dip in I-40 (or old Route 66) between Tucumcari and Cline's Corners. It's more.

Santa Rosa shelters about 3,200 people and at least seven limestone-basin lakes. The former, except for ranchers and public employees, are fed by tourist-related businesses that catered to the late Route 66 trade and continue to nourish both its nostalgic memory and its nemesis, I-40. The small lakes are fed by the Pecos and artesian springs that bubble up through limestone. It's not much of a stretch to imagine these springs in northcentral Florida, except for the marked absence of gators and water snakes. Geckos. Large spiders and voracious cockroaches. Mosquitos. Fire ants. Silverfish. No-seeums.

Despite a tourism drought in the 1980s, Santa Rosa's beneficent waters sprouted a few new chain motels and restaurants. On an earlier visit, I'd noticed those motels, while not as crowded as say, Fort Lauderdale's, were hosting quite a few college students intent on the rites of spring.

Whether or not those youngsters cared, the plastic, art deco face Santa Rosa showed them hid the town's adobe heart, still beating strong and true.

In 1897, early rancher don Celso Baca y Baca built a chapel he named for Santa Rosa de Lima, the first canonized New World saint. The remains of the chapel and Baca's hacienda still stand on Third Street, about a mile from the new Santa Rosa de Lima Church closer to downtown.

The railroad wrought changes here, as it did all over New Mexico, importing 4,000 workers and a smallpox epidemic in 1901. Another major annoyance preoccupied the townsfolk in 1903: the state legislature renamed Guadalupe County, to Leonard Wood County, honoring a Spanish-American War hero. Santa Rosans, having none of it, soon restored the original name.

But for all the arroyo sharks at the motels, history's dry, water's wet, and wet is how to get.

These water babies were intent on the famous local springs and artificial Santa Rosa Lake seven miles north of town to foster their faux-beach illusion.

Back in the present, Santa Rosa Lake wasn't what I had in mind. Back in town, I cruise Main Street a few blocks to Lake Drive and Park Lake, looking for the springs. I find Park Lake, a wonderful free swimming hole with a red sand beach and lifeguards in season. The park includes playground equipment, with a long slide that plunges into the lake. A lone mother and child wearing windbreakers tentatively stroll the beach, but don't brave the water. Nor do I.

Swimming season isn't launched in this lake until the annual Santa Rosa Days and Memorial Day Tournament (translation: ¡fiesta! ¡fiesta!), but that's months away. I leave the peaceful beach to search for Santa Rosa's ace-in-the-hole: the Blue Hole. The 81-foot-deep artesian spring is within sight of Park Lake across a steep-banked stream. The hole's blueness varies with ambient light, but it's clear reef-like limestone rocks are visible at least 30 feet underwater. The bell-shaped, limestone-bordered pool gushes 3,000 gallons a minute, holding a constant temperature in the low 60° F.

Even this time of year, two preschool girls lean over the pool's wall to splash their hands and arms, much to their sitter's dismay. She's torn between scampering to the car for a towel or leaving. Finally, she gathers up the would-be swimmers and makes for the parking lot, as they voice protests. I can't blame them. The lure of the spring must be absolutely irresistible to children. Both Blue Hole and Percha Lake, a few miles out Third Street, are frequented by older children, scuba and skin-divers, which probably includes all the kids in the motels last spring.

Santa Rosa's a ranching center for hard-working folks for miles around. Still, with all its liquid charm, it's lotus-eater land for a few, a recreational aberration on the river not approximated again until Carlsbad. But water lovers better be careful, especially men.

The waters around here are, after all, La Llorona country.

As an awesome apparition shrouded in an ancient legend, the old girl is building quite a cult following in Northern New Mexico.

Fiestas, t-shirts, documentaries, a movie, books: she manifests in more ways daily.

All this buzz for a killer haint akin to a banshee—a wailing wraith —who stalks unwary *borachos* on their way home from *la cantina* too late. She supposedly drowned her own children, and now haunts dark waterways searching in anguish for them. One version of her myth casts her as *La Malinche* (the tongue), the Mesoamerican who translated for the invading Cortéz, and changing her name to Doña Marina, bore him a son, the first in a line of high-ranking Spanish colonial *mestizos*.

People of the Pecos

The continuance of such unions, known as *mestizaje*, the blending of Europeans and American Indians, has much to do with the history of the upper Pecos.

I hope the rest of today's trek from Santa Rosa up the sinuous Pecos might yield a few clues beyond folkways to help explain the essence of the river and its people.

To move up-Pecos, closer to the high peaks the aborigines and my Celtic people prefer for shrines, I backtrack on I-40 west from Santa Rosa, turning south at U.S. 84's Las Vegas exit to I-25, crossing the Pecos at Delia, an old Comanchero village. The river, hardly ever a torrent at this spot, is low, waiting for snowfall. Exposed reddish-orange sand and blue-gray gravel bars along the eroded red banks split the sluggish current, which probably won't rush again until the late spring melt next year. At I-25, I turn south, cross the river again at San José, head north towards ruined Pecos Pueblo, called Cicuyé by the Spanish and Tziquité by the Pecos. Under any name, she is wrinkled mother to many of today's plains-edge towns and the village a few miles upstream that inherited her name.

The river at San José flows a bit higher than downstream, bordered by more fading greenery nearer the mountains. From here, the river's steep banks wind towards the Pecos Wilderness, through canyon pastures and among several Mexican colonial adobe villages, never approaching closer than about a mile to old Pecos Pueblo. I coast to a stop in the Pecos National Monument parking lot and pull out my background material.

Reading 19th century travel accounts about the pueblo, I had earlier crossed a tale of a gargantuan serpent allegedly worshipped there by the now-vanished Pecoseños. Of course, many traditional cultures see water in its riverine form as snake-like, so the tales might be transmuted from earlier Pueblo origin myths. Whatever, the accounts obsess me with the story of a snake the Tewa call Avanyu, but which has many other names. Listen, children. Obviously, there is more to heaven and earth in this fantastic land than is contained in our present philosophies.

The serpent in question is the feathered one, also known in Nahuatal (Aztec) as Quetzalcoátl, a major god in the ruling Moctezumas' Aztec pre-Cortésian pantheon. Worshipped as Lord of the Dawn, inventor of the arts and agriculture, he could be compared to *ki* or *chi*, the life force exalted in kundalini yoga. Aztec scholars and some present-day Indians still debate whether Moctezuma—or the class of Aztec rulers known by that honorific—originated along the Rio Grande and moved south, or was born in the Valley of Mexico and moved north. Signs of Quetzalcoátl here at Pecos would argue well for a Rio Grande-Mexican Valley link, bolstering the theory that New Mexico and Aztlán, the mythical Aztec homeland, are identical.

I've already traced Avanyu's track across Northern New Mexico. Its herringbone pattern writhed into Hispanic folkloric view as *el vivarón*, later proven a dinosaur skeleton imbedded in a red rock sandstone canyon wall near Ghost Ranch in the Chama Valley. At Puyé Cliff Dwellings high above the Rio Grande Valley, the tracks manifested themselves to me as lightning, about which more later. I've encountered Avanyu's petroglyphic tribute pecked into canyon wall tuff at Tsirige Ruins near Los Alamos, in Frijoles Canyon, on boulders at Glorieta Mesa, all over Four Corners Anasazi village ruins, elsewhere. For that matter, the feathered or hooded snake's image was common to the Mississippian and Southeastern mound builders and across Mesoamerica.

Historic record aside, in dealing with an entity as ancient and pervasive as Avanyu, sometimes it's difficult to separate fact from fiction.

The facts: Depending on which historical source I cite, the remnant Pecos Indians numbered from 18 to 30 when they left Cicuyé to join Jémez Pueblo in 1838 after centuries of declining population due to warfare with Plains tribes and more immediate extended sicknesses. Again, depending on the source, the Pecos were Towas with thousands of cousins in Galisteo and San Cristobal pueblos (also now abandoned). Or they were Tewas, related to the Pueblos north of Santa Fe. Considering the centuries Pecos Pueblo served as a major cross-cultural meeting grounds, either version might be true. The migrants left behind many legends, the most haunting of which were a series of snake-related stories told by Hispanos and recorded by various gringo travelers along the Santa Fe Trail.

The old stories claimed an eternal flame, guarded by a giant serpent, burned inside a Pecos kiva. An infant was sacrificed monthly to the snake, which took umbrage when a devoted father fed the snake a goat instead. The offended reptile departed, slithering south towards Galisteo and other Towa pueblos, cutting a deep arroyo as it crawled. Soon after, the pueblo was abandoned.

The tales also told of ancient ceremonial caves up the Pecos River Valley, caverns some have said once ran all the way through the Sangre de Cristos to Nambé Pueblo.

Tracking the serpent legend's scope by employing the exhaustive techniques real hot-shot investigative reporters always use, I'd read a few history books, then punched up some phone numbers.

Wilfred Varela, who works with the U.S. Forest Service at Pecos, said his grandfather, Gavino, recorded a tape before he died in the early '70s at almost 104 years old. *El abuelo* recalled Pecos Valley caves. The old grandfather said the caves open into trans-mountain tunnels through which Nambé people once drove burros to trade with Hispanic settlers in the Pecos Valley.

Anthropologist Dr. Alfonso Ortiz of San Juan Pueblo told a different tale, however.

"The plumed serpent is a universal Pueblo symbol seen as unifying the three cosmic levels: sky, earth and below the earth, where the gods are thought to live," Ortiz said.

"The European colonists were always telling fantastic stories about Indian religion," he said. "There was a great deal of ambivalence about the kivas, probably even some Freudian aspects (to the snake in the kiva legend). They may have used the stories to explain why the Pecos Pueblo population dropped, although we know it was due to diseases and Comanche raids. And the stories also could reflect the Pueblo sense of humor."

That's as in "tell-the-stupid-white-anthropologists-what-they-want-to-hear" humor, not "isn't-a-child-eating-snake-funny?" humor. Obviously, a creature some tribes once believed caused earthquakes wouldn't be sidesplitting to shaky zone residents.

"Every part of a snake's length is close to the earth, and they're very sensitive to any earth vibrations," Ortiz said. "Since they go crazy just before earthquakes, Indian people reversed the direction of causation and said the snakes caused the earthquakes."

What about the upstream Pecos caves?

The caves exist, but were sealed off by the state Game and Fish Department in 1987 at the request of the descendants of Jémez Pueblo's remnant Pecos people, who still use them for ceremonies.

"I hope you won't reveal their location," Ortiz said.

So I won't. A short examination of the European treatment of the Pecos River Valley easily explained his attitude.

The upper valley below the tree line remains intensely green, crammed with aspen, ponderosa, fir and scrub oak, despite our best attempts to trash it. Poisonous mill tailings spill over huge containment areas, yet some campgrounds are open. Snow-caped peaks still dominate the view despite intrusive power lines. Summer cabins and camps crowd the valley floor, but wilderness access is still unblocked.

But what about the energy flow, the sinuous, tenuous connection from the Mother to us breast-feeding human spiritual embryos? The line sometimes symbolized as leading from heart to mouth of a bear, deer or rabbit fetish? Is there still a clear path, a path, as that ethereal old fraud Don Juan Mateus supposedly said, with heart?

I think so.

The ceremonial caves were closed for the same reason Indian people have closed off many ceremonies from snooping outside eyes. Newcomers and sickos were trashing the sacred places, physically, psychologically and spiritually.

I'll not contribute weapons to the assault.

Glorieta Mesa

Not far downstream and across a valley from Pecos Pueblo, in a slight depression on an undulating mesa-top, I once entered a truly lost kingdom. In that netherland, I walked among more than 150 petroglyphs inscribed five millennia or more ago on sandstone outcroppings by Paleo-Indians who may or may not have Anasazi ancestors. Whatever their blood lines, their sites most likely have endured since just after the end of the Ice Age, when leftover glaciers still blanketed nearby mountains and wooly mammoths might have roamed.

Thunderheads were building in the west the May morning a Forest Service ranger and I visited one Glorieta Mesa site in his Blazer. I didn't have to wear a blindfold, but he wasn't too keen on revealing the exact location, since too much traffic around the fragile areas interferes with excavations and site integrity. And the service can't be too careful about the predations of the pot-hunting ghouls, those thieving, pathological *zopilotes* who in future lives will return as buzzards or junkyard dogs.

After we bumped a half-hour along a dirt road through piñon-juniper stands, the ranger pointed out a site. It lay on a broad, gentle slope in an evergreen clump for some reason thicker than those surrounding it, but otherwise revealed no clue to its location.

Since the petroglyphs at both sites were pecked into horizontal outcroppings, they're hard to spot from even 20 feet away, which may explain why they've survived so long without suffering some sort of vandalism.

I photographed a series of zigzag lines (a river? lightning? Avanyu's reptilian ancestor?), concentric circles (migration records, infinity signs?), flowerlike patterns, one of which I could swear was a turtle, and hatch marks (ribs? clan sizes? calendars?) and we descended from the mount, pursued by thunder. I should have listened to the rumblings.

Later that afternoon, I realized I still had the blue corn meal offering I'd intended to sprinkle to help re-sanctify the site, sort of an apology to the spirit guardians for disturbing their slumber. But by the time I reached the mesa road again, heavy rain was pummeling and lightning streaked. Monsoon rains make mesa roads impassable by any vehicle but a four-by, and even then, the going can be tricky. I was denied access by a higher authority than the U.S.F.S.

A suggestion: the Forest Service could alleviate future volunteers' fears about too much rain or seemingly random lightning strikes by advising the use of corn meal, to be applied clockwise, liberally and with respect.

San Miguel

To follow one thread of Pecos Pueblo's diaspora, I hop back on I-25 and off again at Ribera, where I angle south onto State Road 3, the Highway to Heaven.

I call it that for two reasons: the churches at San Miguel and Villanueva and the chance that the narrow, winding riverside road may speed drivers along an eternal journey.

The churches may be dedicated to God, but the road is the Devil's.

Yet initial descent into the valley's rusty rouge valleys at Ribera seems nothing like dropping into the Valley of the Shadow. On the left, the Pecos rushes south through skeletal cottonwood and willow bosques, dormant orchards and pastures already sown in green winter rye.

Winding through the agricultural valley along the river, I pass standing farm implements old and new and homes of native red rock and adobe.

I trace in reverse the route of several conquistadores, some authorized by the Spanish government in Mexico City, some not. Long before any of Pecos villages except perhaps Pueblo, were founded, Francisco Vasquez Coronado, Antonio de Espejo, Castaño de Sosa and others tracked the Pecos north and west to Pecos Pueblo, gateway to the Great Plains or Rio Grande Valley, depending on your inclination.

For my personal Pecos Valley *entrada*, I bump over the rails at Ribera, founded by a Santa Fe family who also helped settle San Miguel del Bado (St. Michael of the ford), a national historic district today.

San Miguel, first occupied in 1794 by colonial Hispanos and by Pecos and other Indians cast out of their tribes because they converted to Christianity, was New Mexico's port of entry during Mexican rule.

Lorenzo Marquez, a Santa Fe resident, and 51 other men first claimed the land. Thirteen of the settlers were *genízaros*, a class of culturally displaced Indian men, women and children who had been captured by raiding Comanches, Apaches, Utes or Navajos. At regular trade fairs, genízaros were ransomed by New Mexicans and "Christianized." During a lifetime of indentured servitude they lost both their language and traditional culture. Others tagged genízaro included a few Christianized Pecoseños who had left their crumbling pueblo and any formerly nomadic Apaches and Comanches who settled along the Pecos and intermarried with the Hispano colonists.

San Miguel's settlers had no doubts as to their identities. They maintained they had founded a genízaro village, possibly because, just as friendly Teutonic and Celtic tribes once fought for the Romans, the feisty borderland genízaros were popular military auxiliaries. As invaluable outlying buffers against Plains tribes, genízaro settlements could wring concessions from church and state.

Genízaro status under New Mexico's simplified version of the complicated central New Spain *casta* (caste) system carried a certain social stigma. But it also meant you were part of the militia warrior class, entitled to war spoils, able to gain land and status. Within three generations a former genízaro's descendant could "pass" into dominant Hispanic (ie; mostly mestizo) society.

A snow-decked cross marks a dirt road out of the Pecos River's canyon east of Puerto de Luna.

The term genízaro, in some circles not one of endearment, officially vanished after Mexican Independence, but dropped from popular usage only a couple of generations ago. But the genízaro village legacy remains.

Some historians contend San Miguel's founding was the beginning of the end for Pecos Pueblo, a few miles upstream. That may be so, but the *molino* of historic irony grinds exceedingly fine. In 1835, a group of San Miguel residents struck out north to found Las Vegas Grandes de Nuestra Señora de los Dolores, today's Las Vegas, N.M. The new town eventually replaced its parent as the most important Santa Fe Trail stop, and San Miguel slid into the river's backwash.

San Miguel Church was completed in 1806 by parish Indians. Its floor covers coffins of wealthier villagers and the first resident priest. I snap a few pictures of the still-used sanctuary, recording its whitewashed walls and simple lines, but don't enter.

Some foolhardy Texans were imprisoned here when they invaded New Mexico in 1847, the same year as the Taos Revolt. Maybe the Texans' bellicosity partly explains the "gringos beware" graffiti on the red roadside rocks that appears periodically, south near Sena and at nearby I-25 rest stops. Or maybe it's due to the frustration river villagers feel at the continuing encroachment of rich outsiders buying up San Miguel County land.

Villanueva

Seemingly isolated from the development juggernaut, at least in the mid-'90s, Villanueva, nine miles south of San Miguel, guards the Pecos Valley from the hilltop that prompted its original settlers to name it Cuesta (slope) in 1808.

The village's Territorial tin roofs blaze like fires in the sun signalling to me, perched high on the windy heights of an overlooking hill. The whitewashed stone church in the village center boasts a wall tapestry hundreds of feet long. Much like the Plains Indians used "winter count" buffalo hides as a chronology to depict significant annual tribal events, the tapestry, woven over the years by village women, depicts Villanueva's history.

Like the tapestry, Villanueva is a slowly growing concern. Fresh adobe bricks are stacked by older, crumbling walls. A small concrete mixer here, some boards there, indicated projects in progress. Although residents don't welcome outside developers, they intend to make sure the town doesn't suffer San Miguel's fate. On the other hand, the villagers decided some time ago not to publish information about their pueblo.

"We just don't want tourists all over the place," a friendly woman who counts me as a local says at one of the village's two general stores.

With that, I get lost.

Las Vegas

But not far. Lazy autumn weather tempts me into a walk around my hometown, Las Vegas, the village that displaced San Miguel. Vegas is a study in contrasts. It still bustles around its adobe Old Town Plaza, while a more recent urban center across the Gallinas River is crammed with Northern New Mexico's own splendid examples of turn-of-the-century architecture. Some are restored, some languish in stone decay; most resemble frosted gingerbread fantasies, thanks to the architectural influences of Midwestern railroad moguls and nearby Fort Union.

Vegas's widespread Victoriana seems incongruous with the many old adobe buildings, but somehow it all works.

The town's dramatic ambience projects from its unique historic cast. Apaches, Utes and Comanches, not Pueblos, claimed the rolling vegas, the western expanses of the Great Plains and the sheltering canyons that devour the Plains. Sheep-herding Mexican colonists, Comancheros and desperados who avoided the capital city looked to Las Vegas for trade and diversion. Mexican and Anglo merchants alike benefited from the village's fortuitous Santa Fe Trail location and from the railroad that plowed through instead of bypassing, as it did Santa Fe.

The resultant cultural mix is more working class and ultimately, more "real" than that of La Ciudad Real, Santa Fe, which suffers at the end of this millennium from what may prove to be a terminal case of social class inequities. In Vegas at the bawling, brawling turn of the previous century, the mix resulted in such highlights as the state's first building wired for electricity and first Harvey House hotel, and some of the country's best-known fighters, the core troopers of Teddy Roosevelt's Rough Riders.

Although earlier settlement attempts along the upper Gallinas River were frustrated by Plains Indian raids, the Las Vegas laid out around their fortified plaza by San Miguel men was much like any other frontier Mexican town of the day. So it remained until 1846, when Gen. Stephen Watts Kearny mounted cannons on the hill now occupied by Highlands University and informed the Mexican citizens they now were Americans, like it or not. Las Vegans shrugged, adjusted their sombreros, and kept providing services for the thousands of merchants and settlers southbound on the dusty Santa Fe Trail and not much changed, except the plaza's rim grew stores instead of homes. But things did change in 1879, when the railroad barons roared in on the Atchison, Topeka and Santa Fe.

Or almost into town. After an overconfident West Las Vegas merchant asked too much money for a lot, the railroaders laid their tracks a mile east of what then became known as Old Town Plaza in the Town of West Las Vegas, and the City of East Las Vegas (or Las Vegas) was born. The two municipalities remained separated by law and differing Hispano and Anglo social customs until 1970 and are by no means socially integrated today.

Playing out the Western boom-or-bust scenario, the railroad tycoons imported their Out East values, scorning local adobe architecture, building instead native stone edifices in styles ranging from Richardson Romanesque, Romanesque Territorial and Queen Anne to Eastlake, Italian Villa, Italianate and Folk Renaissance Revival.

The twin towns slumped after most railroad traffic moved south in 1905, and a local agricultural depression in the Twenties, the Great Depression and the Dust Bowl exacted their tolls.

But more than 70 years of (sometimes benign) neglect actually seems to have benefited Vegas in the long run.

In 1976, Las Vegans adopted an Historic District Ordinance. By 1986, the National Register of Historic Places listed more than 920 buildings here and the town boasted five designated historic districts, including the Plaza and Bridge Street in Old Town and Douglas Avenue, Sixth Street and Railroad Avenue in New Town.

I continue my walk through all this history, because there's nothing so rare as an autumn morning in adamantly non-Santa-Feish Vegas.

If Santa Fe's the City Different, Vegas is the City Indifferent. Not that Vegas is stuck in a time warp, but the Fifties were one of my favorite decades, and I like it here.

I love to approach Old Town Plaza on South Pacific Avenue, passing blocks of low, pastel-painted, flat-roofed adobe homes, joined in the old placita style.

South Pacific, after curving a bit, crosses Moreno, then jogs into the Plaza's southeast corner. Bandito Vicente Silva once lived in the low, stone-faced structure at the corner of South Pacific and Moreno, a building that ironically later housed law offices.

I circle the plaza slowly, shuffling through a few early fallen leaves, then exit down Bridge Street, window shopping the antique stores for nothing in particular. At the corner of the Plaza and Gonzales stands a building in which Silva ran a bar, connected, legend says, by a tunnel to his Moreno Street home. The bar is now the West Las Vegas Schools Administration Building, often substituting for a bank in movies shot here.

If I'm lucky, musicians perched on benches will be picking and strumming acoustic licks out front of the Bridge Street Coffee House, practicing for the upcoming Wildflower Festival and drinking Peter Lamont's good coffee.

No luck, so I walk over to Bennie Gallegos' Ranch Museum.

Gallegos is next door at a house across the arroyo, but shows up as soon as he sees me in front of his place's wooden stockade gate.

Gallegos is a busy man. Sometimes he works on his three acres of ranching memorabilia, mostly wagons, or strums his guitar in the cabin he built on the grounds.

Sometimes he recalls his grandfather, a *pistolero* who guarded world heavyweight champion Jack Johnson when he fought here in 1912. But today he talks about his days as an antique dealer.

"I dealt in real old *santos*," he recounts. "Most of them were by Ben Ortega of Mora, who made at least 800. Almost all of those were for the *moradas*."

So how did Gallegos get his hands on sacred works from the closely guarded altars and nichos of Los Hermanos de la Luz, the Penitentes?

"In the '60s, they were stealing them from the moradas," he says. "My dad was a honcho at one of the moradas and he convinced the brothers to sell all their santos to me. In return, I plastered the morada and replaced their santos with new ones.

"It was a good thing, too. A month later, they broke the door and got into that morada. But since the santos were new, they left them all where they were."

That's the kind of *cuento* (story) I hear in my hometown if I take the time to walk around a bit and listen. I should do more walking, but with afternoons and mornings cooling, it's time to visit my birdwatching spot to see if any annual migrators are yet winging south.

That evening, I return to Las Vegas National Wildlife Refuge. I sit quietly, watching Lake McAllister's chop, listening to the stiffening breeze rattle the dying rushes.

Suddenly, a distant disturbance erupts from the fading light. GARRRONKKK! GARONK! WHIRRRR!

The sandhill cranes are back!

In northeastern New Mexico and along the Rio Grande, we don't need balloon fiesta mobs or the state fair to tell us autumn's arrived. The cranes do that.

Cranes have signaled seasonal change to me since that early autumn afternoon 10 years ago when I stumbled around the crumbled adobes of Tsirige, a pueblo ruin near Los Alamos. Its name means "bird people place," which I attributed to its altitude on the Pajarito (Little Bird) Plateau. Then I heard aerial gronking, and looked up to see wave after wave of cranes flapping south down the Rio Grande Corridor, following the sun as I so love to do.

Later, sidetripping to McAllister, a state Game and Fish Department fishing hole in the middle of the refuge, I'd been startled by a hoarse croaking, like crows gargling. I climbed a gate and peered deep into the drying fields past a fallen, gray, cottonwood husk, but saw no animals.

I should have remembered the cranes.

I always hear them before I see them. Squinting, I pick out a bird or two in close formation, necks extended, skimming along low like miniature stealth bombers. Soon, line upon line undulates by, from bog to pond to lake, clogging the fading turquoise skies with their curiously trilling calls.

(By the way, Peterson's *Field Guide to Western Birds* characterizes their cries as "garoooo-a-a-a, repeated. Also tuk-tuk—tuk-tuk—tuk-tuk," but that's what you get when you let scientists write prose.)

It's hard to beat the refuge for birdwatching and solitude.

On the Central Flyway, it's less crowded than Bosque del Apache in crane season.

The refuge, 8,750 acres of rolling native grassland, cropland, marshes, ponds, timbered canyons and streams, provides habitat for birds ranging from long-billed curlews and herring gulls to rough-legged hawks, herons and 21 duck species. The U.S. Fish and Wildlife Service plants wheat, barley, corn and peas for wildlife food and cover.

The refuge's avian watering spots fill through irrigation ditches from Storrie Lake, the area's primary reservoir, about 15 miles northeast.

Storrie, a favorite windsurfer haunt, is fed by eastern Sangre de Cristo runoff via the Gallinas, which feeds the Pecos.

Soon, north winds will scatter the leaves from the cottonwood grove at McAllister's south end, and the late-departing summer and early autumn residents—blue-winged and cinnamon teal, spotted sandpipers— will pack it up and ship south, to be replaced by more cold-resistant species. These include Canada and snow geese, and I hope, the seven bald eagles I spotted when the lake was iced over last winter.

Star Hill Inn

Birding is equally enchanting at Star Hill Inn, but the inn's specialty is celestial observation. Hidden in a canyon about seven miles northwest of Vegas on County Road A3, a couple of miles west of State Road 518, Star Hill's surrounding mountains block off city lights. Since I'm a sucker for celestial beams, my younger daughter and I paid an afternoon reconnaissance visit last year.

Speaking of beams and diminishing light, there must be some kind of light-related depression that affects me when I want to see stars at night but can't.

Can't be the vampire in me, since I don't even eat steaks rare or otherwise.

I left humid Florida a couple of times because the only way to see the stars down in the mist-blanketed swamps was to the accompaniment of a tap-dancing mosquito chorus or in some airless college planetarium.

But I've found the heavens in New Mexico, bless its relatively clean and bugless atmosphere (especially before and after the windy season). Pristine star-ogling here is easy if you can find some way to block the growing intensity of city lights.

A few years ago, two Las Vegans, Phil and Blair Mahon, figured that out, and now have stargazing down to an art, as well as a science.

Phil, a former Methodist minister who's peered through telescopes since he was 12, was encouraged to launch Star Hill Inn due to favorable responses to astronomy seminars he teaches at Ghost Ranch Presbyterian Center.

Careful marketers, the Mahons rehearsed their star-conductor roles while Phil worked for years at a title insurance company. They became gatekeepers to the heavens in 1988 when they built and moved to Star Hill, which they call "an astronomer's retreat in the Rockies."

Star Hill Inn co-owner Blair Mahon and young visitor.

Hugging 200 acres at the edge of the Pecos Wilderness, Star Hill includes nine isolated, Southwestern-appointed cabins and an observation deck dedicated to star-lovers.

The cottages lie along a piney woods valley at 7,200 feet in the Sangre de Cristos, where ridges block light leakage from Las Vegas, the nearest source.

While Blair and my daughter rested outside a cabin, typically outfitted with a kitchen and sun-proof window shades for daytime sleeping and to prevent night light leaks, I strolled the grounds, past an elevated wooden deck that supports the Mahons' telescopes. Next door is a woodstove-heated, constellation-chart-decorated library, used as a warm-up room during the always chilly all-night stargazing sessions. This, obviously (to a parent), is a warm, sheltered spot for kids to watch videos while mom and dad stare heavenward outdoors.

Just how dark is Star Hill?

Astronomers measure star brightness on an inverse scale of "magnitudes." For instance, the magnitude of Venus, often the brightest object (other than the moon) at night, would measure minus one or minus two. The dimmest object's magnitude could be as low as 10.

While magnitude perception varies from person to person, the skies over Star Hill consistently allow viewing of stars in the eight to 10 range.

Fortress Villages

Next day, I visit a few more Pecos villages, first slipping through passes on I-25 where 19th century builders quarried tons of native rock.

The railroaders who made a killing in Las Vegas after 1879 are long gone, leaving behind little but urban monuments in stone, this stone.

The flashy Easterners may have thought themselves stylistically unique in the land of adobe, but they nevertheless built with materials American Indians and Spanish colonists had used for centuries.

Areas where the rail barons quarried their light brown, purplish- and reddish-brown sandstone are visible near I-25 between Tecolote and Romeroville, south of Las Vegas on the Old Santa Fe Trail.

Earlier native stone works—rock ruins, homes and outbuildings— also are obvious over much of the Pecos drainage.

Throughout much early New Mexico history, Apaches and Comanches raided the eastern frontier, taking slaves and making colonization impossible. But by the early 1800s, Spanish colonials had inched fortified villages down the Pecos Valley, partially to stabilize de-tribalized and otherwise dispossessed Indians.

Plains genízaros used their rock-working abilities when they settled along the sweeping bends of the Pecos at Upper and Lower Anton Chico and Tecolotito. Poised like bluff-top riverside fortresses, the villages cluster together protectively behind high native rock walls and heavy carved wooden doors. Once guardians of New Mexico's easternmost gate to the plains, they also were centers for the always risky, but profitable Comanchero trade.

Today I pull off I-25 to roam a typical Pecos River canyon a few miles upstream from Anton Chico.

The sheltered canyon bottom at Villanueva State Park, near the village of the same name, offers a respite from the autumn winds. Soaking up sun like a rock lizard, I ponder whether I should traverse New Mexico's entire Pecos Valley before I determine its dominant icon.

Pecos might be trickier to tag than it seems, what with the bad luck Pecos Pueblo suffered, and the nasty tailings spills near the sacred caves. Is the Pecos paying some sort of karmic debt reserved only for cursed regions considered national sacrifice areas?

The warmth eventually fades and I pack up my wagon again to head south, following the sun to New Mexico's middle and lower Pecos Valley. But first, I build a small shrine to the beleaguered river, piling up a few rocks in a certain manner and sprinkling them with cornmeal. Some might consider my efforts at evoking pantheistic powers a waste of time, but I figure that, plagued by mine poison upstream and dairy manure runoff and other waste downstream, the Pecos needs all the help it can get.

⟹ Information
Santa Rosa, San Miguel County, N.M.: 1-505-472-3763
Las Vegas, N.M.: 1-505-425-8631
Star Hill, Sapelló, N.M.: Fee. 1-505-425-5605
Villanueva State Park: Fee. 1-505-421-2957

The Rio Bonito

All the way south to White Oaks, the Lincoln County almost-ghost town, I think about The Kid.

That's as in Billy the, or for that matter, as his Hispanic friends called him, El Chivato (young he-goat). That's also as in William H. Bonney, also known as Henry McCarty, a.k.a. Henry Antrim, a.k.a. *¿quien saben?* Who knows, who indeed?

Given Billy's legendary stature, other loose translations of chivato come to mind: maybe Pan or Cornnubus, the Celtic Dark Horned God of the Animals.

Whatever the armed and booted antihero's name, Billy seems to have shot his way into the North American mythos, the Pantheon of Punks.

The hapless Kid may not have been born with a silver spoon, but he must have been weaned by a press agent. All the hokey legends about him would stretch from here to New York, where he may or may not have been born. Billy has busied a century of writers recreating his short life. His reincorporated ghost stalks through scholarly and pulp books, magazine articles, short stories and movies, even a ballet.

Despite the legends, some documented facts can flesh out the skeleton of what's known of his late-19th century life.

Was he responsible for all the deaths attributed to him? Not likely. And did Pat Garrett kill him at Pedro Maxwell's hacienda near Fort Sumner that hot summer night in 1881? I hope not, but we may never know.

In other words, Billy's spirit, inspiration for folklore, was far stronger than his physical aspects: slight body, quick mind and willing trigger finger, none of which in the end could save him.

Far be it from me to glorify outlawry when our culture already is riddled by many of the problems also common to The Kid's time: alcoholism, braggadocio, gunplay, gang thuggery.

But in a time in which the Santa Fe Ring ruled everything and almost everybody was crooked as a scrub oak staff, The Kid may not have been as bent as some.

White Oaks

Puzzling over New Mexico's endless contradictions, I rattle into White Oaks from the north, via the scenic dirt road through the Cibola National Forest and the former Jicarilla Reservation. The village, home to 2,000 people during its golden days, is sparsely preserved. Surviving buildings molder around the long-dead town center. Two notables are a large, intact school house and the Exchange Bank, with a second-story office once occupied by W.C. McDonald, later New Mexico's first state governor.

Recent frame upscale homes dot the surrounding foothills and valley, but as of the mid-1990s, I'd never call it a renaissance.

Founded around 1880 on land stolen from the Jicarillas, White Oaks boomed when Texas desperado John Wilson found gold atop Baxter Mountain, west of the town-to-be. He sold his claims immediately to his two partners, who developed the North and South Homestake mines. The two mines, plus the Old Abe and others produced more than $3 million in their day.

Townsfolk, as memorialized in Morris B. Parker's *White Oaks* may have been industrious and honest, but greed got in their way.

In 1898, townies refused to donate a right-of-way to the El Paso and Northeastern Railroad, pricing town land so high the rails bypassed them. Carrizozo, which since has survived a radioactive dusting from the first A-bomb, was built as a railroad town 12 miles southwest. Fatally wounded by 1900, White Oaks declined with its mines, the post office closing in 1950.

The White Oaks story includes another historical twist: Its honest citizens once tried unsuccessfully to capture Billy the Kid.

In November 1881, hearing Billy was 20 miles north at a roadhouse and stolen-horse processing joint run by "Whiskey Jim" Greathouse, the citizens posseed up to flush out The Kid. In the ensuing error-ridden fracas, a deputy was killed by mistake and The Kid escaped the joint, and for a short time, his fate. Of course, the killing was credited to his already inflated account.

Greathouse later skidaddled to the Gila, and later in the San Mateo Mountains, was shotgunned by a rancher unhappy with Ol' Jim's cattle rustling.

I stop, shoot up the town's few buildings with my camera, then look for a place to drink. Diet.

A small bar advertising itself as a museum stands alone on a deserted lot. A sign warns: "NO SCUM." They don't have diet, the barmaid tells me, without smiling. I scratch the ears of the bar's gray resident cat. The only customers, two Hell's Angels and a pock-faced old-timer straight out of *Treasure of the Sierra Madre,* converse loudly.

The punks are young, leather-vested, tattooed, and like chains. A lot. They are just about Billy's age when things got rough for him and he first killed somebody. If he subscribed to the day's conventional wis-

A serious bar in White Oaks, with the abandoned schoolhouse in the background.

dom, Billy probably thought his victim "needed" it. The punks seem right at home. I do not, and still thirsty, split to visit the heart of The Kid's legend, Lincoln Town, Lincoln County.

Lincoln
Rolling down to Lincoln Town strip, I detour on State Road 214 to Fort Stanton, once a remote U.S. Army outpost. As the highway drops off a rolling plateau into the Rio Bonito's cottonwood-choked valley, I recalled a few facts I'd read in researching Lincoln.

In The Kid's day, the feds at Fort Union contracted crooked suppliers to provide meat for the Mescaleros.

Captured earlier by Confederates, the fort was recovered for the Union and commanded by Col. Kit Carson during the early Apache Wars, after which it was the surrender site for 500 Mescaleros. Its troops were called out several times to "keep the peace" during the Lincoln County War, once to preside over the destruction of Alexander McSween, the Scots merchant-lawyer who dared challenge the authority of the area's leading mercantile house, run by former Fort Stanton soldiers.

In later Indian wars, the fort housed black Indian-fighting troopers known to New Mexicans as "Buffalo Soldiers." Gov. Lew (*Ben-Hur*) Wallace combined a visit to the fort with a trip to Lincoln Town where he and Billy the Kid forged a truce the governor later broke.

Gen. (then-Lt.) John J. Pershing practiced posting while posted at the fort early in his career.

The fort later served as a World War II German internment camp, but it dozed away the postwar years as a state mental hospital. Today the fort, a restored series of 60 or so whitewashed buildings set in an open, shaded campus-like atmosphere, looks, well, institutional.

The contrast between the dead and the quick at Fort Stanton parallel Lincoln County's history.

Near the fort, on a quiet brown hill overlooking the Rio Bonito, rotting white wooden crosses mark the graves of hundreds of merchant marine tuberculosis victims who once lived and died here.

I steal away from Fort Stanton's sad solitude, slipping away to Lincoln, about 15 miles southeast.

Nowhere in New Mexico other than Santa Fe is so much concentrated history so well-packaged and coherently presented as in Lincoln, which its promoters, playing off the tiny town's violent and well-known history, tag "America's Most Dangerous Street." That would be paved U.S. 380, and it's still dangerous if you don't heed the sometimes-heavy traffic that whizzes by. One national travel writer called Lincoln a "uniquely American totem," a mine of "historical McNuggets." Lincoln is to Billy what Graceland is to Elvis, just not as gaudy.

The village does enjoy a mini-Williamsburg, Va., living-history aspect. Employees of the various interpretive sites often appear in period costume.

Restorations include the old, two-story Lincoln County Courthouse, now a state museum, just down the street from general stores owned by two warriors in the Lincoln County Unpleasantness. Across the street, the one-story Wortley Hotel, restored by the Lincoln

An old wagon frames San Juan church in Lincoln Town.

County Heritage Trust on the site of the burned original, functions seasonally as a restaurant and eight-room hotel as it has since it headquartered the Murphy/Dolan forces during The War. The San Juan Mission anchors the town's middle, in what must have been the old plaza. Across the highway stands the circular stone and adobe *torreón*, a defensive tower used by Hispanic settlers to escape Indian attacks, and occupied by Bad Guy sharpshooters during a crucial battle in The War.

The well-kept Territorial and Mexican Colonial buildings emanate a stage-like atmosphere so evocative I walk through a hole in time with but a slight reality shift. That or I've happened upon a very convincing Western movie set.

Not as convincing is the old Lincoln Days Pageant set at the western edge of town. There, the first weekend in August, local volunteers dramatize the bloody events of those anarchistic late 19th-century days.

Caprock Amphitheatre

I missed the Lincoln production, but last summer, I had watched a more elaborate version of the Kid's tale at an outdoor drama at Caprock Amphitheatre, 11 miles south of San Jon.

The amphitheatre is dramatically perched on the high, chalk gray Caprock cliffs, out where the Canadian River Valley's floor smacks into the high caliche.

During the prelude, the audience enjoyed the advance of dark thunderheads from the west, where the sky faded to pearly gray, stitched by yellow-white lightning.

Menacing weather and rainouts were no novelty to the cast and crew, which, depending on what script's in favor that year, stages various versions of a Billy production summer weekends.

Undaunted by thunder, the audience, lulled by a just-completed barbecue-and-beans repast, patiently waited as formidable unseen speakers boomed the theme, locally written "Twilight on the Conchas."

In the gloaming, stealthy swallows, their hungry chirps a staccato accompaniment to the thunder's timpani, chased unseen insects.

Lightning flashed as spotlights illuminated two flag-toting, on-stage horse women who led "God Bless America" and "Oh, Fair New Mexico," our state song.

The young women and horses disappeared and stage lights came up, illuminating Billy the Kid and his unlucky friend Tom O'Folliard, both played by New Mexico drama students. Along the way, the audience met the historic personages of Gov. Lew Wallace, Pat Garrett, Mrs. Susan McSween, the Cattle Queen, and many other long-enduring memories of the real-life Lincoln County conflict.

Young Billy, whose "spirit" rides away on a white horse at drama's end, waited at the theater exit to sign autographs, as did all the characters, to the audience's delight, especially my younger daughter's.

Despite the actors' best efforts, the Caprock, geologically interesting as perhaps the world's largest expanse of flat land defined on several sides by high escarpments, is no destination attraction.

Still, local drama enthusiasts plunge on. There is, after all, that lonesome, magnificent $2.5 million amphitheatre to fill and all that potential business in Amarillo.

Besides, it would be a pity to let down the fans who convinced Quay County Commissioners to wrangle 80 acres of former U.S. Bureau of Land Management land for the New Mexico Outdoor Drama Association. The association's members ramrodded a fund-raising drive, twisted a few legislative arms, turned up some state Parks and Recreation Department funds and completed the beauty in 1985, also the first production season.

I'd like to see the state promote its outdoor dramas more. If we don't, the stunning Caprock Amphitheatre is going to fall back into the caliche from which it sprang.

Billy Theory 101

Despite various dramatic interpretations and historians' emphases on cattle and mercantile theories, there's another, more recent and radically revisionist hypothesis of the Lincoln County War that supersedes earlier assumptions: the Celtic Perpetual Western Migration Theory.

Stay with me here, saddle pals; this twisting trail does lead somewhere.

Celtic-language speakers arrived in Ireland-to-be in separate migrations from the east between 1,000 and 500 B.C. Descended at least partly from neolithic Syths, they were dark-eyed equestrian nomads who swept out of Central Eurasia centuries before the Huns. Syths scalped enemies, impaling their heads on stakes. Driving their cattle ahead and trailing their women and children behind, the aggressive Syths migrated ever westward, a thrust continued by their distant descendants, who helped shape the United States.

The Irish Celts, still bent on subjugating their known world, colonized Wales, England and Scotland.

Ancient Irish tales, notably the Tain Bo Cuailnge, recount how Queen Maeve of Connact raided Ulster, both now in Northern Ireland. Her goal was to rustle a prized brown bull.

Obviously, the traditions of rustling cattle, building sprawling empires and killing anybody who interfered enjoyed a long success among some of Lincoln's English-speaking peoples and their ancestors.

The dancers in the deadly Lincoln *baile* simply were waltzing through an ethnic lockstep, a hopeless *dejá vu* written into their genetic dance cards eons ago.

Think about it: the Irish again squaring off against the Brits and Scots in the same old insular *danse de morte*, with the Irish renegade Henry McCarty-Antrim, a.k.a. Bonney, scoring lead- punctuated music for the Anglo-Saxon cause.

Why did he desert his Irish heritage to take a rebel stand with the Brits and Scots?

Maybe Billy, a closet Romantic, didn't like the odds against Tunstall and McSween. Maybe it was too hard to tell the dancers from the dance. The Kid didn't have many choices; the best might have been hightailing it to Mexico, but nobody really thinks the Billy the Kid Trail, official or otherwise, leads there.

I know where it does lead, however, and as I walk along the rushing Rio Bonito near Lincoln, I ponder whether El Chivato was enlightened for his day or simply another sacrifice to times that were rough and causes that were lost.

Rio Hondo

Reluctantly leaving Billy's ghost behind, I mount up and ride out of Lincoln to the Hondo Valley.

Fruit orchards and manicured horse farms dominate the bottomlands, still green in November. The horse culture, as it did in Billy the Kid's day, defines the Bonito, Ruidoso and Hondo valleys and that means plenty of pasture and shade.

The evidence is everywhere: the race track and the Museum of the Horse at Ruidoso Downs, the lush, full-sized polo field native son Peter Hurd installed in front of his estate at San Patricio, the hand-lettered "horseback rides" signs and saddled mounts waiting by the road for wannabe cowboys. The area no longer is one of New Mexico's best-kept secrets. Even Sam Donaldson, ABC newscaster and like Hurd, a New Mexico Military Institute grad, owns a sheep ranch in Lincoln County, they say.

The most affluent family to settle among the giant cottonwoods along the Hondo, however, may be the Andersons. Robert O. Anderson, a University of Chicago graduate for whom the University of New Mexico's Anderson School of Management is named, made his bundle in petroleum. Part wildcatter, part businessman, he soon owned Hondo Oil, which he later sold to Atlantic Oil. As its board chairman, he built Atlantic into a conglomerate that devoured Sinclair and Richfield Oil and Andaconda Copper to form ARCO, which discovered oil on Alaska's North Slope.

Anderson has shared his good fortune with New Mexico. He directed the University of Chicago-associated Aspen Institute, served as trustee for numerous universities and hospitals, supported the Santa Fe Opera and generally has been most generous to the state. At one time Anderson owned several widely dispersed ranches managed under his Diamond A brand, plus game-hunting ranches, one in the Hondo Valley.

I had an ephemeral tie with the Anderson home at Tinnie: I lived for a year in its blueprint predecessor, half the state away.

One clear, cool, blossomed morning last spring, I breezed down a long, winding paved driveway, past brimming irrigation ditches and through fragrant apple orchards to the rambling Anderson home, an American castle.

I'd gained entry after prying directions from an unhappy cowboy I met at the estate's barbed wire fence by the highway. With his scowl, he sported a black hat and the obligatory striped Brush Popper shirt, Southern New Mexico style.

I knew the history of old Baca house where I lived and had heard about the Anderson's version on the Hondo. The cowboy didn't want to hear it, but went away apparently satisfied I was harmless. I scooted up the road and down the Anderson's long drive, dying to see the place just to compare the two.

Several decades ago, the Baca "mansion," a three-story adobe built by don José Albino Baca between 1850 and 1855 at Uppertown, Las

Vegas, was crumbling to earth. Treasure hunters who believed the Bacas had hidden gold on the property had applied pickaxe and wrecking bar to fireplace and floors. The old place was so neglected, almost anybody in Las Vegas born after 1940 can tell stories of wild parties in the deserted mansion's patio.

Enter Les Bottorph, rancher, horse trader, antiques collector and federal retiree. In the early 1960s he located the last known Baca heir, an elderly matron living in Albuquerque, arranging for La Dueña to visit the decaying estate. Soon afterwards, protesting she wouldn't have done business with any newcomer gringos, she sold Bottorph the home and several acres of thick *bosque* fronting the Gallinas River.

At about that time, Robert O. Anderson, looking for a proper home, also tried to buy the Baca place, but the most he could obtain from the old lady was a set of blueprints. Using those, Anderson built an embellished version at Tinnie. His three-story, U-shaped mansion is similar to, but much larger than the original Baca house.

Bottorph lovingly restored the original home as best he could and occupied it with his wife and family for many years.

I lived with the Baca casa's ghosts for a year in the early 1990s while the family tried to sell the place. By then, Bottorph was in his mid-80s and the house he had revived was sagging once more.

Meanwhile, down on the Hondo, consumed by curiosity, I entered the Anderson's compound. I drank in the sweeping expanse of perfectly trimmed lawn, the latticed gazebo by the acequia, the gargantuan o'erreaching cottonwoods, the panoply of bordering pansies and irises. The dark, cold Baca house had become but an aged imitation of the gracious, rambling dwelling that once had imitated it.

I didn't want to leave the grounds. I, too, deserved to live in the Anderson compound. Now, if somebody would just suggest that to the Andersons....

As no offer seemed forthcoming, I buzzed back to the highway and reminders of the less genteel life.

A few miles toward Ruidoso on the left, a state historic marker points out the site of the murder of the young Englishman, John Tunstall, Billy's friend.

On my right, six miles east of Ruidoso is Fox Cave, once known as Ice Cave, a souvenir shop in a large natural cavern prehistorically and historically frequented by Indians, white settlers, cowboys and, of course, Billy the Kid.

Mescalero Apache Reservation boundary near the site of a proposed nuclear waste storage unit on the reservation's western side.

Mescalero Apache Reservation

All this Lincoln County action, past and present, transpires under the soaring 12,003-foot peak and wilderness-circled massif of a long-extinct volcano invading Texans called White Mountain and Mexicans call Sierra Blanca. Of course, Texans also call Ruidoso (noisy) RIO-doso (Doso River), so I'll go for Sierra Blanca.

The Athapascan (Na Dene) Mescaleros ruled New Mexico's Northern, Central and Southern Plains and Southeastern Desert for decades, until raiding Comanches swooped in. Today, the Mescalero occupy 461,000 scenic acres of range and forests. Their homes for the most part are off main highways, far from prying eyes.

Despite the U.S. government's history of broken promises to Indians, the tenacious Mescalero in 1922 finally received title to their breathtakingly beautiful mountain reservation east and south of Ruidoso.

Here, the tribe joined New Mexico's tourism industry with the elegant, lakeside Inn of the Mountain Gods and Ski Apache atop towering, snowy Sierra Blanca. They also host the public at their rodeo grounds around July 4, when they conduct ceremonies welcoming young women to puberty. All manner of hoopla attend the ceremonial, although it's a serious matter for the participants. The night dance, where eerily trilling ghan (mountain spirits) emerge from the forests, is the most serious.

Then, just as New Mexico officialdom was sure they had the Indians sized up, the Mescaleros threw a curve. Led by their media-wary tribal governor Wendell Chino, they panicked the entire state when they entered negotiations with private energy companies that wanted to "store" nuclear waste "temporarily" on tribal land just west of the White Mountain Wilderness.

The tribe, in an open vote, resoundingly turned down the dump in February 1995. Chino's staff said it would look for other economic development options, but were accused by several tribal members of mounting a drive that reversed the "no" vote six weeks later. Chino and his tribal council have promised the tribe's 3,900 members hundreds of jobs, annual dividend payments, new schools and roads from the proposed storage site's revenues.

Cloudcroft

Five miles east of Mescalero village, I take back-country Indian Highway 244, which rolls through seemingly uninhabited Mescalero forest and cattle country to Cloudcroft, my favorite New Mexican southern mountain town.

Not far from Cloudcroft and tons of U.S. Air Force avionics equipment is the U.S.'s southernmost alpine forest. It shelters a grove of towering aspen trees with trunks so thick I can't reach all the way around them. The only other such aspen beauties I know thrive in a canyon bottom south of Valle Vidal, in Northern New Mexico.

Although autumn leaves are faded now elsewhere in the mountains, this golden grove blazes with trembling fury in the desert wind.

I prefer the Sacramento grove, but I know why both are there, magic sites in remote forests, seemingly planted deliberately to invoke the spirits of the place. I always take plenty of cornmeal when I'm lucky enough to return here.

By late morning, I'm strolling Cloudcroft's boardwalks. In addition to two blocks of fakey turn-of-the-century "Western" main street and a Forest Service headquarters, Cloudcroft glories in one of New Mexico's premiere inns, The Lodge.

The Lodge was built in 1899 by Alamogordo and Sacramento Mountain Railway magnates as a log pavilion to attract heat-struck El Pasoans. The 8,640-foot-high village of Cloudcroft sprouted around and below the lofty inn.

Today, the Lodge is rambling, renovated and pricey. Its Bavarian look is topped by a distinctive copper turret. Just off the parking lot is the forest-fringed golf course on which one of the hazards, warns the scorecard, is bears.

The inn's history is almost as interesting as its present-day views and nook-and-cranny architecture.

The Albuquerque Journal-Democrat, in an 1899 story, noted the Lodge's "… fireplaces with wide, hungry mouths," one of which was hungry enough to burn the place to the ground in 1909.

The El Paso and Southwestern Railroad rebuilt it, using surviving windows and fireplaces from the old hotel.

Rebecca, the hotel's resident ghost, also survived, so to speak.

The ghost, whom I suspect to have been made-to-order for the imposingly haunting inn, reportedly is that of a beautiful, titanium-haired hotel room maid. Her lumberjack boyfriend murdered her after finding her in the arms of the hotel manager, a traveling salesman or whomever you'd like to name as the alienating party.

In the days when the hotel used a plug-in switchboard, Rebecca often "called" from room 101, but when the operator sent maids scurrying there, it was unoccupied. These days, with fewer chances for electronic shorts in the equipment, Rebecca sometimes appears in the lobby near the snarling stuffed brown bear. She's still elusive, but her winsome Celtic images adorn a lobby tapestry, stained glass in the restaurant, and cards and refrigerator magnets in the hotel gift shop.

Rebecca's Honeymoon Suite, which went for about $165 a night in the mid-1990s, includes a gold-crowned, mirror-topped bed and a whirlpool for two.

Like Rebecca, the railroad has long departed Cloudcroft, although a carefully preserved trestle (with a new interpretive center) still spans deep Mexican Canyon southeast of town. And the logging industry still flourishes in the surrounding forests. I always keep a careful watch for runaway logging trucks on these curving roads. You never know.

Logs are big in Cloudcroft. Displays explain the area's rail and logging heritage at the Sacramento Mountains Historical Museum, housed in—what else?—a log cabin across U.S. 82 from the Chamber of Commerce masquerading as a log cabin.

Hummingbirds as well as tourists favor Cloudcroft in summer, although the casual resort stays busy almost year-round.

Soon snow will blanket nearby Snow Canyon Ski Area, laying a white foundation over excellent cross-country trails along the rim ridges and canyons south of town. The village is ringed by popular campgrounds and stately forest. It abuts hiking trails of varying degrees of difficulty, including many of the 27 miles of the former rail spur from Alamogordo to Cloudcroft.

One of those, Rim Trail, offers expansive views of the dusty Tularosa Valley and White Sands National Monument thousands of feet below. Both desert microclimates visible below tell me why El Pasoans and other lowlanders still flock to this woodsy mountain retreat.

Wilderness Waterfalls

Motoring south of Cloudcroft on State Road 6563, I veer left down FS 164, along the inviting canyon of the Rio Peñasco, one of the Sacramento Mountains' few year-round streams.

Hidden away here, but still subjected to heavy use, flows one of New Mexico's treasures: Bluff Springs Falls, a tumbling cascade surrounded by national forest.

Brazos Falls, which flows for about two weeks during the May snowmelt, plunges about 2,000 feet from the plateau above.

I park in the sloping dirt lot, cross the wooden bridge and sit a while under the falls' prickly spray in the afternoon sun, remembering other New Mexico waterfalls.

***

It's difficult to envision a land as arid as New Mexico spattered by misty natural waterfalls, especially during the bone-dry weeks before the monsoons or the crisp autumn days before the first winter snow.

For the most part, our leaping waters are out of sight, out of mind, well-hidden in national forest canyons.

But New Mexico's mountainous regions all boast waterfalls, from Sitting Bull Falls, to El Salto (the jump), a few miles north of Taos.

They range from a rain of thin trickles and veils such as the sprays here at Bluff Springs to substantial, but seasonal sensations, such as 2,000-foot Brazos Falls, on private land near Tierra Amarilla.

Wherever they're found in New Mexico, even falls that barely trickle roar a sort of defiance against the destiny that someday may overtake us as it has past civilizations in this land of limited moisture: desertification—the smothering of a formerly flourishing, watered land by arid conditions.

Whenever I stumble upon a fall while hiking, I'm always captured by its awesome beauty, its assault on my senses, the way its kinetic, ionized energy contrasts with the stolid nature of the not-too-distant deserts.

And awe, as New Mexico's landscape constantly reminds me, is an attitude that often translates to religious feelings in any culture.

I once discussed falls with Alfonso Ortiz, the cultural anthropologist and author from San Juan Pueblo.

"All waterfalls are spiritually significant," he told me.

"For Indian people, they're associated with spirit dwelling places and certain natural phenomena. For example, some people believe rainbows grow out of the little prisms that dance in the light around a falls," he said.

When he told me the legend of Nambé Falls, who should slither back into view but The Serpent?

"The serpent god, Avanyu," he said, "was vomiting water into the Rio Grande Valley to drown San Ildefonso and Nambé. The elders called on the Twin War Gods to help, and they battled Avanyu at Nambé Falls, where they killed him.

"The outline of the serpent's body appeared where it was slain, and is still etched on the rocks at the falls, although the modern-day dam obscures its head," Ortiz said.

Falls engage the senses in mysterious manners, most hypnotic.

I once sat in a forest two miles from Brazos Falls, watching tons of water crash into a ledge, then plunge to the rocky valley floor another 1,000 feet below. And as I listened to its thunder, I remembered why I spend so much time in the woods.

Brazos Falls, which runs only a couple of weeks a year, projects its voice through the wilderness, sometimes roaring like air and fire colliding in a jet engine, other times muttering like a distant surf.

At the more serene and more isolated Bluff Springs, I see no serpent tracks, but I watch for bears. Always.

I finish my picnic, stash the trash, labor up the steep grade to the relatively flat primitive camping area above the falls and cop a few photos.

A few darkening clouds have blown in on a south wind, and I don't want to be trapped on the dirt forest road in a freak early snowstorm. I'm always sorry to leave the spring-fed falls, but it's time.

Zipping back to Cloudcroft I turn left down U.S. 82, through High Rolls, where my family and our friend Nati Rodriguez once spent a delicious warm day climbing cherry trees, picking and eating until my face and hands were stained red.

Just below High Rolls, a tunnel, one of the state's three, worms through the mountain. This one was chiseled to accommodate the pioneering Charles B. Eddy's now-vanished "Cloud-Climbing Railroad." Today it serves the heavy auto traffic generated by heat-struck lowland refugees heading for cool summer pines and winter recreationists on their way to tube, sled and ski Cloudcroft.

From Cloudcroft to Alamogordo is a somewhat abrupt transition, although the highway descends gently enough.

The easiest way to prepare for what's to come is to keep sight of the gypsum sand haze from White Sands National Monument below and about 10 miles north of "Alamo."

At a pulloff just down-mountain from the tunnel, a marker describes the vast dome of marine limestone that once spanned the desert from here to the San Andreas Mountains, far in the obscured distance to the west. When the Rio Grande Rift widened, the dome collapsed, falling 5,000 feet in some places.

The Tularosa, the Rio Grande Rift's easternmost valley, with 6,000 feet of valley fill but no significant stream cutting through it, is a closed, perpetually dusty, salty, mineral-rich basin.

Three Rivers Petroglyphs

Alamo's an interesting enough town, but after reserving a motel room there, I motor north along the wide street also known as U.S. 54. This stretch from north of Alamo to Vaughn is one of the narrowest, meanest, steep-shouldered, aggressive-truck-driver-infested highways in the state.

Still, I'm determined to see Three Rivers Petroglyphs, especially since they could be sacrificed to the Mescaleros "temporary" nuclear dump.

A few miles west of the petroglyph site is Mrs. McSween's spread. This courageous woman saw her husband shot by legalized ruffians while U.S. Army troops passively looked on. She survived him and most of the other Lincoln County warriors, relocating on the Sacramentos' west side to become one of the state's leading ranchers. She was so successful they called her "The Richest Woman in New Mexico."

The Three Rivers Petroglyphs National Historic Park five miles east of U.S. 54 actually includes two sites depicting how Mogollón culture evolved. I reach one by a mile-long, fairly easy walk through a lava rock ridge ceremonially emblazoned with geometric and animal forms by Jornada Mogollón people from about 1000 to 1400 A.D. The other lies along an easily strolled path past signs that interpret the surrounding pit houses and simple above-ground rock foundations of once-standing homes.

After a water break, I continue past the petroglyphs on the forest road, bearing left at the second dirt track. It's rough and rutted, eventually ending at a primitive Forest Service campground near White Mountain Wilderness. Multiple stakes and miniature red and yellow surveyors' flags stud the cactus-strewn range, evidence that the Mescalero leadership is serious about the nuclear waste dump. A short dirt road branching to the right miles before the campground leads to the Mescalero Reservation's western fringes and some "Keep Out" signs.

Returning to U.S. 54 and heading south, I stop for soda at a gas station in tiny Tularosa, a Hispanic village founded in 1862. Today Tularosa's a sleepy, shaded farm community, with a few tourist shops, several annual fiestas and, so says a friend, a speed trap.

I'm a pistachio fan, so I pull off at Eagle Ranch's gift shop a few miles north of Alamo. This successful agribusiness is another clue to irrigation's importance in this otherwise bone-dry valley.

Alamogordo

Finally entering Alamo, I take a few minutes in the deepening afternoon shadows to walk around Alameda Park. At its north end a miniature diesel locomotive and passenger cars pull kids on 15-minute rides over 16-inch tracks in warmer weather. The Toy Train Depot, a ticket office and museum, once was an actual depot in Torrance, N.M. in 1898. It then was moved to Corona, where it was a Southern Pacific depot until 1974, when it was moved to Alamo.

The Depot houses more than 600 feet of model train tracks, hundreds of toy and model trains, and a 1,000-square-foot HO gauge exhibit that illustrates the railroad's 1940s layout in Alamo and environs.

At the park's south end is Alameda Park Zoo, where I kick through fallen cottonwood leaves and view such animals as the endangered Mexican Wolf, one of several in the state.

In touting Alamo, its Chamber of Commerce mentions its journey "from arrows to rockets in less than 100 years." That's accurate enough if the journey includes the railroad that spawned and still runs through the town.

Seeking a definitive desert sunset from a high vantage point, I visit the rocket part of the chamber's boast: the Space Center near New Mexico State University's Alamo campus to view the Clyde B. Tombaugh Planetarium and Omnimax theater, just like the one at John F. Kennedy Space Center Museum near Titusville, Fla. I don't catch a show, but walk through an exhibit inside the imposing museum's expansive reflective facade to see moon rocks, a rocket sled and satellites. Outside a rocket collection noses towards the wild blue yonder. Ham, the first *chango* in space, is buried under the prickly pear just south of the museum.

As I exit, the sun is poised to drop behind the Organ Mountains. The orange cliffs east of Alamo show purplish-red in the declining illumination. Why, I wonder, weren't these mountains also known as the Sangre de Cristos (blood of Christ). They certainly bask in as impressive a sundown light show as do the Sangres near Santa Fe.

Oliver Lee State Park

After breakfast I venture south, out to Dog Canyon, a microclimate with a history.

Dog Canyon, the deepest in Oliver Lee State Park was a favorite escape route for Apaches needing a quick return to their Sacramento Mountain refuge after military skirmishes or hunting trips on the desert floor. Far up the well-watered canyon, on a ledge called *la ceja* (the eyebrow), they held defensive positions as long as they wanted, raining fatal boulders down on attackers, including the U.S. Army. An old coot called Frenchy (Francois-Jean Rochas) held out against Indians and greedy new ranchers for years, building a network of stone corrals and a rock house by the arroyos west of the canyon. The corrals and house now are overrun with mesquite and ocotillo. The combative rancher-politico who ended up with the land, Oliver Lee, built a ranchhouse that still stands. It was used as a set in the Walt Disney movie "Troublesome John," but now opens only during ranger-guided tours.

This canyon also must have been overrun with wildlife. I spot two mule deer does as I walk near the campground, and see coyote scat near Frenchy's Cabin. The reclusive desert doves whose plaintive calls lend such an eerie mood to this southern wilderness are everywhere calling this cool morning.

White Sands National Monument

Trying to make White Sands National Monument on U.S. 70, I leave Dog Canyon about 10 a.m. I slow for traffic at Holloman Air Force Base and recall a factoid from my Las Cruces days. Holloman and White Sands Missile Range bracket White Sands National Monument west of Alamo. The highway's sometimes closed for up to an hour for missile tests, so I always check before taking off across that miserable expanse from east or west. Today I'm lucky.

My favorite time to visit the gypsum dunes at White Sands is very early morning during the July-August rainy season. That way I avoid both the afternoon crowds and the heat. I bypass the museum on my morning trek and head deep into the heart of the dunes, where I can observe the freshly washed sands in a state reminiscent of their existence eons before humanity tracked across their uneven mounds. After the sun starts to heat up the sand, I usually break for the mountains or one of Alamo's shady parks.

Today, after a cursory half-hour loop through the deserted sands, I regain the highway and pass the dunes' western edge, where 19th-century lawyer Albert Jennings Fountain and his young son disappeared, allegedly murdered. As my wagon labors up the steep *bajada* towards the jagged Organ Mountains that conceal Las Cruces, I wonder about the progress of the Air Force's attempts to expand its bombing range and NASA's plans for a spaceport near the Jornada del Muerto 40 miles north of Las Cruces.

Just before the crest of San Augustin Pass, I pause at an interpretive pulloff that includes a missile aimed at WSMR's desert expanses.

So desolate and all-of-a-same is this huge sinkhole of a valley, I can't think of a better spaceport location. Heck, in some places, if an astronaut peered out her porthole, she wouldn't be able to tell if she were on moon or earth.

Playing Tom Petty's "Freefalling," I coast back down the Organs' east side, yearning for my Las Vegas home, a hot bath and a little evergreenery. I daydream about the sacred aspen circle high over Alamogordo, but decide against prolonging my highway time. I must hustle home for Turkey Day Weekend. And besides, while the road goes on forever, I do not.

⇒ Information
> *Lincoln State Monument, Lincoln: Fee. 1-505-653-4372*
> *"The Real Billy the Kid," outdoor drama, near San Jon, N.M.:*
> *Fee. 1-505-576-2455*
> *Billy the Kid Outlaw Gang, Taiban: 1-505-355-9935*
> *Ruidoso: 1-505-257-7395 or 1-800-253-2255*
> *Cloudcroft: 1-505-682-2733*
> *Inn of the Mountain Gods, Mescalero Reservation: 1-505-257-5141*
> *Three Rivers Natural Recreation Site, north of Alamogordo:*
> *1-505-525-4300*
> *Alamogordo: 1-800-545-4021*
> *Space Center, Alamogordo, N.M.: 1-800-545-4021*
> *Oliver Lee State Park: Fee. 1-505-437-8284*
> *White Sands National Monument: Museum free. Park entry fee.*
> *1-505-479-6124*

The Lower Pecos

After breakfast, I watch Alamogordo slide off my rearview mirror. With holiday promises breathing down my neck, I push east across the Sacramento Mountains and down to the Llano Estacado.

Llano Estacado

Nobody ever accused Southcentral and Southeastern New Mexico of striving for tourist center designation, especially along the Texas-hugging strip from Portales to Hobbs. Here oil and natural gas wells and cracking plants, potash mines, and a desolate landscape prevent the manufacturing of Chamber of Commerce baloney.

In fact, I've heard the Llano's stark eastern portion called the Stinking Quarter, maybe because its northern edge touches Stinking Springs. More likely, it's due to the sulfurous layer of Oil Patch by-products that blankets the Central and Southeastern Plains. From Clovis south, add to the malodorous mix the smells of manure, money and manipulation wafting from large dairy farms recently fled from California's stricter antipollution laws and higher taxes.

But in New Mexico's Llano, as all over this diverse state, the desert harbors its secrets. Here thrive friendly people much given to Western horse culture, plus several institutions of higher learning. Its hidden oases, both rural and urban, also will flourish as long the sinking water table floats high enough.

Oil isn't the only liquid being pumped from the Llano's limestone depths. Without water, oil is worthless. If these bustling towns strung out across the southern Permian Basin continue to develop, eventually another uniquely Western bust will empty town and country from New Mexico to Wyoming. Just as water depletion drove its inhabitants from Chaco Canyon, so could a depleted aquifer end contemporary North American Southwestern civilization, European phase. And on the Llano, everybody's aware of that fact, which hones life's nicked, sunburnt, windblown edge.

But for now, hey, water's abundant enough, as is oil and gasoline, so I go for the gusto. I zip south of I-40 again, soaking up warm autumn fading-to-winter sun. This is primo touring weather in this part of the state, but I don't try it from late spring to mid-autumn while it's hellaciously hot—triple-digit days—from Clovis to Hobbs, Carlsbad to Fort Sumner.

Deep into the Llano, I stop to stretch and consider the limitless 360-degree horizons. Across the highway, roosters crow in an abandoned marble orchard, graveyard guardians. Hardly the Four Horsemen, but it seems a nice touch, particularly forceful in this otherwise empty and potentially deadly country.

This is reportedly the world's flattest land, although occasional arroyos indent the gently rolling surface here and there.

Known as Little Texas, the reach that stretches to the Texas border might as well be. It looks like West Texas. They talk like Texans here. The women even wear their wind-defying hair like ladies from Lubbock, as a friend of mine observes.

At first glance, maybe at second or third, much of this region appears denuded, overgrazed, drought-blighted, mined, devastated. But in somebody's eyes, the Llanos's not wasteland. Ranching, farming and energy bucks flow here while the flowing's good.

The question is how much longer humans can go with that flow. Homonids first populated the Great Plains eons ago, but in typical Western fashion, the plains have time and again rejected human subjugation. Water—in river, *pozo* (waterhole) and *playa* (seasonal lake)—drew wandering bison herds and pursuing hunters here.

In later centuries, Apaches, Comanches driving stolen Texas longhorn herds to trade with New Mexican Comancheros, and range-busting Texas ranchers drifted through. Settlements may thrive on oil, but they owe their existences to deep-drilled groundwater, which fills metal "trick tanks" on the range, cools oil rig drilling heads, and irrigates peanuts, alfalfa, wheat and sorghum across the Llano.

Two types of towns dot New Mexico's Southern High Plains: those with farms irrigated only by deep ground water and scant rainfall, like Clovis, Portales, Lovington and Hobbs; and those irrigated from wells as well as from a nearby river, usually the Pecos, like Fort Sumner, Roswell, Artesia and Carlsbad.

Clovis

Clovis, creature of the railroad, was founded on the Llano in 1907 at Riley's Switch, a major junction renamed for a European heathen king who converted to Christianity and fought barbarians.

Gringo ranchers and farmers willing to try irrigation moved here just after the turn of the century, but they didn't really prosper until deep drilling struck the Ogallala Aquifer in the '40s.

Since 1942, Clovis also has benefited from a fluctuating U.S. Air Force presence and the sort of fast food and convenience store franchise development that plagues most American towns in the 1990s. On the other hand, the military presence probably has added to the number of fine Asian restaurants. Buzz haircuts in this town are worn by fliers, not homeboys.

But as are almost all other New Mexico towns, Clovis is connected to Big City Go-go Reality, a.k.a. Communications Central in Albuquerque and The World via cable and the state-wide *Albuquerque Journal,* several national TV networks and public TV and radio. It boasts lots of red-brick homes and a community college with a free historic museum.

Adobe houses, vigas and other Northern New Mexican icons are anomalies in this cowboy town. Along the bricked segment of downtown's Main Street, scattered Art Deco buildings indicate spotty prosperity, while the now-deserted Hotel Clovis, nine stories of orange and yellow brick, argues otherwise.

I cruise Main looking for the studio where pioneer rock 'n' roller Buddy Holly recorded the first multiple-track vinyl pop hits. Wasn't vinyl another offshoot of the petroleum industry? I finally locate the historic site at the now-closed Norm Petty Studios on Seventh Street. A large evergreen tree obscures the studio's front and its side yard is guarded by a large dog, but it's open for tours for anyone who calls first.

Other than Petty's studios, Clovis' major claim to fame is the appropriation of its name by archaeologists to label a group of early humans, Clovis People. Evidence of their Neolithic presence was found south of Clovis, around a former gravel pit called Blackwater Draw.

Blackwater Draw

The draw (known elsewhere as an *arroyo* or wash), once a lushly vegetated pond shore, lured Paleo-Indians, a Folsom Culture branch later known as Clovis People, to its life-giving water 11,000 years ago.

Only a few wooly mammoth bone fragments are on display at the dig site off State Road 467 where in 1932 workers discovered the first of several wooly mammoths. The best interpretive displays are at Blackwater Draw Museum nine miles south of Carlsbad. The museum houses several large dioramas, one of which reminds me that the tusked giants were, pardon the term, mammoth. We need some monument to those long-gone people for having the bravery to face such an awesome beast. Actually, I guess they left their own monuments behind, to be buried by centuries of sand.

Ongoing digs at Blackwater, a living historical preserve, have yielded camel, horse, bison, ground sloth, saber-toothed tiger and dire wolf fossils from the pond that dried up 7,000 years ago. Of that once-flourishing biological community, only descendants of bison and Paleo-Indians walk the earth today.

The Clovis People hefted their formidable, monster-killing spears with the fluted rock heads and moved on because water disappeared from the Llano during the same climate change that desiccated their spring-fed pond.

Later, Folsom and Portales Paleo-Indian bands, peoples who arrived around 10,500 and 9,500 years ago, respectively, camped by the dried lake bed, but they too, migrated. Even later, as water tables lowered, some bands dug wells at Blackwater, the oldest in the New World. It was for them, as it will be for those who dig wells today, a temporary solution.

Where the thirsty tribes wandered next intrigues me. Did they join others to become the people who were there when the Pueblos' Anasazi ancestors moved down into the Rio Grande Valley? Did their descendants meet Alvar Núñez Cabeza de Vaca as he wandered as a mad healer through their arroyos, or avoid Coronado as he struggled north up the unknown Rio Grande? Or did they just get lost?

Portales

Not far south of Clovis across an agriculturally productive, irrigated section of the Llano is Portales, home of Eastern New Mexico University and a few more red brick homes. The university houses the Roosevelt County Historical Museum, the Natural History Museum and the Miles Mineral Museum. The campus is still a bit shady, and due to the region's lower altitude, a lot greener than Santa Fe this time of year.

Previous comments about odors notwithstanding, a dairy near Portales produces mozzarella cheese for the national Pizza Hut chain, and that smells delicious.

Just south of Portales, however, trees are replaced by pump jacks, like iron grasshoppers devouring the land, wheezing, groaning and clanking away as far as south of Hobbs. We need the oil; very few in this internal combustion age deny that. But the energy-extraction industry contributes its own brand of visual atmospheric degradation, and this part of New Mexico is one of the state's several *de facto* sacrifice areas to the God of Go.

The god's unique by-products are a rotten eggs odor and a yellow ocher haze that hugs the horizon, shimmering purple-gray at sunset.

The all-encompassing haze, like the mythic fog that Celtic shamans conjured up on demand to mask their movements, also results from a below-ground energy.

Albuquerque, Santa Fe, Farmington or Las Vegas, even Taos, can look a bit grimy of sky when inversion layers strike and TV weather prophets warn Albuquerqueans it's a "no-burn night."

In the Stinking Quarter, I doubt if any night should be a burn night. I drive through the haze from Portales to Lovington, through a forlorn landscape of squalid, mostly deserted ranches, some with pumpjacks overrunning old corrals. More prosperous ranches line the dimming horizon. The only music on radio is country; I play country's predecessor on tape by the Chieftans and Van Morrison.

Lovington

I'm glad to reach Lovington just after dusk. Strung out by too much driving and cranky, I make a cursory tour, which doesn't take long. I soon learn Lovington has a couple of motels, a few gas stations, a large courthouse and a museum. The motel where I sleep is run by smokers, for smokers. I cough a lot. Strains of "Third Rate Romance, Low Rent Rendezvous" blare from the windowless lounge. The chartreuse haze returns at dawn, probably there all night. I'm greeted by a stench when I open the motel room door. Despite the town's proximity to the well heads, gasoline is expensive. I search for the plaza, expecting I'm not sure what. What I find, here in Anglo Country, is a British-style square dominated by four-story Lea County Courthouse. The nearby county museum is closed, although I note the pumpjack and windmill proudly showcased in its cyclone-fenced yard. Somehow, I get a message. *Paso por aqui,* pilgrim. Pass through.

Hobbs

To where? Hobbs, then back to the Pecos as soon as possible. I'm a fish out of water here, and all the sandy scrub country—ancient sea bottom some of which is called the Querecho Plains—between Portales and Hobbs hasn't alleviated that feeling. Nor does a sweep through Hobbs, a refinery town, pure and simple.

The community's pride is New Mexico Junior College east of town, with its on-campus Lea Cowboy Hall of Fame and Heritage Center. Hobbs also enjoys an old-fashioned Main Street with a working pumpjack and an oil cracker spurting flames not three blocks away in case anybody forgets where they are.

Carlsbad

Saline lakes and ponds, ancient sand dunes and wide-open potash mines predominate on either side of four-lane U.S. 62/180 between Hobbs and Carlsbad. On this particular speedway, oil trucks and other big field rigs would just as soon run me over as look at me.

I drop with relief down Carlsbad's eastern bajada into the Permian Basin's lowest area and once again encounter the Pecos River. The river, widened here for several miles, is bordered by ample lawn and shaded by cottonwoods. I relax, glad to be out of the trucks' target range.

I pull off at the Santa Fe Railway station just across the Bataan Bridge, admiring the broad river view, docks and the new riverwalk recreation path. The air smells soothingly moist, even in late November in the Chihuahuan Desert.

The best way to learn about the desert that fringes Carlsbad is to visit the Living Desert Zoo and Gardens, on a bluff overlooking U.S.

The Pecos Flume at Carlsbad carries water from the river back across itself to an irrigation lake.

285 just northwest of town, as I did on a hot summer day a few years ago.

My tour took about three hours, winding along a gravel path past animals in appropriate habitats, from the Guadalupes to the southeast to the sandhills east of town. I rested frequently in the shade and applied lip balm regularly. Since I don't operate too well at temperatures over 100° F., I wasn't overly impressed with the zoo, although it's obviously a gem in the desert. It's a kid-friendly zoo, however. A friend recalls an early spring visit when her preschool grandson stared down a (caged) cougar at close range, so near he could hear the animal purring. A crow played a game with her husband, placing pebbles on a ledge, then re-placing them when they were tossed back into his cage.

Intense heat aside, I had to admit the zoo rivaled Tucson's Desert Museum. Still, the fenced elk, deer, buffalo, the caged kit fox, coyote, black bear, bobcat, porcupine, rattlesnake, bald eagle, great horned owl, turkey vulture and other animals on display deserve a freer life.

The Pecos dominates Carlsbad, which recently established preliminary senior water use rights over upstream Roswell. Carlsbad claimed Roswell irrigators were depleting Pecos water by using underground wells. North of town, the Pecos Flume, looming like a Roman aqueduct over the river, is a reminder of water's value in the desert. When it was built to replace washed-out earlier wooden flumes, it was the largest concrete structure in the country. It carries Pecos water across the river itself to Lake Avalon on the east bank. Contented fisherfolk stand casting in its shade.

Also under the flume are the hot springs that motivated the town to change its name from Eddy. Their mineral content supposedly matches that of a famous European spring in Karlsbad.

A few hundred feet from the flume, in what now looks like a large parking lot, I find the rock Eddy House, with a wooden windmill and a *chosa* (dugout) of the type early European settlers excavated for temporary homes.

Carlsbad's Museum and Fine Art Center house a Taos Founders collection, ranching artifacts, a mineral collection, Tarahumara Indian and Peruvian artifacts and Mimbres and Pueblo pottery.

Despite its dependence on the river and its extractive industries, Carlsbad's economy is diversifying. It still favors the energy business, however. The U.S. Department of Energy's Waste Isolation Pilot Plant south of town, has sweetened the economic life here somewhat, adding 1,000 jobs directly related to the plant's mission. Although it's called a "pilot plant," WIPP is a $1.2 billion series of underground vaults earmarked for permanent disposal of defense-generated radioactive waste. Although WIPP's opening has been delayed for ten years due to environmental and safety concerns, it's now set to open in 1998. I doubt it will.

Controversial elsewhere in New Mexico, WIPP earns nothing but cheerleader praise from Carlsbad's politicians and will boost area income for some time.

WIPP or no WIPP, as an increasing number of retirees are learning, Carlsbad's weather's not bad, not bad at all. It's blessed by mild winter temps and the Pecos meandering through, moderating the desert's baking influence. Of course, hardly anything moderates the late spring-early summer desert before the monsoons blow up, so I still favor my mountains.

The numerous aquatic diversions, including several fishing lakes, obviously boost the taxbase. In addition to river-shore offerings, the town's also a comfortable jumping-off spot for the climatic extremes of the desert, the dry Guadalupe Mountains, or Carlsbad Caverns, where it's 56° F all the time down in the hole, but hot as the hinges of hell upstairs in summer.

Sitting Bull Falls

Speaking of the Guadalupes, I'd planned for years to visit Sitting Bull Falls there. I read up on the place while I finish my coffee break in Carlsbad.

Sitting Bull, the Lakota chief, supposedly hid some cattle in the canyon carved by the falls, but since he was in Canada at the time of his alleged bovine indiscretions, that's unlikely. The canyons around Sitting Bull historically were known as cattle rustler hideouts, however, and a trip into their reaches demonstrates why.

I take U.S. 285 north of Carlsbad to the site of now-inundated Seven Rivers, turning left on County Road 137, which traverses Rocky Arroyo, a deep, watered canyon that once sheltered the family of Ma'am Jones, the rancher and innkeeper who took in Billy the Kid upon his arrival in Pecos country. The formidable Ma'am reportedly is buried in tiny Rocky Arroyo Cemetery, among the other Joneses and a handful of Smiths and Campbells.

I pause a few minutes at the graveyard, then find a delightful, shaded spring and waterhole not too far away, with a tire swing suspended from an overhanging tree. Just the other side of the spring however, the odor of progress wafts in again on the stiffening desert breeze, and the perpetual pumpjacks reappear soon after.

I push on, avoiding road-hogging cattle trucks, almost taking the wrong backcountry turn at a "Y" intersection (bear left, traveler), wondering why the only animals I've seen so far are roadkill: a skunk, deer, coyote and raccoon.

At Sitting Bull, the first hint of something special ahead is signalled by a series of charred fire rings by the road, evidence of the area's heavy summer use. Suddenly, rounding a curve, I splash through live water, the runoff from the falls a quarter-mile ahead, but yet hidden.

By the time I reach Sitting Bull Canyon the sun has climbed enough so most of the huge amphitheater that holds the park's parking lot, barbecue grills, restrooms and picnic shelters is sunlit. That doesn't compensate for the blustery winds, however, which blow the car door shut

Even its Upper Chihuahuan Desert setting doesn't keep Sitting Bull Falls from sometimes icing in late autumn.

on my leg and blinds me with gritty dust. I see no drinking water, so I strap on my canteen, arm myself, pile on a couple more layers and trudge uphill for the falls, out of sight and sound of the eerily deserted parking lot.

The hissing falls' approach is via a paved, guard-rail-bounded path, bordered by yucca, creosote bush and prickly pear, a few of which bear munchy scars from hungry bears or javelina. I can't see the falls until I round the last of several blind corners, so I'm alert for any unusual grunts from the brush.

The falls' several misty ribbons glint, plunging past steep carbonate walls to a microclimatic miracle, a canyon filled with willow, reeds, oak and bigtooth maple. Cold nights have frozen a few ribbons stiff, but the remaining waters fight the winds, falling to the sheltered, pool-pocked canyon floor. Some tuff basins, still lined with green vegetation, are deep enough for a good soak. Not today, but certainly before the arrival of the summer crowds that turn this otherwise secret spot into a circus.

I snap as many photos as I can before my hands numb, then wait an hour in the car—just in case the mountain lion or bear I keep visualizing needs an afternoon snack—for the wind to abate. It doesn't, so I retrace my route, intending to make Roswell by dark.

Seven Rivers

I turn north onto U.S. 285 and am 40 miles from the falls, just passing artificial Brantley Lake, which had swallowed the abandoned site of once-savage Seven Rivers, a cowboy town that's probably better off dead. Archaeologists report that when the Seven Rivers' graveyard was dug up before the water rose, scarcely a skeleton was without an injury, an indication of a violent death. Alcoholism apparently was rampant in the town, as it was all over the frontier. The dam's public opening in 1989 probably was the best thing that ever happened to this submerged village.

A tan roadside flash interrupts my reveries. I stand on the brakes, as does the man in the southbound car in the opposite lane ahead of me. Four adult mule deer—two bucks, two does—prance slowly, heads high, across the highway, east to west, then streak into the mesquite. I retrieve camera, maps and books from the floor and pull off for a few minutes thinking time. Seven Rivers, four deer. My Indian friends would know what to make of it, but I don't. I chalk the incident up to simple good luck.

Artesia

The respite is fine, but shadows are running long. Just north of Carlsbad, I'm assaulted by dairy stench again and not long after, see both massive hayricks and more grinding pumpjacks.

They dominate to Artesia, an oil and railroad town. The discovery of oil in the underlying Abo Field in 1923 projected Artesia into the 20th century. The town's core originally was homesteaded by a former Yankee soldier, J.F. Truitt, who settled at a spring on boss rancher John Chisum's spread. His was one of the many artesian wells that burble up here and to the north which lend the town its name. Water-dependent refineries, cattle and farming support the town's economy.

Speaking of underground resources, the good citizens of Artesia were taking no chances during the Cold War. They built Abo Elementary, a combined school and fallout shelter.

Artesia's free Historical Museum and Art Center is housed in an old cobblestone residence on West Richardson Avenue.

I don't have time for a peek, moving on up the road to Roswell, looking for a decent cup of coffee.

Roswell

Roswell, of all the Llano towns, is my favorite, the closest thing to a city on New Mexico's Plains. Downtown Roswell bustles like an active urban center, with several nine-story buildings and a courthouse square.

The Mescalero Apaches, who once wandered these lands, were more or less confined to reservations by the time the early Anglo pioneers arrived.

Servando Trujillo, my Mescalero friend who's entering his 70s at this writing, once told me about growing up "off-rez" in Roswell.

"I remember my old grandfather sitting day after day in his rocking chair in a back room in our little house," he said, staring into the fire we were tending. "He just rocked and chanted the old songs, that's all he did."

Two ranching families, the Chisums and the Leas, greatly influenced Roswell's growth as the Indians retreated.

John Chisum, who controlled pretty much all the range in this part of New Mexico, arrived from a failed Texas business, following his longhorn herds to the Rio Hondo, which flows through town. One of the locals he offended was The Kid, who liberated a few of Chisum's cattle to repay a debt he claimed Chisum owed him.

Led by Capt. Joseph C. Lea, no relation to Oliver Lee, the Lea family bought out other interests and soon owned all of Roswell, which they registered as a townsite. Their cattle empire spread north and west. The Leas were instrumental in relocating a military school from Fort Worth, Texas to Roswell in 1891, where today it has grown into New Mexico Military Institute. NMMI's crenulated sandy brick ramparts tower over what once was Roswell's northern limits, but today marks the beginning of the new commercial strip.

As all over the Llano, the ranching heritage around Roswell remains strong, with prosperous spreads fronted by black iron gates adorned with cowboy, horse and cattle motifs.

A couple of blocks south of the institute is the extraordinary Roswell Museum of Art, a pleasant surprise here in cow country, not to say that cowboys don't have "kulcha."

A dozen potters are assembling their pre-Christmas sale displays when I arrive, but they aren't the only show in town.

The museum exhibits several landscapes and portraits (including self-portraits) by Roswell native and Hondo Valley resident Peter Hurd and his wife Henriette Wyeth, who lived upcanyon. The permanent collection includes pieces by Georgia O'Keeffe, Andrew Dasburg, Marsden Hartley, Ernest Blumenschein and other well-known New Mexican painters.

Here also are examples of Luís Jimenez's acrylic art, including an artistic comment on the old "End of the Trail" sculpture, in this case, a Plains Indian mounted on a horse with flashing red neon eyes. Jimenez's pieces are realistic, yet surreal acrylic art pulsing with fluid weirdness and glowing gases.

The museum-associated Goddard Planetarium, the state's largest, is named for one of the original rocket scientists, Robert Goddard, who, backed by financier Harry Guggenheim and aviator Charles Lindbergh, experimented near Roswell in the 1930s. Not keen on science, I scan the exhibits quickly.

The UFO Enigma Museum at 6108 South Main, near abandoned Walker Air Force Base, for a dollar purports to explain the much-publicized 1947 "Roswell Incident." So does the free International UFO Museum and Research Center at 400 North Main. CNN, ABC's "Good Morning America," "Omni" magazine and other media have shown a marked interest in the incident. Why shouldn't we?

The privately owned Enigma is next door to where the "action" took place: the alleged secret packing of flying saucer debris and alien bodies for shipment from the old military field.

I talk later with John Price, Enigma's director, on what I think might be a related matter.

Seems I'm checking my map and notice, not 10 miles east of Bottomless Lakes State Park an extensive geographic feature marked "Camino del Diablo," Devil's Road. The "road" is at least 20 miles long and depicted by a series of curvy lines running parallel east and west. I strike out across the Llano, finally bumping down a dirt road past many pumpjacks and oil "leases for sale" signs. I startle a sizeable antelope herd and a few crows, but after searching that dirt road for an hour, find nothing vaguely resembling the map's depiction. I mean, is this thing, whatever it is, some UFO landing strip? An extraterrestrials' communications system antenna? A lava formation submerged by the sands that marked this portion of the Llano near shifting Mescalero Dunes?

Price isn't sure he's heard of the place, but refers me to Elvis Fleming, noted Chaves County historian and author, who clarifies the mystery.

"I've heard old-timers say they used to drive their wagons along the Camino del Diablo, so it may actually have been some sort of road," he offers. I ask neither Fleming, who teaches at Eastern New Mexico University's Roswell campus, nor Price about my UFO theory. Some things are just too fantastic. I guess I could talk to a geologist, but I love a mystery. I think I'll just let it lie.

Other neat Roswell things:

a) The annual County Fair. I went one year while living in Cruces in the late 1980s. It was large enough to be boisterous fun, small enough to be relatively non-threatening to my younger daughter, then about three. Cowboys and punk gangs don't interact too well and the punks don't usually come out on top, as I observed during a brief fracas on the midway. Score one for Chaves County.

b) The fact that a new, nonsmoking coffeehouse is trying to make it in a small shopping center on South Main.

c) The many city parks and playgrounds, a small zoo and a nearby wildlife refuge.

What is there to recommend the Stinking Quarter? Some nice people, several campuses, excellent museums, the hum of industry amidst desert waste, sinkhole lakes to match Florida's finest, four mule deer and a sacred falls. Maybe that's not sufficient for some people, but it's good enough for me.

⇒ Information
Clovis: 1-505-763-3435
Petty Studios: 1-505-763-7565
Blackwater Draw Museum: Fee. 505-562-2254 or 562-2032
Lovington: 1-505-396-5311
Hobbs: 1-505-397-3202
Carlsbad: 1-505-887-6516
Living Desert Zoo: Fee. 1-505-887-5516
Artesia: 1-505-746-2744
Roswell: 1-505-623-5695

The Lower Rio Grande

R eacquainted with my family and expecting a couple of weeks of fine, dry New Mexico early-December weather, I drift south again on a day that dawns frosty and starflecked across the northern prairie.

La Frontera

By lunch, my legs and lower back are killing me, but the desert sun burns my face, so I push ahead. I skirt Belen and the lower valley's Hispanic villages: Jarales, Sabinal, Abeytas, until the Bernardo exit and U.S. 60 east.

Crossing the river the Spanish called Rio Bravo, I wonder if the feathery, invasive, water-sucking tamarisk (salt cedar) thickets choking the banks equate to the East Coast's kudzu curse.

The Rio Grande, great lazy, lifeblood river of legend, cuts through a region of New Mexico that socio-political experts are beginning to recognize as *La Frontera,* the border frontier.

I'd define that zone, and I'm not the first, as neither Mexico nor United States: a 20- to 40-mile wide swath on either side of the 2,000-mile U.S.-Mexico border where the culture differs uniquely from that of either bordering country.

In addition, in New Mexico, an internal frontier for centuries has followed the rivers and tributaries. Due to that riverine human influx, I would extend the zone along the I-25 corridor north to Santa Fe and on to Taos and Costilla via state roads 68 and 522. It also runs north and east along I-25 by way of the Pecos River and Las Vegas and Ráton.

It's easy to tell when I'm in *la zona frontera's* southern extremes. The U.S. Immigration and Naturalization Service is everywhere. Border Patrol agents in dark green uniforms roll by in pale green vans. The INS, known as *la migra,* stops everybody at checkpoints scattered along the interstates in three directions from Las Cruces.

As a native-born, taxpaying, registered-and-voting U.S. by-God citizen, I resent being stopped in my own country and questioned about my national origins by armed persons. Actually, I've only been detained once, and that only for a few seconds beyond what I'd consider a routine stop. The fact that recent newspaper accounts of federal investigations have shown a few *migras* to be infected by greed doesn't add to my confidence in the outcomes of these borderline confrontations.

Of course, 20 miles south into the Mexican side of la frontera, checkpoints are manned by Uzi-armed guards, so I guess it's unfair all around. But we might think of a more civilized way of checking for illegal drugs or defending the borders along our vulnerable southern continental underbelly.

Salinas Pueblos National Monument

To investigate the border's vagaries, I drive into history, from Salinas Pueblos National Monument near Mountainair, west to Socorro and south to Las Cruces. And since winter's already dusting the high mountains, I've picked a fine time for a road trip down memory lane. Actually, Memory Lane's in Silver City, but that's a different story.

Not far from Salinas National Park headquarters' in Mountainair stand the decayed remains of three once-major Tanoan pueblos—Abó, Quarai and Gran Quivira—and the inhabited remnants of several frontier villages that once marked the northeastern borders of Spain's colonial empire.

The Tanoans, strategically living near large salt beds, probably were related to Indian people at the vanished pueblos at San Cristobal, Pecos, Galisteo, and San Marcos. Tanoan-speakers also later settled at Santo Domingo, Jémez and briefly at Santa Cruz (Española), until they moved to Hopiland.

At the saline-dependent pueblos, near where limitless plains roll up to the Manzano Mountains, ancient Mogollón people from the south and Anasazi from the north met and merged. Eventually, they were joined by Tompiros and Tiwas from the Rio Grande Valley. From 1100 A.D.

until Spanish Colonial days, the Estancia Valley was the Los Angeles of New Mexico's Indian world.

But by the 1670s, at least six pueblos perished from drought, famine, disease and Apache raids. Many Pueblos fled north to Galisteo or down to the Rio Grande Valley.

What lessons are learnable here, where meadowlarks trill among the ruins of Pueblo and Hispanic cultures?

Once when I was investigating the lofty church ruins at Abó, I was approached by a friendly National Park Service interpreter.

"Do you know why the Spanish were able to build their churches so close to the Indian kivas?"

"Syncretism," he answered himself, smiling like an abbot saving a soul, "the ability of the Church to combine two different forms of religious practice. The Indian people simply added Catholic saints to their own hierarchy of gods, and the Church tolerated that."

That's true. At Abó and Quarai kivas were built within the church compounds. Or maybe the churches grew around the kivas. Whatever, syncretism also may have worked along other lines not anticipated originally by the Church.

For instance, so affected were Hispanic frontier dwellers by the Plains Indians over the years that some almost became acculturated Indians. One 1930s study showed villagers from Manzano, resettled after the Pueblo Revolt by Hispanos, borrowed not only the use of Indian bows, arrows, lances, moccasins and buckskins, but also adopted Comanche ceremonies, including the scalp dance. *Así es nuevo méxico.*

Abó is on a pass opening to the Rio Grande Valley. Its people traded with Acoma-Zuñi, Tanos from the Galisteo Basin and Plains Indians. Today wind roars through the ruins of San Gregório de Abó Mission and a large, unexcavated pueblo, which thrived beside a perennial stream.

Red-walled Quarai was content beside its spring when Oñate approached it in 1598. Today it includes two excavated kivas, one of which is square. The site encompasses the most complete surviving Salinas church structure, the ruins of La Purísima Concepción de Cuarac Mission and an artifacts display. Enough remains of the church that I have no trouble hearing mournful echoes of long-vanished priests intoning early morning offices. Visions, after all, can be aural as well as visual.

Gran Quivira (Cueloze), a 3,000-room pueblo which boasted two churches, was famous for its black-on-white pottery. Syncretism didn't sit too well with the friars of the site's San Buenaventura Mission. Burned and filled-in kivas there attest to a Christian determination to stomp out the Old Religion. But above-ground rooms converted to kivas indicate the pueblo priests fought back, just as the Celtic priesthood defended their Horned God, Cornnubus, against the Roman Christian invaders. Both priests and pueblo retreated in the face of famine and Apaches in 1672. So much for syncretism.

All of these somber, isolated ruins impress me with a sense of the vast scope of history, of the many voluntary and involuntary migrations of both Indian and European peoples. Faced with desolation on such a grand scale, I wonder why we think contemporary civilization, hooked on diminishing fossil energy, is static, and not just another turn on the wheel of time? I always bring plenty of cornmeal here, as if I could restore the balance we lost somewhere along our way to progressive living.

Socorro

I flee the smell of disaster lurking around the pueblo ruins just as the Piro Indians fled the twin disasters of drought and hostile Indian raids, abandoning the Salinas Pueblos to trickle down to the Rio Grande. There they settled in a string of new pueblos near what was to become Socorro.

In their oases north of the dry *Jornada del Muerto*, Juan de Oñate met them in 1598 at Teypana Pueblo. He renamed the pueblo Socorro (assistance) because of Piro generosity, it's said.

The Piros paid for their early alliance with the Spanish. From the early 1630s, Apaches angry with anyone who supported the Spanish wreaked vengeance on the trans-Rio Grande pueblos. The onslaught forced the Piros to flee west to Senecu, Alamillo and Pilabo pueblos, all vanished today.

In 1628, Franciscans built San Miguel, a mission church they called Nuestra Señora de Socorro del Pilabo, north of Teypana. Here, above the marshy Rio Grande bosque, the brothers planted New Mexico's first vineyards.

But during the Pueblo Revolt, even San Miguel Mission was razed. Most of the Piros followed Gov. Otermín to Guadalupe del Paso (Juárez, Mexico), where they built Socorro del Sur. Later, many descendants of these Indians moved north to Tortugas, a village near today's Las Cruces, where *their* descendants live. I intend to anchor this trip with a visit to Cruces, but for now, I'm trying to locate Socorro's original plaza.

That's difficult, because Socorro (del Norte) was abandoned for 136 years after the Pueblo Revolt. I circumambulate the current plaza, looking for the best light, trying to ignore the Indian kids sitting on the gazebo steps, silently watching my every motion.

Hispanos resettled the town in 1816 and soon rebuilt the old San Miguel. By 1821, Socorro's profile included three terraces and several plazas.

On the bottoms near the river, livestock grazed. On the second level, crops surrounded several placitas and the main plaza, three blocks north of today's plaza and two blocks from the church. Nobody knows why the original plaza was so far from the church, but later buildings probably filled in the original plaza. The third level included pastures stepping up towards the warm and cold springs that still bubble from Socorro Mountain.

I can only approximate the oldest plaza's layout, so I walk a few blocks east to the Val Verde Hotel to order breakfast and read up on my Socorro history.

Beginning about the time of the U.S. Civil War, a sequence of events common in New Mexico's history swept over isolated Socorro. The military presence at Fort Craig, then the railroad, provided impetus for a boom that lasted several decades.

In 1867, prospectors found silver in the Magdalena Mountains northwest of town and built a silver smelter. The railroad rolled through in 1880. By 1890, Socorro, the center of a rich mining area, was the territory's largest town.

But disasters lurked on the dusty horizon. In 1893, silver prices plunged. An 1895 flood destroyed the lower town, and in 1896 the smelter fizzled out. Floods in the 1920s and '30s also closed the last large employer, Golden Crown Flour Mill.

Although today's New Mexico Institute of Mining and Technology opened as New Mexico School of Mines in 1893, it didn't pack enough economic clout to resurrect the town.

The revival actually began after U.S. 60, the "Ocean-to-Ocean Highway," was routed through town.

In 1919, developers built the Mission Revival-style Val Verde Hotel near the Atchison, Topeka and Santa Fe depot. Once boasting the state's first telephones and furnace heat, today the building strives to match its former glory, housing businesses and the Val Verde Steakhouse. The Val Verde's wrought iron gates, shaded *portales* (arched porches), deep, lushly landscaped patio and old interior murals mixed with contemporary art hint at what the Eagles were singing about in "Hotel California." After breakfast, I clump around the wood-trimmed, high-ceilinged rooms, viewing artwork. Outside, the fresh morning air scents the patio.

On a wall by the street, a ragged Festival of the Cranes poster reminds me of another of the area's glories, the river-bottom wetlands. Twenty miles south of town is Bosque del Apache National Wildlife Refuge, where migratory snow geese, sandhill cranes and endangered whooping cranes generate so much excitement that Socorro hosts the annual festival each November.

Lectures, exhibits, workshops and a wildlife-related fine arts and crafts show liven up the town, while guided tours of the nearby Bosque del Apache Wildlife Refuge provide special access to Rio Grande wetlands.

***

I fill my gas tank before setting out south for San Antonio, named by 19th-century Hispanic colonists for one of the Saline relocation pueblos, San Antonio de Senecu, which had flourished 20 miles south.

A lot of places named San Antonio have shown up on my travels, so I look up the saint's pedigree. Turns out there are two of him. San Antonio Abad is patron of brushmakers, domestic animals, anthropologists and grave diggers. San Antonio de Padua specializes in finding women good husbands, good fortune or lost objects. Perhaps he's also patron of lost places.

This San Antonio, on the very northern fringe of the old trail the Spanish called *Jornada del Muerto,* Journey of the Dead Man, garnered its 15 minutes of fame during World War II. Los Alamos scientists masquerading as prospectors gathered at Rowena and Adolph Baca's Owl Bar and Cafe to sweat out the stressful hours before the test of the world's first atomic bomb a few miles across the Rio Grande. The bar's still operating, the bomb's on hold. San Antonio also was the boyhood home of hotelier Conrad Hilton, who with his sister met the trains and lugged baggage to his family's boarding house.

After helping myself to a famous and fiery Owl Bar chile cheeseburger, I turn south on State Road 1, the remnant of old U.S. 85. and eight miles later, left onto Bosque del Apache National Wildlife Refuge. It's famed as a bird-watching sanctuary, but it's not birds I seek. The first Bomb blew a few miles east of here, and I intend photographically to beard the nuclear beast in its lair.

The refuge, except for the nearby dry mountains and its lack of basking alligators, reminds me of Merritt Island Wildlife Refuge, just north of the Cape Canaveral Space Shuttle launch site on Florida's east coast. At both refuges, visitors drive along canal banks to view spectacular avian displays.

And near both, rocket scientists working with inconceivable power have altered history.

Across the bosque at Trinity Site, Americans detonated the world's first atomic horror in July 1945. This marsh is as close as visitors can approach the site except during semiannual official tours. There's not much to see except ash-black volcanic hills and the Oscura Mountains some 20 miles to the east, but it's as near as I care to get.

I perform a brief ceremony and to be on the safe side, sprinkle cornmeal across the road behind me as I leave.

Under the Oscura Mountains' western peaks (background) the United States exploded the world's first atomic bomb at Trinity Site.

Before State Road 1 rejoins the interstate, a marked washboard dirt road leads from it east to the crumbling adobe ruins of old Fort Craig, back to the days before America's arsenal was nuclear.

The fort, with units relocated from older Fort Conrad to the south, was built on gravelly Rio Grande sand bluffs to help control Indian raids along the Jornada, once part of the Spanish Camino Real, the Royal Road from Mexico City. But the fort's troops were defeated several miles east by Texas Rebels at the Battle of Valverde in 1862. The Rebs forged north to later defeat at Glorieta Pass. It was a tough time for the isolated Union troops, who also were attacked by marauding Navajos that year.

In the mid-1990s, enthusiasts began to stage annual commemorative battles at the long-neglected fort, now a state park.

From here, abandoned Jornada trails, dry as they were four centuries ago, straggle to the village of Doña Ana along the Rio Grande's east bank. A New Mexico State University range scientist told me he'd seen some trail remains from the air: lines of weeds growing in moisture-saving indentations impressed by cart or harness animals, slightly darker than the surrounding fragile desert. Of course, irrigation from Elephant Butte and Caballo lakes today softens the desert's harsh face, and from the West Bank communities of Arrey, Derry and Hatch, the Rincon Valley's chile, cotton, onion, lettuce and alfalfa fields in season green the otherwise brown and tan land.

The Jornada, however, already home to an extensive experimental range project headed by NMSU and a large NASA facility on the north end of the Organ Mountains, is due to zoom deeper into the Space Age. White Sands Missile Range intends to expand north, and plans are in the works for a commercial rocket launching complex 40 miles north of Las Cruces.

Mesilla Valley

After a lunch stop at Truth or Consequences, where the many hot springs that spurred the town's founding remain busy, I continue south on State Road 185, a back way through Radium Springs and under Robledo Peak, which marks the Mesilla Valley's northern boundary.

I pull off onto a riverside byway just downstream from Leasburg Dam. The desert wind hums across the rio's slurping ocher deluge, while a rooster brags and chickens cackle answers to curious squawking cactus wrens. A sleepy bullfrog rumbles from under salt cedar sanctuary, a roadrunner raises his sucking-popping song, thrashers, hatches and mourning doves pour music into the warm afternoon. Nothing unusual, just routine New Mexican enchantment.

Fort Selden, where Gen. Douglas McArthur spent part of his boyhood, is just over a bluff east of here, but I had often seen the ruins at the now-state park when I lived in Cruces. During its annual living history days, I had seen plenty of people in period dress, plenty of horses. By late afternoon, with the Rio Grande on my right, I was gliding south through the Mesilla Valley's extensive pecan orchards, stark this time of year.

The Mesilla Valley is a surprise even to native New Mexicans who may never have visited this far south. By spring, 14,000 acres of dark-barked pecan trees will bud and green. Globe willows and poplars will shade neighborhood streets in Las Cruces and mulberries

Quetzalcoátl's stylized image adorns a water tank in Las Cruces.

will harbor irritating grackles at New Mexico State University on the city's south end. Las Cruces is the state's second largest city, and with two slowly developing downtown historic districts, may someday eclipse Santa Fe in historic restoration.

One impediment blocks such growth. Water in Cruces is hard, mineral-laden and as far as I'm concerned, suspect for drinking. Although the city's water supply is from groundwater wells near its east mesa, my advice is to buy bottled.

As a tourist destination, Cruces benefits from three outlying historic areas: the Organ Mountains to the east and the villages of Tortugas and La Mesilla just south and southwest, respectively.

Dripping Springs

As the almost-winter afternoon wanes, I remember my involvement in an Organ Mountain spook story in 1989, and decide to pay the mountains another visit. I cautiously approach the old Cox Ranch headquarters, now the A.B. Cox Visitor Center.

I'd exited I-25 at University Avenue in south Las Cruces, heading east 9.5 miles. The paved street skirted "A" Mountain (Tortugas), passed alongside a desert subdivision then abruptly disintegrated into a dirt washboard road.

Why do the mountains spook me so? It isn't that I'd been alone near this same spot years ago, high up in a deserted, dry canyon. And it isn't that it had been Halloween Eve, with the sun dropping fast behind Las Cruces' arid West Mesa, some 20 miles away.

It isn't even the thought I entertained that previous late afternoon about departed souls gathering here from the deserted TB sanitorium about a quarter-mile higher up Ice Canyon, in the heart of the 9,000-foot high Organs.

No, maybe it was something about my trusty Canon 35 mm camera jamming three times in a row for no apparent reason that had set me stumbling through the shadows back down the dusty, rocky old ranch road as fast as dignity permitted.

Now, in mid-afternoon, from what I consider a safe vantage point, I scope out the early darkening canyons with my binoculars. I need these photos and I'm going in, because while the old Dripping Springs Resort might harbor its share of shades, it's also a naturalist's delight and fun for a photographer.

Administered by the Bureau of Land Management and the Nature Conservancy, the area's 2,850 acres includes the former owner's home, now the visitor center.

The old ranch land rambled over diverse habitats, from Chihuahuan Desert shrub to wooded riparian areas. It's home to at least nine rare plants, five endemic to the Organs, and two species of land snails found only in Ice Canyon.

As I enter this naturalist's (and supernaturalist's) wonderland, I wonder if La Cueva, a giant tuff formation pocked with caves, is too dark for a photo. La Cueva had sheltered Archaic Indians—some surely engaged in primitive agriculture—as early as 5,000 B.C.; then members of the Jornada Mogollón culture; and much later, roving Apaches.

La Cueva's sandy caves also once housed an eccentric Italian peripatetic and reputed healer, Giovanni Maria Agostini, known locally as *El Ermitano,* "The Hermit." Tecolote Peak, near Las Vegas was renamed Hermit's Peak to honor his tenancy in Northern New Mexico, where he lived before his pilgrimage south to the Organs and death in his lonely cave, where he was lanced by an unknown murderer one night in 1869.

An abandoned corral near the Organ Mountains east of Las Cruces.

I won't have time to visit the springs if I don't trudge on, so after signing in at the visitor center at road's end, I hoist my canteen and hike up the 1.5 miles up Ice Canyon on the exposed, rocky old ranch road (and up to about 6,200 feet) to the ruins of Van Patten's Mountain Camp. Built in the late 1800s, it was originally a long, Territorial-style adobe. The "camp" blossomed into a 30-room, two-story edifice that hosted such notables as Pat Garrett, Pancho Villa and Albert J. Fountain, all of whom died violently. Hmmmmm.

Walking back down the trail from Van Patten's, I turn left at the "Y" near the picnic tables to the "dripping springs," most of the year but a meager trickle. A few yards farther the winds sough through Boyd Sanitorium's ruined remains, including a once-screened dining hall and the doctor's stone house. Although I've never understood how Doña Ana County's constant dusty spring winds could benefit TB victims, the stone terraces and acequia testify to poignant attempts at gracious living and dying within the narrow canyon's towering walls.

I glug from my canteen, shiver in the thin sunshine and hurry back down to my car. Tonight the pilgrims are coming back down Tortugas Mountain near town, and I don't want to miss it.

Tortugas

Eugene Van Patten of Van Patten's Mountain Camp married an Indian woman and was adopted into the Manso-Piro-Tiwa people of Tortugas, who helped build his camp.

Hands in my jacket pockets against the chilly December evening, I watch as their tribe seemingly launches rivulets of lavalike fire down bald, cactus-studded Tortugas Mountain.

The fire stream actually is a series of blazing *luminárias* (not *farolitos*) fueled by stacks of burning tires. The bonfires, visible for miles, are lit by Tortugas village parishioners to guide their descent from the mountain. The pilgrimage is part of the Feast of Our Lady of Guadalupe, the ancient Marian vision Pope Pious XII called "The Empress of the Americas."

Yet despite a centuries-old history, the people of Tortugas, descendants of the Manso-Piro-Tiwa Indians, have struggled for 30 years to gain state and federal recognition of their tribal heritage. Much of their sacred land on Tortugas Mountain has been appropriated by the U.S. government and NMSU.

"We have a lot of indigent Indian families here, and we're trying to get federal money for housing for them," said Lamberto Trujillo, a tribal member, when I talked with him late in 1994.

Trujillo was aware of the politics of increased Indian gaming activity in New Mexico.

"We might open stores or factories, something to put people to work, but the council has never mentioned gaming," he said.

State recognition notwithstanding, federal recognition has been elusive due in part to changing U.S. Bureau of Indian Affairs regulations, Trujillo said.

"We filed under the criteria in the 1978 BIA law, but they changed it early in 1994," he said. "We had done genealogy on the 22 families and a history, but they wanted a little more blood, you might say."

The BIA requires the following of a tribe seeking recognition: a continuous historical presence; inhabitation of a specific area; a historical political influence; specific membership requirements; a list of all known members; no members of any other tribe on tribal rolls; and no previous Congressional termination.

In 1994, 145 groups applied for federal tribal recognition, BIA historian John Dibbern told me.

Since the BIA launched its recognition process in 1978, it has acknowledged nine groups and denied 13, with seven more acknowledged by Congressional act or other legislation, he said.

Tortugas' situation is complicated by the Manso-Piro-Tiwas' complex history, recorded by historian Patrick Beckett and genealogist Terry Corbett in their jointly authored 1990 monograph, "Tortugas."

The Manso, said Beckett, a bookstore owner with ties to the village, met the Spanish as early as 1582. They descended from the Jornada Mogollón culture, which existed roughly coincident with the Anasazi.

In his monograph, Beckett said they apparently ranged from present-day Hatch to south of El Paso, Texas, east into the Franklin and Organ mountains (originally the Sierra de los Mansos) and west to the Florida Mountains near today's Deming.

Nuestra Señora de Guadalupe de los Mansos mission church at Paso del Norte (today's Juárez, Mexico) was established for them in 1659. Piros from the Apache-harassed Senecu Pueblo assisted the priest.

During the 1680 Pueblo Revolt, the Mission Indians at Paso del Norte were joined by Piro from the middle Rio Grande, Tompiro from earlier-abandoned Salinas pueblos east of the Rio Grande, and Tiwa from Isleta.

Meanwhile, as intermarriage continued at Guadalupe Mission, Manso and Piro merged into one band, Beckett wrote in "Tortugas."

"The common thread that held these people together," he wrote, "was their identity with the Guadalupe Mission and its patroness."

From 1680, the Mission Indians also lived closely with their Hispanic neighbors, so "many customs and religious beliefs of both groups became intertwined and indistinguishable from each other," Beckett noted in his history.

In other words, as was happening all over New Mexico, a third, mestizo ethnic group, sometimes known as *la raza*, was emerging.

When the Mesilla Valley opened to settlement in the mid-1800s, some Paso del Norte Mission Indians moved north, soon shifting their ceremonies to Las Cruces' St. Genevieve's Church.

There, as Los Inditos de Las Cruces, they carried on the Guadalupe Mission's cultural heritage, Beckett said. They later were joined by Ysleta del Sur and Senecu families who claimed Tiwa and Piro ancestry. The combined group bought land next to the already established village of San Juan de Dios de Tortugas, just south of Cruces.

In 1910, Los Inditos moved their traditional Guadalupe Day ceremonies to Tortugas village just south of Las Cruces. There they formed the nonprofit Los Indigenes de Nuestra Señora de Guadalupe, which included a few non-Indians married to tribal members.

In 1917, they built a chapel in the Guadalupe area of Tortugas where Guadalupe Church now stands. The resultant merged villages and the new San Juan-Guadalupe parish today is known as Tortugas.

A 1940s feud between some Mission Indian descendants and other corporation members resulted in lawsuits. Eventually, one litigant group claiming Mission Indian descent initiated federal recognition actions.

Recognized or not, the tribe continues its Indian traditions, including the Guadalupean ceremonies.

Those ceremonies include a four-mile pilgrimage to Tortugas Mountain, feasts, various Indian dances and installation of new *mayordomos,* the ceremony's sponsors.

They also include the annual San Juan Fiesta in June at which I once was "arrested" for dancing with my preschool daughter. In the old manner, I had to "bail" myself out of the wooden "jail," with all proceeds earmarked for the church.

Despite internal dissent and external indifference, the tribe is pressing ahead. I wish them the best of luck.

La Mesilla

A few blocks from Tortugas, adobe La Mesilla slumbers in the sun.

Although I'll probably be hung out to dry on a chile rack by loyal Mesillans for suggesting this, La Mesilla is like a miniature, hotter Santa Fe surrounded by miles of orderly pecan groves and chile fields. The down side is the next-door neighbors: east across the railroad tracks is Las Cruces, a miniature Albuquerque in the making.

Actually it was Mesillans' choice to forfeit the incoming railroad to Las Cruces, which meant Cruces grew while Mesilla happily languished. As a result, Cruces got NMSU, chain restaurants and a downtown outdoor mall that livens up during the Whole Enchilada Festival and the bustling, colorful farmers' markets held there Wednesday and Saturday mornings.

But Mesilla retained its plaza, historic adobe buildings and a tourist-luring ambience that just won't quit. Heck, some days there are more Texas than New Mexico license plates visible around the plaza.

Before the Gadsden Purchase in 1853, the Mesilla Valley was divided between the U.S. and Mexico, with La Mesilla, then on the Rio Grande's west bank, planted firmly as an ocotillo in Mexico.

Founded in 1850, half of Mesilla's original population fled there to escape U.S. rule after the 1848 Treaty of Guadalupe Hidalgo. The Mexican government approved a La Mesilla land grant in 1853, but almost simultaneously sold the area to the United States. Disgusted Mexicans flocked farther south.

Soon, even Ma Nature confirmed the inevitability of the fate of those who stayed behind.

Situated in the Rio Grande's sandy, river-bottom flood plain, Mesilla sits on a slight rise noticeable enough for Juan de Oñate to have called it Trenequel, or dike. For years, residents of Mesilla, the "little table," visited Cruces only by ferrying across the Rio Grande. But in 1863 the river cut a new channel west of town, converting the table into an island. In 1885, the river's eastern channel dried up and so did the ferry service. Like the swamp-circled island it once was, Mesilla emerged from the mud of relative obscurity to take its place in New Mexico's history.

Mesilla was briefly the Confederate territorial capital of Arizona during the U.S. Civil War. After the conflict, the California Column marched from the Bear State to New Mexico, bringing with it Col. Albert Jennings Fountain. Fountain, who married a Mexican woman, immersed himself in local range war politics to the extent that he and his small son were murdered.

Fountain's relatives today maintain the Gadsden Museum in a home on La Mesilla's eastern fringe. The small museum keeps unique hours. The guide, a Fountain great-granddaughter, beguiles me with all sorts of curious stories about the ghosts of days departed.

On a windy night, some of those ghosts probably still stalk Mesilla's plaza.

A few might have been created in 1871, during a bout of Doña Ana County politics-as-usual, when several people were killed after zealous Democrats and Republicans scheduled simultaneous rallies on the plaza, then rioted.

Recalling all this history makes me hungry, so I stroll around the plaza trying to decide which restaurant to frequent tonight. I remember the fine fiestas my wife, younger daughter and I had enjoyed here, mariachis blaring from the gazebo in the plaza's center.

In a low adobe building on the plaza's south edge is El Patio Lounge and Restaurant, founded in 1935 by one of Col. Fountain's grandsons.

El Patio is justly famous for its reasonably priced Mexican-American food. There are more *nouveau* interpretations of the same cuisine—I'm talking black beans, white cheese and small portions here—across the plaza at Pepper's, also arranged around an old home's now-sumptuous patio.

Just off the plaza is La Posta Restaurant, once a Butterfield Stage Line way station. Here Mexican-American food is served at yet another enclosed patio courtyard, this one complete with serenades by squawking exotic birds.

The Billy the Kid Gift Shop, across the street from La Posta, once was the county courthouse and the only jail that could contain its namesake.

I opt for Pepper's, wondering while I eat where I'll check in for the night. I want an early start before visiting Kilbourne Hole southwest of Las Cruces, to me the most sacred spot along La Frontera's eastern boundary.

I reluctantly arise around five a.m. and am coffeed-up and on the interstate by six. I turn south off I-10 at Cruces' airport, then speed along the access road past the county fairgrounds, prison and a couple of panicked jackrabbits.

Where the paved road dead-ends, I veer left onto a dirt country road, drive for dusty miles until I cross a railroad track, turn left, crawl a few more miles parallel to the track, steering left after tooling through a ranch yard where the dogs still sleep. Soon the dirt road is streaked with black northern offshoots of the 25,000-acre Aden Lava Flow to the south. At a point where I know the lava soon rises to a substantial bluff, I enter BLM land and drive south, around the shadowed rim of an extinct volcano, Kilbourne Hole. The crater is one of several in the miles-long ancient, pocked Aden Flow. The volcano's inner crater, which I spy from its south slope, is partially plugged inside.

After walking across a couple of football fields-worth of jumbled boulders to the cone's northern wall, I attempt the steep vent, once site of lots of fiery action, now chocked with massive lava blocks and boulders. From the cone's peak, I peer into Mexico. Vultures wheel high above, hoping I'll lie down and be their lunch. I nip at my water jug, intending to disappoint them.

Some friends once told me they'd been hailed by La Migra out here. The rangers were concerned that civilians might be injured if drug runners decided to pass through the lava beds, highly likely since the almost unguarded border's only a few miles south.

But the prospect of close drug "mule" encounters disturbs me less than whatever had been hanging around Ice Canyon in the Organs yesterday.

The spirit of this dead volcano is airy, but lurking darkly, emitting unseen images into the dusty air, something that may have manifested itself to the unfortunate hermit at La Cueva moments before his murder. To focus the scattered feeling, I sprinkle cornmeal, adding a little tobacco for the fire spirits, satisfied this was about as sacred a spot as I'll find in Doña Ana County. I stash my meal, sprinkle a little water on the lava to thank its rocks for being so fine for sweat lodges, snap a few photos, pay a few more respects, and point my wagon towards Deming.

⇒ Information
Salinas Pueblos National Monument: 1-505-847-2585
Socorro: 1-505-835-0424
Bosque del Apache National Wildlife Refuge: 1-505-835-1828
Dripping Springs: Fee. 1-505-522-1219
Las Cruces, Tortugas: 1-505-524-8521

The Mimbres and the Gila

Blasting across Southern New Mexico, I remember Vegas in its early winter graybare raiments, the sweet mountains of home dappled by patches of lingering snow. To shake fatigue, I mentally click onto the road game unfolding through my windshield, but it doesn't matter. I've morphed into a road drone and I've been driving for months. All I really want to do now, floating across the Upper Sonoran Desert a couple of weeks before Christmas, is detour towards the white-capped Gila Mountains and my home far beyond. But several photo stops beckon first, the name of the cash flow game.

Deming

After inching through the giant, irritating carport on I-10 known either as *alta de la migra* or the INS checkpoint, I streak like moonshiner Mitchum in "Thunder Road" for the big curve east of Deming, my speakers booming The Traveling Wilburys' "Going to the End of the Line."

Eventually, the jagged Florida Mountains protrude on the south. Site of multiple mines, and gunfights between miners and Indians, the neighboring Floridas shelter Spring Canyon State Park. The equally stark Little Floridas conceal Rockhound State Park.

Even in this dry climate, I keep a weather eye. Seasonal storms move fast, and again I repeat our state's *caveat emptor:* "*¡Asi es nuevo méxico!*"

The first town west of Cruces edges into view over the flat horizon ahead. Deming's icons are more obvious than those of the Pecos. Here a sturdy windmill, railroad cars and retired Southern Pacific Steam Locomotive No. 1221 dominate the Luna County Chamber of Commerce Visitor Center at the city's eastern entrance. Deming was founded in 1881 where the Atchison, Topeka and Santa Fe and Southern Pacific lines met and still do. Railroad and interstate run over the same ground as the 19th century Butterfield Line stagecoaches that lumbered from La Mesilla to Lordsburg to the Golden Gate. Harassed by Apaches and Rebel Texans, Butterfield's Saint Louis to San Francisco route lasted a few years before he struck camp and moved the route north.

The Chihuahuan Desert valley surrounding Deming's irrigated chile, cotton and sorghum harbors an underground river born in the Gila Mountains to the north. It seeps into the valley floor 20 miles north of Deming, running under the town, benefiting water table and crops, finally emptying into Laguna Guzman in Mexico, at least on the maps.

In essence, that frustrating water loss applies to *La Frontera Ocidental:* New Mexico's southwestern frontier with Mexico, also known as Big Sink, West. Rivers that run respectably in the mountains fizzle out in the intimidating desert, which, by the way, does NOT foster saguaro cacti. (Those are ocotillo or prickly pear or teddy bear or cholla. But they're not saguaro this far east.)

In Southern New Mexico's Chihuahuan Desert, every drop not claimed for irrigation or industry or which doesn't evaporate first, ends up far from any ocean.

Neither the delicate water situation nor the early '90s discovery of an alleged drug lord in their midst deter retirees from flocking to Deming. The seniors, lured by the town's tidy aspect and moderate weather, learn about dust-laden spring winds, scorching summer and early autumn heat after they've lived here a year. But hey, Deming's cost of living is way below that in the Twin or Windy cities up on the northeastern plains.

Fans flock here the last weekend in August for the Great American Duck Race. For years, the duck racing champion was a man who signed his name Robert Duck.

Deming shares a patriotic history with other New Mexico towns. During World War II, C.G. Sage, Deming newspaper publisher, commanded the New Mexico National Guard's 200th Coast Artillery, the heroes who endured the Bataan Death March. The war also brought a

U.S. Army Air Base bombardier training site, today known as Deming Airport.

Speaking of the military, Deming's Luna Mimbres Museum is in the sturdy former National Guard Armory on South Silver Street. The brick fortress was thrown up in two months immediately after Pancho Villa's March 1916 attack on tiny Columbus, N.M., 32 miles south. Who says government can't move fast?

Columbus, N.M.– Palomas, Mexico

I gas up in Deming and find a sunny park bench to go over my notes from previous border journeys to Columbus and Palomas.

On one several years ago, I had been helping Servando Trujillo and a group of associates build a ceremonial sweat lodge in the desert near Columbus. I had driven in past Tres Hermanas and was climbing out of yet another dry arroyo when I heard the familiar gronk of sandhill cranes. I watched them push north, probably content after they'd fished the hidden lake near Palomas, Mexico.

Those cranes were bringing me a message. Flying from south to north, in my medicine man friend's cosmology, they moved from the direction of healing to the direction of the spiritual. I simplistically thought they might have meant healing powers were spiritual. I should have thought again. For that smug assumption, Spirit slapped me in the face with an embarrassment, just to be sure I was paying attention.

Busy with several students, Servando had asked me to lay out the coordinates for the lodge we were to build. I lined up the winter sun and several peaks, marking where I thought the east and only door should open. The group worked fast and well, and soon a wicki-up-style, canvas- and rug-covered 20-person lodge squatted in the middle of the spindly ocotillo.

The fire pit was dug, lava rocks and wood stacked inside. The flame blazed swiftly and after a couple of hours, the eyes of the rocks Servando had imported all the way from Pecos fiercely glowed crimson. We crawled in and closed the flap on one of the most jangled lodge atmospheres I've ever encountered. Afterward, I left for Cruces wondering why I bothered with these disconcerting cross-cultural spiritual expeditions.

Several months later, I bumped into Servando in Santa Fe's Guadalupe District. We talked a while, drank coffee. Then he told me:

"Say brother, you remember that sweat lodge we built down in Columbus?"

"You mean the weird one?"

"Huhhh. Yeah, I guess it was weird. They called me down there to conduct another one, and you know what? I found out the lodge door was facing south."

"You mean somebody moved it?"

"No, that's the way we built it. Hmmmmmm. Didn't you lay out those directions, brother?"

Mortified, I didn't answer, so he elbowed my ribs and laughed.

"Don't worry. Next time we'll use a compass," he offered. Good ol' Indian teasing, right up there with often-sardonic Indian humor on my list of little-known cultural characteristics.

But I took my mistake as a sign. For me, there wouldn't be a next time. After 10 years and about 45 lodges in four states, including several at Ute and Lakota sun dances, I was out of the sacred circle, or so I had thought.

And so I had intended. Indian philosophy, religion, contemporary culture and history seemed natural enough subjects for study, and hopefully, personal involvement, when I had first settled in New Mexico.

Although I attended every announced dance I could, I lived here several years before I met any Indian people outside of my Taos High students, and several years more before I participated in, rather than observed certain ceremonies. I'm thankful for what I learned and was impressed by the many bright people I met on the righteous Red Road. But following several latter-day medicine people around, watchfully assisting them for several years, had taught me something. While many good, already spiritually secure, non-schizoid people follow healers, the shaman's often-charismatic, professional presence attracts both elevated and disturbed individuals, and many looking for McAnswers to life's biggies. The Red Road can be riddled with potholes and deviled by detours.

During the few years I shared my very limited esoteric knowledge, I was distressed by how deeply the people I met in our New Mexico and Florida lodges craved some sort of spiritual guidance. I was in no mood to play guru to pseudo-hippie pilgrims, let alone serious seekers. Besides, I'd heard a few traditional Indians criticize whites for adopting aspects of Indian religion, an ethnic zinger I'd come to see as valid. While I'd never regret the time I spent with my friends in ceremony, I decided it might be more appropriate if I searched for my own tribe, the Celts, and my derivative bands. Maybe I could discover the Celtic equivalent of the Good Red Road.

At last: Roots, the White Generation.

Years after the Moving Lodge Flap episode, I had traveled south again for a free-lances interview. I circled Columbus, a National Historic Site, before contacting any news sources. First I drove through 49-acre Pancho Villa State Park and climbed cactus-laced Coote's Hill, its dominant geographic feature, noting the clapboard train station no engine has visited for generations. Inside the station, now a museum, hung a clock stopped by a bullet as Villa launched his raid on Columbus, 4:11 a.m. exactly, March 9, 1916. In this Mexican Revolution footnote, Villistas torched this tiny village, killing 17 Americans.

Two water towers waded across the sea of cactus patches to the north. Ocotillo, agave, barrel, bunny-ear, cholla and prickly pear stretched to the horizon west of town; a roadrunner scooted from cover and zipped away.

To the south, Palomas, just across the border into Mexico, seemed a hazy extension of New Mexico, or were we an extension of them? Except for the spanking new migra border station and U.S. Customs office, the artificial lines of the Gadsden Purchase's southern boundary probably would be heeded by neither Nature nor mortal.

That's good or bad, depending on which side of the border you come down. I thumb through my negatives, trying to decide if Columbus needs another visit.

I know events there have involved booming Deming with the border's problems. Deming's school board is caught between educating both Mexican and U.S. students in Deming or setting up a separate school district at Columbus. That option probably would include building a high school at Columbus, population 700, one of New Mexico's three official border crossings with Mexico.

Similar conflicts swirl like dust devils these days all along the border, but in Columbus-Palomas in the mid-1990s, the spin is binational cooperation.

Since 1992, parents from Columbus and Palomas, population 7,000, doggedly have sought to carve their own educational turf from Deming's. Their combined efforts might someday help a pilot international school district flourish here. Parent-run, binational Columbus Independent School Association members say they're opposed by retirees, who don't cotton to taxes for education now they're beyond all that irritating child-raising stuff. Ah, America, the land that devours its own young.

Nevertheless, in 1994 CISA prodded Deming into approving an independent Columbus School District, subject to state approval.

On my last visit, I had talked with Jack Long, CISA's executive director and a Columbus village trustee. Long, co-publisher of *Las Fronteras,* a bilingual weekly newspaper, sees CISA's work as international community development.

He showed up in Palomas, Mexico, where fellow board member Victor Tzitzumbo, CISA president and a U.S. citizen since 1980, had driven me for an interview. We were talking in Tzitzumbo's garage office, slugging down Mexican Cokes when Long arrived.

Tzitzumbo, who had laughed at my original reticence to cross the border, thought the failed lawsuit was a waste of taxpayers' money.

"Of the students who commute from Columbus-Palomas to Deming, about 450 are U.S. citizens living in Palomas," he said. "Only 17 cross on U.S. visas. Most of their parents are U.S. citizens living in Palomas because it's cheaper, and they don't have a car, so the kids have to get up at 5:30 a.m. to make the bus."

It's not that there is no school close to the border: Columbus and Palomas have operating elementary school buildings, but many Columbus and Palomas primary students attend Deming schools.

Since Columbus lacks secondary schools, all Columbus and many Palomas secondary students are bused daily to Deming, where they make up about 10 percent of Deming's 5,000 public school enrollment.

Deming educators tried several alternatives to ease overcrowding, including limiting out-of-district students. That touched off a Columbus-Palomas rebellion in 1994, when 17 Palomas kindergarten students, 15 of them U.S. citizens, were dropped from Deming schools. After parents produced notarized affidavits that the kindergartners had temporary U.S. guardians, 12 students were readmitted.

Nevertheless, irate CISA members say the 60-mile round-trip to Deming is too long, and the rigid bus schedule kept Columbus-Palomas secondary students from after-school activities in Deming, unfairly setting them apart from other students.

"Besides, it's hard to have school pride when you can't play sports," Ramón Garcia, CISA member, U.S. citizen and a Columbus village trustee, said at lunch in a Palomas cafe.

Pete Aguilár, a Mexican national who owns La Farmacía (the pharmacy) in Palomas, said education was crucial to cross-cultural understanding. Aguilár, CISA's treasurer, attended Columbus and Deming schools and New Mexico State University.

Like other CISA members, Aguilár was sure education is the key to prosperity.

"It's very important for Mexican people to be close to American people, to understand them, to talk their language. NAFTA won't have any effect on Palomas if we don't have the schools," he said.

International events may be lining up in the renegade school district's favor.

In 1991, Luna County designated Columbus a *colonia,* a border community without potable water, adequate sewer system or safe, sanitary housing.

That qualified Columbus for federal infrastructure improvement grants, worthless without a decent education system, Long said.

"We've had an industrial park in Columbus with the infrastructure in place for 14 years, but we only have a few *maquilas* (twin plants). We believe one of the big negative factors is no schools," he said.

Despite the daunting task ahead, CISA's members are optimistic.

Long had ticked off other examples of on-going cross-border cooperation here.

Item: For years, Columbus's fire department answered Palomas calls, finally helping the Palomas Fire Department to self-sufficiency.

Item: Medical emergencies in Palomas requiring rapid transport are transferred across the border and taken to Deming or the nearest appropriate U.S. hospital.

Item: The villages' baseball and basketball teams have competed for years.

"We've already had 10 acres donated for a school site," Long had said. "We're going to pull it off. I guarantee it."

The Dusty Bootheel

After my Columbus-Palomas jaunt, I had headed for a rectangular waste called the "Bootheel," ("Boothell" to some), southwest of Deming. The Heel is bordered east and south by Mexico and west by Arizona. Hidalgo County ranchers, like their peers state-wide, favor the classic wide open spaces.

For generations, a persistent few farmers have watered trees, cotton and other cash crops along the county's ditches, fed by water pumped up from below. Other pumps, remote from ditches, brought water to livestock.

Today, the Bootheel profits from cattle, upland cotton, grain and alfalfa sales, a Phelps-Dodge copper smelter, and government and service industries. Tourism is negligible; the nearest services are in Lordsburg, Hidalgo County's largest town. The closest commercial jetports are El Paso or Tucson.

Other than ranching and farming, the Heel's tax base depends on a remote Phelps-Dodge's copper smelter, which provides about 40 percent of the county's tax base and a Los Alamos-like middle-class housing project for its workers in the middle of the desert near the plant. Phelps-Dodge, citing higher copper prices, announced in 1995 that it would pump up its New Mexico operation.

The isolation ranchers treasure has its problems. Smugglers and drug runners sneak across the border as they have for generations. La migra snags thousands of undocumented Mexicans, mesoamericans, and probably Asians, here annually.

The Heel's southern border is laced east to west by thin, sensor-loaded four-foot-high wire. Across the border from Antelope Wells international crossing, the road leading to Janos, Chihuahua, quickly dribbles out into a sandy track. The scene is much the same, minus legal border crossing, across mountains to the west all the way to Arizona and beyond.

The historic Gray Ranch occupies a large chunk of the Bootheel. The problems of a 500-square-mile cattle stocker ranch might seem trivial to travelers and truckers roaring along U.S. I-10, the Bootheel's northern and most populous boundary. But this unending dust generator also generated a war of words among powerful conservation groups and federal and state agencies in two states.

The Gray is a working ranch, home to cattle, other livestock, stockmen and women and their families. The ranch also produces much rare flora and fauna, of great interest to some.

The area once inspired reporter Bruce Selcraig, of *The New York Times Sunday Magazine,* to describe "a field of grama grass three times the size of Manhattan" whipping in the desert wind "like a sheet on a clothesline." He also noted that his car radio found neither an AM nor FM station all day.

That's why I'd brought my ever-present tapes, my own sound track behind the Western movie unfolding beyond my wagon window. And while I sure couldn't see but a couple, that scene encompassed the Bootheel's 718 plant species. Of those, 71 on the Gray Ranch are listed either as rare or endangered. The Bootheel's isolation from humans has meant refuge for 75 mammals, 150 species of breeding birds and 52 kinds of reptiles and amphibians. Three of its inhabitants are on the federal endangered species list: Sanborn's long-nosed bat, the bald eagle and the ridge-nosed rattlesnake.

The area also shelters at least 13 significant ruin sites from the prehistoric Casas Grandes culture.

The Heel, blessed with but 10 inches of rain annually, enjoys a rarely disturbed desolation invested with a haunting beauty. Sprawling across the Animas Mountains and the Continental Divide, flanked by the arid north-south running Animas and Playas valleys, the Gray has no live water. Ranch windmills pumping wells and scant rain nourish livestock and wildlife alike.

Before 1900, the broken and mostly arid terrain of the valleys that line the Bootheel harbored the Clanton outlaw gang and numerous disgruntled Apaches. Geronimo's final surrender was near here in 1886. Old miners told stories about mysterious Indian-frequented hidden caverns with running water and buried treasures. The Mexican Gray Wolf's last known trackway into New Mexico was up the forbidding Animas Mountains and nearby rural valleys. Although conservation groups tout the area as one of the country's few remaining ecologically complete ecosystems, irrigation foreshadowed the growth of farms and ranches and death to the wolf.

The Gray once was part of an enormous ranching empire owned by George Hearst, California mining magnate and publisher William Randolph Hearst's father. In the early 1950s, a subsequent owner, Kern County Land and Cattle Company, sold off 321,000 acres of the original spread, which became known as the Gray Ranch.

The Gray made national headlines in the late 1980s when the Nature Conservancy, wealthy, nonprofit environmentalists, bought it to resell to the feds. The Conservancy has preserved more than 17 natural areas across New Mexico, hundreds across the U.S., and more than 3.5 million acres worldwide.

But the Conservancy's attempts to buy the Gray met stiff resistance from the Bootheel's politically active Sagebrush Rebellion folks.

When the ranch was on the block, several New Mexico and Arizona counties formed the Coalition of Arizona/New Mexico Counties for Stable Economic Growth. Their goal: defend the interests of ranchers, miners, timber companies and others who feel they are under attack by environmentalists. Government land ownership is not a popular concept among many of the county's 157 ranching families.

The coalition's outlook was shared by some in other, well-established bureaucracies, like the state Land Office and the state Agriculture Department. Their interests were water, oil, or precious metals, or livestock in the area's lower elevations.

A 1990 state Ag Department report by a top Republican administrator noted that the Pedregosa Basin, in which the Gray is located, is considered by many petroleum geologists as one of the areas in the U.S., outside of Alaska, with a high potential for oil and gas development. New Mexico, of course, generates millions annually for education and services from oil and gas royalties: no drill, no bill.

***

A small private plane buzzing over my park bench took me back to a Bootheel flight I had shared a few years ago with pilot Ernie Hurt, an area rancher who held no brief for government land ownership.

The Hurts went way back in the Bootheel.

Hurt family patriarch, Erastus Franklin, homesteaded 60 acres near Deming in 1909. His scions in 1983 bought the present ranch, once William Randolph Hearst's middle headquarters for the old Victoria Land and Cattle Co. In its previous incarnation, VL and C included the Gray Ranch as its south headquarters.

Before our flight, while he safety-checked his Cessna, Ernie had told me about his years-long conflict with the Bureau of Land Management over the status of the historic old adobe in which he and his wife live and use for ranch headquarters.

The BLM wanted to sell the land to the Nature Conservancy which at that time was trying to buy the Gray. Then the conservancy would sell it back to Ernie at a profit to the organization.

That kind of acquisitive talk made Ernie and his neighbors edgy, sometimes downright cranky. I hoped it wouldn't affect his flying.

"They tell me the profit will go to the Gray Ranch, but I know where it'll go," Ernie said. "It'll go right back to the BLM and we'll never see it again here."

The BLM, from which he leases thousands of acres of grazing rights, was not one of Ernie's preferred charities.

"The BLM says it maintains the land in good condition. But they have added more people in their Las Cruces district office in the past few years than they ever had in the field. And you know what they do? They sit there and push papers."

Paper-pushing is anathema to Hurt, a New Mexico State University grad; as was most of his family.

Ernie trusted the single-prop Skyhawk II to lift us over the rough Animas Mountains. Like Sky King, Ernie buzzed back and forth across the Playas, Hatchita and Animas valleys on his way to his various cow camps. He flew it down south to Antelope Wells and to his brother's Alamo Hueco Mountains place. And he flew to Deming, where he owned a radio station.

Airborne, Hurt reassured me. He didn't assuage my fears that a single prop didn't offer good enough odds if we had to set down out here. Who'd look for us in this wilderness anyway?

"They've probably picked me up on the (U.S. Customs) aerostat blimp at Deming by now," he said.

Oh, great, I thought. Itchy-fingered flyboys. Or girls.

"If they're not sure who it is," he continued calmly, "they'll scramble and sit on my tail, then follow me down to make sure I'm legal. Of course, they can't stay on my tail long because they're too fast."

This lanky, serene man was no stranger to border weapons systems. His brother's ranchhouse once was entered by a Mexican *federale* in hot pursuit of some drug dealers. His bro's guns were confiscated and he was under arrest at the end of an automatic weapon before the little misunderstanding was cleared up. Life on La Frontera, oh yeah.

It ain't much of a border, anyhow. As we swooped out of the craggy, thirsty Animas Mountains, down Walnut Creek Wash into the morning sun and south a bit, we spied a thin strand of barbed wire stitching the sere tan desert like a suture. The seam is interrupted at Antelope Wells by a forlorn international crossing. There the Cowboy Border is embellished only by two small customs stations, a livestock holding pen on the U.S. side, and a few squat adobe living quarters on both sides. A Mexican and an American flag, their poles planted in their respective national soils, droop in the early morning calm.

We swooped down in a tilted curve, overflying Mexican airspace by a quarter-mile before circling back stateside and bumping down on a rodent hole-cratered dirt strip near the living quarters. Hopping over a few barbed wire strands, my pilot greeted the border guard on our side by name, Roger Morris, who looked and sounded Hispano. A conversation ensued about the types of bugs an entomologist had come to study at this dusty, remote crossing. Morris fetched a nature book to show Hurt pictures of some small red-ringed snakes he'd collected lately. Morris didn't object to my taking pictures as long as I didn't snap him or the living quarters, "For security reasons," he said.

In those days, and maybe these, Morris might well worry.

He told Hurt: "I couldn't tell who you were at first. I thought you were some Iraqui terrorist or something."

I asked if he had any ground-to-air missiles.

"Yeh," he said. "I throw rocks."

Not much later, we zigzagged along the runway, dodging the chuckholes, hoping we wouldn't be upended during takeoff.

Aloft, I snapped photos like crazy, leaning out the window, hoping my thin door wouldn't open.

Ernie started to talk again as Animas Peak came into view.

"You see how you couldn't run much cattle on this land anyhow," he noted, indicating the Animas' deep canyons and severe slopes.

The morning thermals started shaking us up a bit, but Ernie wasn't worried.

"I try to stay pretty high, so if the engine goes out, I'll have enough room to coast down," he said. I wasn't comforted.

We flew over Phelps-Dodge's copper smelter, sequestered far from outside eyes in the alkaline Playas Valley's dry lake bed near the Mexican border. Its stacks spit smoke clouds and fumes a thousand feet into the otherwise clear desert morning.

Ernie winged right to point out a fence line demarcating two pastures.

"The green side is ours," he said. "If you were doing one of those fence-line photos, you'd think the guy ranching on the other side was overgrazing. But that might not be true. He might be intensively grazing that paddock for a season. If you came back next year, our side might look like that and his would be green. Photos don't give you, like Paul Harvey says, 'the rest of the story.'"

We bounced and clanked down his headquarter's dirt strip. After securing the Cessna against the winds, Ernie had to spend the afternoon drilling for water for his stock, so he left me with a few final thoughts.

"You know," he had said, "I've joined the Cattlegrowers Association and some other groups, even though I'm not real political. I try to explain the situation to people, but if you get into that, it takes up all your time, and you don't have any time for ranching."

Crops, cattle, contraband.

For the Bootheel, isolation may prove to be a blessing or a curse. Only time will tell.

***

I gather notepad and pens, rise and indolently stretch in the sun. Time to ride. I want to make Silver City for lunch in a little Chinese restaurant near Western New Mexico University's hilly campus.

I wish I had time for Lordsburg, the last town west of Deming on I-10 before Arizona's state line. But I had driven through before, and know it as another railroad creation where roses thrive year-round in geothermally heated greenhouses. Two genuine, but mostly for-tourists ghost towns, Shakespeare and Steins, are a few miles from Lordsburg, as are some nasty alkali flats.

A few black-bottomed clouds slide in from the southwest, turning me, at last, towards the north and the blessed mountains.

Silver City

Once by the copper mines at Central and refineries elsewhere southeast of Silver, it's a pleasant ride into the old town its settlers built in the middle of a swamp, La Cienega de San Vicente. Not only did those bravos stake their claim to the marshy pastureland, they founded their town in the middle of the lands of the Gila and Mimbres Apache.

The Apaches grudgingly relocated eventually, but Earth Mother must have resented the holes miners gouged in her side. As if in vengeance, Pinos Altos Creek washed away most of Silver City's Main Street a couple of times, finally gouging a 55-foot-deep, gaping arroyo where businesses once bustled.

That arroyo's now Big Ditch Park, still cut through by Pinos Altos Creek. Businesses moved east and west of Main, which now exists only in interrupted fragments north and south of the ditch, replaced by Bullard as the town's major street.

A few other historic fragments surface in this brick-loving town conceived in Hispanic colonization, born of mining fever.

Several involve Billy the Ubiquitous Kid, here making his final appearance in these pages.

Apropos The Kid: little's left of his boyhood pre-outlaw world but three corners at the Hudson and Broadway intersection. His home was on the northwest corner; northeast, the jail from which he escaped by shinneying up the chimney; southwest, the Star Hotel, a foster home after his mother died. She's buried in Memory Lane Cemetery northeast of town, but her wooden tombstone's on display in Lincoln.

I lose my map in the backseat junk and can't find her resting place among the lanes, but a roadrunner, Mercury of the Mountains, zings across the old poplar-bordered graves.

Using the Silver City Museum as a rallying point, the city's brochures offer three one-hour walking tours of the old downtown: La Capilla delves south into adobe-lined, Mexican-settled Chihuahua Hill Historic District; the Business Historic District tour veers east into the midst of the Great Washout's successors west of Big Ditch; and the third, Gospel Hill, threads through Silver's Victorian boom residences, many near the museum.

After my Chinese food, I nose around downtown, happening onto a coffeehouse and a developing student quarter downhill from Western New Mexico University. A mug of Seattle-exported dark coffee and a good conversation later, I've learned Silver is strewn with abandoned mine craters. Downtown's contrasts: occasional colorful art deco facades and elaborately columned Victorian stores add to a recovering-bust-town ambience.

Private contributions help fund Silver restorations such as the magnificently cupolaed, three-story H.B. Ailman House, now the Silver City Museum. From the topmost cupola I scan campus and mountain vistas.

Ailman was one of the silver rush's victors. In 1878, after a prospecting trip, he was the first northern European to describe the Gila Cliff Dwellings. He and partner H. M. Meredith cashed in big when they sold their silver-rich Naiad Queen in 1880. The wealthy partners moved into Silver, bought a general store, a sawmill and built sumptuous, nearly identical Mansard Italiante-style neighboring homes.

Their Siamese Twin act dissolved when plunging silver prices and a severe drought helped in 1887 to crash a bank they had bought. They sold their twin houses for debts and left town.

The spacious rooms of Ailman's former home accommodate the city museum's displays of Victorian-period fashion, furniture and businesses, plus a gift shop featuring regional crafts and Mimbres-design contemporary pottery. Ailman's partner's home eventually met a severe fate: disassembled, its bricks and other materials helped construct other town buildings.

I stroll past a few more homes, tinseled, draped, candled and ready for the upcoming holidays, until, noting shadows shifting, I switch gears. I need to buy provisions for my trip through the Gila Wilderness to the Gila River. The Gila Cliff Dwellings National Monument is far from convenience stores or Furr's.

Pinos Altos

On the Cliff Dwellings road, six miles north into the cool high pines for which it was named, tiny Pinos Altos maintains vestiges of its mining-related history. Founded by gold miners in 1860, it was abandoned by 1862 after frequent attacks by Mangas Colorado's Apaches, survived another boom, another bust. Being restored by the artsy set, the town's old buildings include the Buckhorn Saloon and an interesting log cabin museum with a decent selection of locally produced monographs. One resident tells me large trucks again rumble by from a recently reopened gold mine not far up the wilderness road, so maybe the bust-boom pendulum is swinging again for this historic mountainside village.

The Gila

From Pinos Altos to the Gila Cliffs is only 37 map miles, but it's two full hours (really!) on the national forest's paved but narrow, twisting roads. Mountainside State Road 15 eventually drops to Lake Roberts in the Sapillo Creek Valley, then with 19 miles to go, climbs to dizzying vista overlooks and plunges several thousand feet to the sparkling Gila River, then rolls upriver to the West Fork cliff dwellings.

Gila Hot Springs lies just beyond the confluence of the Gila, New Mexico's last major free-flowing river, and its east fork. The settlement, surrounded by mountainous national forest, includes older private summer cabins and year-round homes in the immediate river valley and a cluster of trailers and modular buildings clinging to the valley's western slope. Among those, across the highway from Doc Campbell's Trading Post, is the only overnight lodging I can find in this narrow, back-country valley: a two-story, barn-like modular building heated by piped-in thermal waters. The reasonably priced lodgings include kitchens. The trading post's prices are about what I expect this far from civilization.

During the few years I lived in Las Cruces during the late '80s, I had considered the Gila too dry, too boring, too fire-prone, usually opting instead for desperate, heat-fleeing outings to the greener, cooler Sacramentos.

Several later trips changed my attitude.

For one thing, I read a few Gila-related works by early settlers and prospectors, something I wished I'd done much earlier. The 569,792-acre Gila Wilderness, the nation's first, thanks to conservationist Aldo Leopold, was set aside from the 3.3 million-acre national forest in 1924.

The adjacent Leopold Wilderness reserves another 211,300 acres. Both support bear, cougar, javelina, Rocky Mountain Bighorn Sheep and elk, mule deer, beaver, and ringtail. Thanks to its southern location, it's also home to an astoundingly varied seasonal and permanent bird population. All that natural input insinuated itself into my consciousness, finally demanding a satiating road trip.

Not that the wilderness gives a damn if I appreciate it or not. It's much too busy doing elemental things, like flooding and stirring up blizzards. Shortly after my most recent visit, a persistent rain washed a 30-foot chunk out of a bridge to the Cliff Dwellings, stranding several hunters for a couple of weeks and closing Cliff Dwellings Road for more than a month.

This time, I settle in to warm, ground-floor digs at Campbell's comfortable "barn." The rooms are TV- and phoneless, so I venture out in the nippy dark to the trading post's porch to call home. A decent-sized skunk regards me briefly over its shoulder, quickly ambling away in the pale moonlight, past the artesian spring-fed pond where I'd heard bullfrogs with boomboxes for lungs celebrate the summer night on an earlier visit.

Next morning, before sunlight touches the high caves, I revisit the Cliff Dwellings, hiking up their narrow, frosty fronting canyon. Guardian crows insult me from reddish sandstone hoodoos at the canyon's entrance. It's frigid in the glens of Douglas fir, ponderosa, piñon, Arizona walnut, towering gambel oaks, canyon grape and yucca along the canyon's forested floor. I gradually ascend the trail, taking advantage of wooden benches for welcome breaks, then cross the creek and climb 200 vertical feet up volcanic tuff.

This bridge crosses the Gila River to the mesa that shelters the Gila Cliff Dwellings. Floods sometimes close approaches to the dwellings.

Once, during one of the site's uncrowded periods, I sat at the mouth of one of the seven caves, gazing at the canyon's far wall with an El Paso-born park ranger, a Tiwa (Tiqua), who said Apaches used the facing mesa-top for burial sites.

Not so for war leader Geronimo, who was born and grew up near here. Doomed after his surrender until he died to endure first Florida swamp, then the Great Plains internments light years from his desert mountains, he swore to return to his homeland. I have no doubt he has. Or does.

The ancestral residents of the 700-year-old, cave-sheltered adobe and stone ruins might have been related to the pithouse-digging Jornada Mogollón. I already had visited one of their ruined villages at the Three Rivers petroglyphs.

The Mimbres Mogollón possibly dispersed to join the Anasazi to the north or the Casas Grandes culture to the south. The T-shaped doorways they fashioned in their cliffside village certainly hint at Anasazi influence. The official line: the former Mimbres settled in Hopi, Zuñi or other northern Arizona or New Mexico pueblos along the Rio Grande. I suppose they also could have settled at one of the Salinas pueblos. If so, there was a good chance my Tiwa ranger friend's distant ancestors once hunted this very canyon.

I brew coffee in the Mimbres-clone mug I bought earlier at the Silver City Museum. The Mimbres produced unique black-on-white pottery decorated with geometric and stylized human and animal figures that are well known today.

At the Gila visitor center, I browse a modest literature, map and poster collection, thinking Christmas, buying likewise. As I load my wagon, I remember the pack train I saw here last summer, heaped with tourists and supplies, bumping its way up a nearby ridge to the back country. I wish I could have shared that journey. They wouldn't be too happy up there today, with the mountain snow level lowering daily and the El Paso mariachi stations I picked up in Silver playing Christmas carols.

I can return home via a side trip to Mogollón, the Gila-spanning Catwalk, Reserve and the San Francisco River, but since Catron County's Commissioners recently suggested that all right-thinking citizens bear arms, maybe I'll detour. Could there be more wrong with ornery Catron County than resistance to federal Mexican Spotted Owl protection?

I avoid Reserve, passing instead via more tourist-friendly Lake Roberts, through thick pine forest and around an orange hoodoo-haunted river bend to Mimbres, then climb the long switchbacks upgrade to Emory Pass. Over the forested Black Range and down to the old mining towns of Kingston and Hillsboro lies the road home.

⇒ Information
   Deming: 1-505-546-2674
   Columbus: 1-505-531-2236
   Silver City: 1-800-548-9378
   Gila Wilderness: 1-505-536-9461

The San Juan

The weather degenerates in the next week, confining me to Las Vegas. The holidays mesh in the usual colorful blur, leaving me disgusted with materialism, claustrophobic and eager to roam.

I avoid the New Year's traffic and sulk in my office, waiting. Finally, early springtime's soothing moist air lures me from couch and computer, launches me on a Four Corners amble.

From Las Vegas, the Four Corners is a long, grueling journey, but everybody from my Apache-Lakota holy man friend to chi-chi Santa Fe spiritual dilettantes assures me I just must see Chaco. Naturally, I've waited as long as I can for this visit to Kokopelliland. After all, considering the Columbus lodge affair, I might not be in favor in the spirit world. To get to Chaco I must head west across a mean patch of ground and then it's north toward the San Juan.

El Malpais

On an earlier Four Corners trip, I had glimpsed what must surely be a manifestation of the Dark Side. Just west of McCarty's, the scarred northern limits of the El Malpais lava beds seemed to pour over I-40. The dark badlands stretch south in a wide valley bounded by Acoma's sandstone escarpments on the west and the Oso and Zuñi mountains to the east.

If it had been summer, a visit would have been instructive: I could have suffered through a preview of what Hell is all about.

New Mexico boasts several malpaises (badlands). One of the most recently formed, as young as 1,500 years old, lies west of Carrizozo, near the man-made hell of Trinity Site. Older flows slurped over Doña Ana, Harding and Union counties.

The heat that forged the 155,000 acres of lava valleys at El Malpais flared up at least three times, from as long as three million to as recently as 1,000 years ago, making the area at once the adolescent and senior citizen of New Mexico's lava lands.

A map from the Grants visitor center in hand, I backtracked five miles and turned south on State Road 117. At the Sandstone Bluffs Overlook, I viewed 25 miles of flows hardened into black sea foam.

Down the road, I was awed by La Ventana, our state's largest natural sandstone arch, dissolved by erosion and a narrow corridor formed when lava flowed near the sandstone cliffs.

For more volcano visions, I returned to Grants and took State Road 53 south.

On that route, about 15 miles after the village of San Rafael, the original site of now-demilitarized Fort Wingate, I passed an Acoma-Zuñi Trail segment, probably laid down by the Anasazi, who constructed lava rock bridges over the more formidable Malpais fissures. Although its builders marked the trail with rock cairns, some markers are hard to see.

I soon was climbing into Zuñi mountain ponderosa country. About here, County Road 42, unmarked on my state map, cut left to Junction Cave. The fair-weather track, passable by most vehicles for the first quarter-mile, leads to several volcano-related sites and a bat cave I avoided. I remembered Martin Cruz Smith's *Nightwing*. Those rabid, plague-ridden Mexican vampire bats still spilled over the borders of my memory like invading killer bees.

Junction Cave, a 17-mile-long lava tube, definitely lies in four-wheel-drive country. The tube also houses Big Skylight and Four-Window caves.

About five more miles west on State Road 53, I turned left onto the powdery black-cinder road to the Ice Cave and Bandera Crater. The wind had sprung up and I was thankful for my large, garish cowboy bandanna, which I tied on, desperado-style.

Coronado reputedly was shown the Ice Cave by the Zuñi, but he didn't have to cough up the bucks the attraction's present owners demanded.

Still, as Robert Frost reminded us, what's fire without a little ice?

I trudged past the old trading post, wandered amongst a bizarre stone and wood forest of heaped, mangled lava rock and twisted trees, and found the steep wooden stairs leading down to the algae-encrusted pool in its icicle cave.

I clicked away. Maybe my camera's equipped with a digital divining rod: those water shots were the best I captured all day.

West of the Ice Caves, and about 35 miles east of Zuñi on State Road 53 loomed El Morro (the headland), an isolated, pale sandstone mesa also known as "Inscription Rock." El Morro's a *cuesta*, sloping gently and gradually upward on one side, then dropping abruptly. In a cove near the steep end, a green, cattail-ringed natural pool and water-stained sheltering cliffs have sculpted a sweet-scented oasis that for eons has attracted animals and travelers.

Many left their marks here.

Located on ancient Zuñi-Acoma Trail, the shady nook first was inscribed by the Zuñis' Anasazi ancestors, who logically called it *"A'ts'ina,"* or "place of writings on the rock." They lived in two now-ruined pueblos on the mesa top, sometimes carving mountain goats, birds and other figures on the walls below.

Later, Spanish colonists pecked out their imprints, most including some variation of *"paso por aqui:"* I cruised through here. One such tourist was Oñate, returning in 1605 to his Rio Grande Valley base after yet another fruitless search for the Pacific Ocean, which successive Pueblo con artists, lips pursed, chins pointing, persuaded him was always *poco mas alli*, just a bit more along, sort of over there, señor. Still later, Manifest Destiny disciples, including U.S. Army cartographers, sundry Union Pacific railway surveyors and California emigrants, passed by, many tempted to scratch on the rock evidence of their literacy, complete with dates of passage and home states.

As for the Acoma-Zuñi Trail, I had returned to it after a refreshing imported lunch by El Morro's spring and a good back-scratch by a hidden boulder.

Zuñi

About a half-hour west of El Morro, I had slowed down to enter Zuñi, New Mexico's most populated pueblo, and the first visited by gold-struck Spanish explorers.

Today there's treasure in Zuñi all right, but it's in the form of innumerable fetishes and excellent silver and turquoise jewelry for sale in pueblo shops.

Our Lady of Guadalupe Mission, completed in 1629, holds down the center of the old village. Although visitors are welcome to the village itself, the Zuñi Council of late has decided to release less information about the pueblo.

Having located a well-stocked shop and perused case after case of fetishes until the room spun, I ingested a bit of coffee, then ventured north 36 miles and an undefined expanse of time up State Road 602, through undulating, craggy, piñon-juniper hills to Gallup, the jewel of old U.S. Route 66.

Indian Country

This springtime, however, I roll into Gallup from the east, past Fort Wingate and Red Rock Amphitheater. Yep, around here it's redrock country, dominated by sandstone that dissolves over millennia into fantastic shapes.

This, as area tourism touts are fond of saying, is indeed The Heart of Indian Country, at least of this particular corner of Indian Country. Indian Country being pretty expansive, extending as it does from Florida to Washington State, from Canada to Mexico, I don't think the boast holds up under a world-class challenge, but it's doing the job for now. Hogans are everywhere, as are signs advertising "We buy sheep, lambs, goats."

I check into my favorite Gallup chain hotel, the one with the indoor pool and hot tub, and plan my next week's itineraries and logistics.

Navajo Nation Zoo (Northeastern Arizona)

Early next morning I brew a dark cup of my own coffee, pack the wagon, and set out to see a few sights on *Dine' Bikeyah,* the Navajo Nation.

The 200,000-member Navajo tribe, which holds more land in New Mexico and Arizona than there is in West Virginia, is the largest U.S. Indian tribe. About 7,400 square miles of Navajo Nation is in northwestern New Mexico, where about 78,000—or 37 percent of the tribal members—live.

I start at the Navajo capital, Window Rock, Ariz., 30 miles northeast of Gallup.

Window Rock also is home to the Navajo Nation Zoo and Botanical Park.

A haystack butte towers over the Navajo Nation Zoo at Window Rock.

Anyone who thinks Native American claims about enjoying a special relationship with Nature are just publicity puff should see this zoo. It'll change minds. Not that the animals inhabit living quarters any larger than say, the Albuquerque Zoo. But the quarters they roam are natural: no concrete floors, no phony rocks. In fact, the corner where the black bear, bobcat and rare Mexican wolf live incorporates a high rock ledge. Churro sheep and elk browse in the shadow of monolithic red sandstone "haystack" rocks.

Today the zoo, founded in 1962 after somebody abandoned a bear at the Tribal Museum, also shelters cougars, coyotes, prairie dogs, mule deer, pronghorn antelope, rattlers and gopher snakes, tarantulas, salamanders and a desert tortoise.

A dirt path describes a rough circle among the rocks and by animal homes, leading me clockwise around the zoo. Since my Pueblo-Ute, Apache and Lakota friends assure me clockwise movement draws power into a ceremony, I assume the layout is purposeful, constructed with intent. I'm pretty sure of it when I spot the two styles of *hogans*. One is conical, forked-stick, roughly built "male," patterned after a sweat lodge and used mostly for ceremonies. The crib-logged "female" hogan is a log-cabin-type structure in which much of children's learning about Navajo life occurs. A small sweat lodge stands in the parklike center of the zoo, near a barely running stream.

The zoo's printed handout offers another clue: "The male (forked stick) hogan opens to the dawn, as is proper for all Navajo dwellings. The supporting forked sticks are placed in the cardinal directions. The opening in the top allows the smoke from the fire to escape, but also symbolizes the hole dug by the Badger when the People escaped into the Fourth World from the floods of the Third World."

Speaking of water, there's none in action yet this early in the year, but near the female hogan is an experimental drip irrigation system that waters about two dozen native plants, including wild geranium, elderberry and firewheel (blanket flower).

Some may think it remarkable the Dineh include human dwellings and religious structures in a space dedicated to wild animals.

But the zoo's layout restates the widely held American Indian belief that humans are not on earth to dominate, but to live in harmony with and respect for all life.

Other diversions include the tribal museum, near the Navajo Nation Inn, and nearby Window Rock Park, site of Navajo Tribal Council Headquarters. Legend has evil creatures banished through the hole in the Window Rock during the Time of Creation.

In summer, St. Michael's Mission's museum opens. Founded in 1898, the mission, two miles west of Window Rock, was the first contact many Dineh children had with belicani (outsiders), in this case Franciscans, for better or worse.

Anywhere in the heart of Indian Country, depending on the weather, local vendors may be selling anything from sheep to crafts from the backs of their pickups. They're out there today.

Their merchandise sometimes includes world-famous Navajo rugs. The Navajos, who legend says learned weaving from Spider Woman, are renowned for the dramatic patterns of their weavings. Communities created different styles, often named for their places of origin: Two Grey Hills, Burnt Water, Crystal, Teec Nos Pos and others. These sell at the monthly Navajo Rug Auction in Crownpoint.

Hubbell Trading Post (Northeastern Arizona)

After Window Rock, I'm ready for a little more of the Four Corners, before mirages shimmer from the blistering caminos and RVs crowd the road.

On an earlier Gallup visit, I'd eaten lunch at Rio West Mall, jammed with hundreds of Navajo kids socializing and adults shopping.

That may not seem exciting, but actually it was a chance to engage in a self-indulgence I'd discovered when I taught English in the distant Marshall Islands: the vaguely disorienting thrill a White Boy feels when familiar cultural markers fade and he's a minority surrounded by a majority culture not his own.

Cheap thrills notwithstanding, 55 miles northwest of Gallup, past Window Rock, across miles of ponderosa-dotted Navajo Nation Forest is the red sandstone Hubbell Trading Post National Historic Site. The post is an historical equivalent to (and in some ways an Indian Country predecessor of) today's malls.

For generations, cultures have met and learned from each other at the post.

John Lorenzo Hubbell wanted it that way. Hubbell, whose father was a Connecticut Yankee trooper and whose mother's Hispanic family hailed from the Albuquerque area, founded the post in 1878, a short decade after the disastrous Navajo internment at Fort Sumner.

From the first, the wary Navajos were drawn by Hubbell's ability to speak their language, his honesty and genuine interest in their welfare. They flocked from the windblown reaches of their reservation to trade with the dark-haired, bespectacled Hispano they called "Old Mexican" or "Double Glasses."

Hubbell repaid their confidence by interpreting government rules for them, writing their letters, teaching the importance of quality in their rug-making and silversmithing, and sometimes holding school classes. He developed Ganado, the Navajo rug pattern named for the settlement nearest his trading post.

Once, when a smallpox epidemic swept the reservation, Hubbell, immunized by a childhood bout with the disease, nursed the ailing Navajos, who were convinced he had powerful spiritual connections.

Such connections, along with hard work, must have helped Hubbell expand his trade to encompass an empire that included stage and freight lines and several other businesses, including curio shops in Hollywood and Long Beach, Calif.

Thirty-seven years after Hubbell died in 1930, his daughter-in-law sold his extensive jewelry and rug collection and the post to the National Park Service, which administers it as a living museum.

Today, the site includes a museum-visitor center, the three-room post, stables, corrals, a collection of freight wagons and farm implements and Hubbell's former home.

The post's uneven, oiled wooden floors still squeak as visitors tread them. Its dark interior, not much lighter today than when it was lit by the kerosene lanterns hanging about is as welcome a respite from outside dust and glare as ever.

Navajo women stand behind the high wooden counters, ready to sell anything from corn flakes, bananas and Spam to Navajo rugs, colorful bolts of cloth and jewelry.

Not-for-sale harnesses, horse collars and canvas saddlebags hang from the ceiling rafters in the area known as the bull pen, near the pot-bellied stove. In an adjoining room, near a case of old rifles and the glassed-in Hubbell book collection, a saleswoman patiently explains the value of Navajo rugs to tourists.

The owners of the steady stream of modern-day conestogas that fill the parking lot aren't the post's only visitors.

In the corner by the bull pen, a family of Navajo tourists talks with a clerk.

"We'd heard about this place for a long time and just thought we'd visit," one of the visitors says. "Pretty amazing."

Amazing, indeed.

Not as large as Gallup's mall, not air-conditioned, no paved parking lot, no pizza stands or yogurt shops. But for years, this has been one of those hidden internal frontiers where the fates of two peoples were decided, in this case, mostly for mutual benefit.

Canyon de Chelly (Northeastern Arizona)

Since my informant in Window Rock recommended the beauty of Indian Route 12 to Canyon de Chelly, I opt for that road and am not disappointed. I skirt the Chuska Mountains' western slope, gliding past tempting small lakes and stippling green, undulating pastureland, a pleasant contrast to the desert between Gallup to Window Rock. Dramatic mesas, buttes and spires spike the land like stone punk haircuts.

At Fort Defiance, which enjoys several restaurants and gas stations, hogans give way to tan government housing and Quonset huts at the high school. I'm not careful enough here, where Indian Route 12's changes aren't well-marked. Back on the right track, at the sign to Navajo and Lukachukai I ascend on Indian Route 12, slowly rising through piñon-juniper country and sculpted reddish rock until I reach Navajo, which apparently has renamed itself Navajo Pines. The small town, gateway to willow-bordered Red Lake, includes a small supermarket and gas stations. Not far north, the roadside earth turns the yellowish-green I associate with yellowcake, a uranium indicator.

A few miles north I round a curve, top a hill and am greeted by a large, turquoise-tinted lake surrounded by lodgepole and ponderosa pine. This is Wheatfields Lake, where for a fee, visitors boat or fish, or picnic for free. Today, scores of Navajos are engaged in one or another of those activities, despite the brisk winds.

Cutting through a few miles of high country forest, the road descends again into piñon-juniper until shortly after Navajo Community College, where I turn west onto Indian Route 64.

After about 15 miles across open range, and in my case, past several stray horses and a loose sheep herd apparently attended only by a lone black dog, I glimpse layered, striped orange and rust sandstone mesas to the north and the shadowed walls of a large canyon to the south.

Finally, a few miles northeast of Chinle, Del Muerto, one of de Chelly's major tributary canyons, yawns to the south. A few miles past the small town of Del Muerto, where the rock turns green, purplish and red, I cross de Chelly River and immediately bear left to enter the visitor center parking lot.

In the canyon just below the National Park Service visitor center is Cottonwood Campground and an amphitheater. The camp's three loops, with fireplaces, tables and restrooms are free for those who arrive early enough to snag a spot. The cottonwood groves, empty now, are a favorite recreation area and the only campsites for barren miles around.

I've just cleared the canyon rim near White House Ruin, slipping and sliding down the gritty path through a short tunnel in the redrock sandstone when a thundering horde rushes by.

It isn't buffalo, but groups of Navajo kids streaming down Canyon de Chelly's steep cliffside trail, sometimes risking precipitous shortcut leaps, jostling each other, laughing. Some 600 feet below, melt-swollen Rio de Chelly winds like a dirty vermillion yarn across the greening valley floor.

It is, after all, spring, and families who move to the canyon rim in autumn so their kids can attend the huge consolidated school in Chinle are ready to bottom out for the summer, to tend fields and flocks. The kids obviously are ready, too. If the rouge-rimmed valleys are greening, it means the wheel of the seasons is turning and it can't be long until summer.

And vacation.

I'm glad for them; glad they can repeat a relatively recent ritual of return; glad they continue in the footsteps of their ancestors, even if their canyon now is a national monument.

As they do at Hubbell Trading Post, some 40 miles south, Indian people continue to use their resources here, and the land inside de Chelly is Navajo Nation-owned. Except for day trips along White House Ruin trail, visitors aren't allowed into the 26-mile-long canyon without a Navajo guide, who generally charges $7.50 an hour for a three-to-seven-hour trip.

Still, if I had the time and money, I'd take that trip or the truck tour the Park Service offers, because much of what we *belicani* (Navajo: strangers) learn about American Indian historic sites and still-vital Indian subcultures remains hidden unless we make an extra effort.

I rest on a trailside rock, batting at tiny biting insects and reflecting on the extra effort needed just to get to the canyon, 1,000 feet deep in places.

De Chelly is a Spanish corruption of the Navajo word "tsegi," or "rock canyon." It seems obvious that the Navajo have lived here a long time, but as in much of Indian Country, the obvious can be misleading.

The canyon's whorled-rocksides (compressed ancient sand dunes) and fantastic freestanding spires and volcanic plugs now are part of *Dine' Bikeyah*. But its first known permanent inhabitants were Anasazi, Pueblo ancestors known as Basketmakers, who lived in circular below-ground pit houses, grew corn and squash, and wove yucca carrying baskets and sandals. After 700 A.D. they moved up the canyon walls to multi-storied "apartments," where the Spanish might have met their descendants. The ruins of their homes still speckle the walls of Canyon de Chelly, as they do at Mesa Verde, Chaco, Frijoles Canyon and elsewhere across the Southwest.

But at de Chelly and Chaco, the vacuum of the deserted canyons soon was filled by an invading people, the aggressive Navajo, cousins to the Apache, both peoples relative latecomers to the Southwest.

The Navajo raided Pueblo, Hispanic and American Rio Grande settlements until Kit Carson boxed them into de Chelly, eventually relocating 8,000 of them to Fort Sumner in 1864. Four years later they returned to the Four Corners, where many became shepherds, jewelers or rug weavers. Others held piecework jobs until royalties from oil, gas and uranium mining companies and World War II brought a new way of life.

Still, more so than many Eastern tribes, the Navajos have retained a defiantly self-sufficient lifestyle, "traditionals" choosing to remain in family groups clustered in rural back-country hogans, coming to the scattered settlements only to trade or school their kids. Others, the "progressives," have adapted to a more urban life, and work tribal and other jobs at population centers such as Chinle, Fort Defiance and Window Rock, where they enjoy such amenities as video rental shops and Basha's, a large supermarket-deli-hardware emporium along the lines of Jewel Osco.

Back at the canyon's top, at a windy rim overlook, I notice a man—Pueblo, probably Hopi, but definitely not Navajo—standing for several long minutes, gazing at the deep valley below. I imagine longing in his face. Maybe he's yearning for something his Anasazi and Hopi ancestors found in this canyon, something that may return to his people as the wheel continues its spin.

Or, given the glacial rate with which the federal government has moved in trying to relocate Navajos from land the Hopi claim west of here in the Hopi-Navajo Joint Use Area on the Navajo-surrounded Hopi Reservation, he may be yearning for something forever lost.

Shiprock

After consulting my map and considering the theological and astral implications of an area bounded by routes numbered 13 and 666 and a wash called "Many Devils," I turn north up a paved road towards 7,178-foot Shiprock Peak, the towering volcanic neck rising southwest of the town named for it. The Dineh call it *Tse B'it a'i,* winged rock.

Large, dark-winged birds circle the pinnacle, holding me for a few minutes. I tear away, stopping a half-hour later at a shopping center restaurant west of town for mutton stew.

Bustling now with tribal business, Shiprock's even busier in October, when it annually hosts the Navajo Fair, the area's oldest and most traditional. The event features Navajo songs and dances, a parade, rodeo, intertribal powwow, Miss Northern Navajo pageant, livestock and agricultural shows, a midway and carnival, farmers' market, food booths and arts and crafts. It coincides with a nine-day *Yei-Be-Chai* healing ceremony, also known as the Nightway Chant.

Navajo Mine

I motor by the Navajo Mine-fed Four Corners Power Plant with scarcely a glance. Since the power plant's emissions are visible for miles, and are in fact one of the few human-made artifacts discernible with the naked eye from space, I've already determined which way the wind is blowing from high on the mesa north of Shiprock.

The Navajo Mine on New Mexico's portion of the Navajo Reservation is the center of a vortex of sorts; here metal meets earth, culture meets culture, and scientific theory and reality run smack into each other.

Here, in a never-ending dance, huge drag line rigs constantly growl and rip the earth from a buried ancient reef to get at valuable coal deposits.

I recall in 1990 standing on the mine's mesa south of the San Juan River, where the bustle of equipment contrasts with the quiet grazing of nearby Navajo sheep. I watched while Luci Davis, a New Mexico State University graduate student, patiently sampled the soil.

I talked with her and her supervisor for an hour one summer morning. The power plant was spewing bigtime, and I could barely make out the Shiprock 15 miles west.

Davis, born to the Ute Clan, born for the Bitter Water people, was gathering data for her range and soil science master's degree from NMSU's Ag College.

Her laboratory was the mammoth 32,600-acre Navajo Mine. One of the largest U.S. surface mines, it surrenders million of tons of coal annually, all fired in the nearby plant, a vital energy source for Southern California, Arizona and New Mexico.

Davis' involvement with nurturing floras for grazing was a logical extension of her ties to her family and their Hereford ranch near Burnham, south of the mine. The scope of her education also was an extension of that family.

"My parents are very traditional," said Davis, youngest of six children. "They never went to school. Ranching has always been a big part of my father's life, and my mother has always been home. But they told us as we were growing up what an education would mean to us."

The Davis children, like most Navajo kids, were sent off to school. For Luci, that meant Bureau of Indian Affairs' Nenahnezad Boarding School at Fruitland, then Farmington's public schools.

"The shock to a six-year-old of being shipped off, your mother leaving you at a place you don't know, that was hard. But we grew up away from home and that brought out our independence," she recalled.

After obtaining her undergraduate degree in 1985, Davis worked as an Extension Agent for the Navajo Department of Agriculture at Window Rock. But she kept remembering a taunt from her older brother, Albert, who holds a master's degree.

"He told me when I was growing up that 'none of you girls will ever get your master's.' I ask him now why he said it, and he says 'I did it to motivate you,'" she said.

Another motivation, Davis said, was the location of her parents' ranch.

"Burnham has some potential for coal mining," Davis said. "Since my parents live off the land, it really hurts them to see it being mined. And there's a chance that the Navajo Agricultural Project will move out to Burnham. It's a question of who'll be there in 25 years. My parents always told us 'you're going to be the ones to make those decisions, so get out and learn about the situation.'

"It hurts me, too, to see the land treated like that. I want to know for myself all the processes involved in mining; reclamation and later, grazing. Then I can go back and help my parents and the community to understand a positive way to go," she said.

Just as she needed her brother's teasing to motivate her to try graduate school, Navajo people need motivation from within, Davis said.

"Navajos relate better to their own people as role models. We need that extra trust and familiarity," she observed.

That familiarity motivated Davis, reinforced her concern for the Navajo people, caught in their own whirlpool at the twirling center of cultural change.

"I just hope some other Navajo students can look at what I've done and decide they can do it, too," Davis said.

I take a well-deserved break at a Farmington motel's hot tub before my next strenuous journey. Tomorrow I might be glad I rested.

Chaco Culture National Historical Park
Today I will need all the energy I can muster to tour Chaco.

Once in a great while comes along a story so great in scope, so sweeping in implication, a writer struggles to understand the whole by examining its parts.

Chaco Canyon is one of those stories.

It's the out-of-the-way kind of place that attracts really determined visitors, almost as to a shrine, although its remoteness seems to deter hardly anyone. Even in windy early April, the canyon crawls with tourists.

There's a reason: to experience one of the cores of Anasazi culture in the Great Southwest, Chaco's a must.

Chaco is 62 miles south of Bloomfield, by way of State Road 44 and dirt State Road 57, the worst of the two entries, although it's closer to Bloomfield. From Nageezi, an alternate route is paved, then dirt County Road 7800 to the same State Road 57.

The 26 miles of dirt road morphs like a Kafkaesque beetle from graded clay to sandy bottom to killer washboard several times. The final descent into the long canyon narrows to a boulder-lined single lane with blind corners.

While I survive the ride in, once on the paved loop road at the hot, dry, unshaded canyon's bottom, I discover few amenities other than drinking water, coffee and a few snacks at the extremely informative and well-run visitor center. The afternoon heat is such that I can't believe I'd been in blinding snow a few short days before.

Not that the Chaco experience doesn't have several up sides.

Confronted with such Spartan simplicity, my mind is freer to wander, to contemplate, along with myriad archaeologists and anthropologists, why the Chacoans, ancestors of today's Pueblos, abandoned their homes so long ago.

Those thoughts are the exception, because it's not easy to concentrate on much of anything here. Chaco is too disconcerting, too immense in the scheme of things: too large, too ancient, too germane to the span of human inhabitation of Southwestern North America.

Here, 1,000 years ago, a series of peoples that merged into one people worked, played, worshipped and slept, chasing dream shadows across silent canyon walls. They probably never dreamed that some day they'd abandon their canyon, moving towards today's Rio Grande pueblos and Acoma, Zuñi and Hopi.

In succession across a three-century sweep, they crafted various-sized multi-storied masonry rock settlements under high, rocky cliffs. They irrigated now-dry cornfields and flourished in an oasis surrounded by harsh, high desert plateaus.

Not only did they carefully construct some 75 rock and adobe towns and 400 settlements from 900 to about 1180 A.D., they built them to endure. Endure they have, generating admiration for the work of superb architects who planned and built the masonry town and kiva walls.

The northeast-to-southwest canyon protects 13 major town ruins, with a half-dozen more on surrounding mesa tops and scores more strung out for miles in all directions.

Chaco's architectural time line runs from Early Basket Maker to Classic Pueblo periods, with styles overlapping, as did the civilizations that produced them.

I climb a steep trail to enter Pueblo Bonito's plaza, but it's crawling with touring college students, so I retreat for now. Pueblo Bonito and Chetro Ketl, less than a mile apart, are the largest, most complete ruins. Huge, multi-storied edifices compete in grandeur with the cliff that backs them. Intricately arranged rectangular rooms open onto the vast plaza and its numerous kivas.

West of Bonito, so close to Chaco Arroyo it's in danger of being washed away, is D-shaped Pueblo del Arroyo. Just down the paved road is Kin Kletso, near which the able-bodied can scramble up a worn, narrow path to the windy mesa top, on which are more ruins.

Awe, of course, is one of the building blocks of religion, and one interpretation of Chaco is that in at least one incarnation it was a religious center, populated at any given time by but a few families. How else can we explain why people who didn't use the wheel built more than 400 miles of arrow-straight, 30-foot-wide roads from the central great pueblos to at least 75 smaller outlier sites up to 90 miles away? What else explains the "sun dagger" seasonal observatory high atop Fajada Butte, which anchors the canyon's southeastern end?

Yet the only time I actually "feel" the people who once lived here is alone in a massive room block at Pueblo Bonito. Here, for the first time in my years of Southwestern ruins-hopping I am totally enclosed by walls, backed by other walls, topped by other walls, deep inside the living areas of a vanished civilization.

What went on in these rooms? Excavations have shown them to have been, successively, living quarters, granaries, trash bins and tombs.

Chaco's vast spaces swallow up my time sense, its immeasurable distances, reaches, perforating my memory. My mental fabric tears, the continuous weave of consciousness is violated, only gaps remain.

Whatever their other uses, these rooms define a horizon of sorts and snap things into perspective.

I emerge from the ruins and Chaco to sink into a dreamless sleep in Farmington. I seem to hear a ceaseless wind all night, however.

Aztec Ruins National Monument

Morning dawns, coffee disappears and I'm on the road to Aztec, east of Farmington.

The debilitating 12th-century (1130-1180) drought that sucked the vitality from the Anasazi cities that once dotted the Four Corners area wasn't as violent as a tornado, but it was just as destructive.

Yet, unlike cyclonic furies, the drought spared, even helped preserve the architectural wonders of a civilization that might easily be compared to that of ancient Greece.

One of these, a site today known as Aztec Ruins, near the town of Aztec, slumbered for centuries beneath tons of earth. Surviving longer than Chaco, its prototype 65 miles south, because it was watered by the reliable Animas River, it was noted by early Spanish explorers, but

Eerie light plays inside the reconstructed kiva at Aztec National Monument.

wasn't excavated until the early 20th century by archaeologist Earl Morris.

Aztec, so-named by Anglo settlers because they thought it resembled Mesoamerican ruins, never was occupied by Aztec Indians, although its Anasazi inhabitants probably traded with Indians far to the south. "Aztecans" were cousins both to the Chacoans and the Mesa Verdeans who lived about 40 miles northwest.

Aztec Pueblo, consisting of the first-built and now-excavated 400-room west pueblo and the still-unearthed east pueblo, was occupied during two periods. The first lasted about 50 years after the pueblo was built around 1111 A.D. until the drought that devastated other area pueblos also took its toll here.

After three decades of drought, after the last Chacoan stragglers had abandoned their canyon and moved south and east, Aztec was reoccupied, this time by Mesa Verdeans or people influenced by their cliff-dwelling culture.

But by 1300, Aztec also stood empty, its inhabitants, like their ancestors, heading for the better-watered Rio Grande basin.

What's so special about Aztec?

For one thing, its midpoint location on one of the well-engineered Chacoan "roads" means it was in the overlapping cultural orbits of two important Anasazi centers during a period during which both peaked.

For another, its latter-day excavators were enthralled by what they found at Aztec, including the skeleton of a six-foot-two-inch man, who lived among people most of whom were five-foot-two or shorter.

Intrigued by Aztec, archaeologist Morris in 1934 restored the village's most prominent landmark, a "great kiva" built in the Chacoan tradition.

That stunning restoration, which I visit the day after Chaco, changes things.

Humbled in its vaulted chamber, I now picture the Anasazi not just as a people who built large, but relatively crude homes and kivas but a people standing proud among the world's great civilizations. This kiva demonstrates just how classical the late Pueblo Classical period (1100-1300 A.D.) really was.

The kiva, with morning light pouring through its 15 surface room windows and two doors opening north and south, might easily be the Delphic temple in which Cassandra's oracles received their sacred intuitions. In comparison, the restored kivas at Pecos National Historical Park are so many ground squirrel burrows.

Supported by four thick columns that each stood on four limestone disks weighing 375 pounds each, the roof alone weighs some 95 tons.

The spacious chamber invites flights of fancy. For instance, did the large man whose skeleton was unearthed in the northern room block conduct ceremonies or business in this sacred space?

Pueblo mythology, like that of the Mexican Aztecs, tells of a tall, light-skinned, bearded man who taught the people many things, then vanished to the east, the direction the Anasazi moved, promising to return. The Aztec and their predecessors called him Quetzalcoátl. This pervasive feathery snake has slithered by before and no doubt will again.

Did the giant's fame spread south, or his descendants migrate from this river valley paradise that may be Aztlán to Tenochtitlán, today's Mexico City?

Whether or not his spirit returned as Quetzalcoátl, the morning star, he was a man of stature probably living in a dignified, ordered civilization that reflected a respect for all that is. We would do well to elevate similar precepts today.

Four Corners Outdoor Dramas

Weary from tracing my version of the Anasazi Saga, I lunch in Farmington and reflect on the summer I was introduced to two Anasazi-related dramas.

I'd waited several years before taking in *Anasazi: The Ancient Ones* and its newer sequel, *Hopi: People of Peace,* both by Farmington-area native Sharon Hatch French. If only I'd known what I were missing.

Anasazi, staged at the city-run Lions Wilderness Park Amphitheatre in Farmington, using broad-sweeping drama and traditional and original music, relates the story of Sarah Mara Boots.

Boots, a half-Navajo, half-Paiute girl whose parents were killed by raiding Indians, was raised by a Mormon missionary family. She later was reclaimed by her Navajo grandmother, Black Shawl, played by French, whose humorous use of Navajo *patois* lifts the show out of some historic dark moments.

Boots, played that year by Michelle Jordon, spent the rest of her childhood on Navajo land, eventually marrying Mormon missionary

Ira Hatch. The couple, instrumental in the eventual return of T'aa Diné (Navajos) from their Fort Sumner exile, were French's great-grand-parents.

Encouraged by veteran director Merril Lynn Taylor, the show's cast carries the audience through both tragic and joyful events surrounding Sarah Mara's relationship with her grandmother, as the youngster grows to womanhood learning Indian ways.

While *Anasazi* is staged on spectacular sandstone cliffs in an en-hanced natural amphitheater, *Hopi* is presented in a kiva-style circular stage backdropped by a small Hopi village at Salmon Ruin near Bloomfield.

Written and produced by French and staged with the cooperation of the Salmon Ruin Museum, the show unfolds in a space reminiscent of a miniature Paolo Soleri Amphitheater.

Hopi follows the lives of Boots' children, whom their father left with his Hopi friends when Sarah Mara died giving birth to their fifth child.

The story is told from the point of view of Joseph, one of those ethnically mixed children, who was acculturated forcefully into white society at one of the dreaded Indian boarding schools. Joseph, like his mother, Sarah Boots, was suspended painfully between two worlds. He walked alone along one of our invisible cultural borders, enduring the tortured fate of those once known as "breeds."

His Indian family included Tuvie, who "gave" the Mormons the Navajo land on which they built a town named for him—Tuba City—and his wife Pulaskanimki, played by the multi-talented French.

Joseph, drunk and distraught, returns to his home village, Oraibi, where he is guided through a flashback of his life by a mysterious spirit woman he names Sapling.

The unfolding scenes, while they portray no less tragic and poi-gnant situations than does *Anasazi,* include more wry "Indian humor," which French wrote into the script to great advantage.

Both shows play well in the great out-of-doors, with profes-sional-level lighting, sound and costumes adding to high production values.

In fact, *Anasazi's* stage is on the site of an ancient campground.

There's no more appropriate use of such sacred space than interpre-tive dramas mounted by the local people, many of them Native Ameri-cans, who now honor that space.

Sharon French, playwright and actress, on the set of her "Anasazi" outdoor drama at Farmington.

That was confirmed by the brilliant greenish-blue asteroid that streaked like a Roman candle behind the towering sandstone cliffs at *Anasazi* the night I attended.

Jicarilla Apache Reservation

By now, trapped in a time warp from which home seems unobtainable, I cross the Jicarilla Mountains to Dulce for a final detour on this journey's home stretch, anxiously Vegas-bound.

Isolation.

You gotta love it.

Well, you don't gotta, but I do, and my traveling hints often take wanderers where they don't recognize their car radio's station call letters and cable TV is an infant science.

In fact, so back in the mountains is one of my favorite places, the feds used part of it a couple of decades ago in an underground experiment called Gas Buggy to determine if nukes could improve natural gas production.

Turned out nukes couldn't, but that didn't faze residents of the 850,000-acre Jicarilla Apache Reservation, 35 miles east of and across the Continental Divide from Chama on U.S. 64. Nor did continued unsubstantiated reports of UFO activities in the piney hills around Dulce, the tribal capital.

Isolated or not, the Jicarillas have augmented their economic development by insisting on their right to levy taxes on fuels extracted from their lands. Simultaneously, they've carefully developed a type of nonintrusive, low-profile tourism that today provides a much safer yield than anything measured in megatons.

Now their travel brochure promises "untouched acres of outdoor recreation"… at "primitive camping areas … nestled around four mountain lakes." And they deliver on their promises.

Dulce, flung across and under several enfolding limestone-streaked mesas, is relatively quiet except when its 1,800 or so inhabitants and crowds of visitors enthuse a bit during high school sports events, rodeos, July's Little Beaver Roundup and the mid-September Stone Lake Fiesta.

The Jicarillas, probably the last Athapascan people to enter New Mexico, didn't come by their present homelands easily.

Nomadic wanderers until just before European contact, they hunted mountains and mesas, establishing a mutually beneficial trading relationship with Taos and Picurís pueblos. The Pueblos taught them to grow corn and build rancherias, flat-topped adobe houses, which they did as far east as west-central Kansas and as far west as Rayado until invading Comanches drove them deeper into the Sangre de Cristos by the mid-1720s. In 1733, a Jicarilla mission opened at Taos.

During a transition period, the Jicarillas lived around Taos and Truchas in the winter, ranging to Mora and Pecos in the summer. They engaged U.S. troops several times in the 1850s, but a generation later accepted the reservation life promised by the U.S. government, although Washington didn't get around to establishing their present reservation until 1887.

Settling in on land once occupied by the Anasazi—with ruins and pictographs to prove it—the Jicarilla set about making lemonade from lemons, building up both their fossil fuel and tourism businesses.

Today, in an ironic twist smacking of sweet revenge on the machine that hastened the bisons' demise, the tribe invites visitors to overnight at the Jicarilla Inn when they ride the Cumbres and Toltec Railroad, based in Chama. And they'll throw in a Jicarilla cultural presentation upon request.

Too late, I note the Inn doesn't have a hot tub or pool.

In fact, in a display of tongue-in-cheek, underappreciated good ol' Indian Humor, the young Indian woman behind the front desk laughs and says if I want a hot tub, I can run my bath water deep. I don't chuckle, but the rest of the night crew breaks up.

Then she helpfully suggests a sunset drive along paved roads to four high-country lakes, a route on which I circle in the gathering dusk, all the while in view of snow-capped peaks, all the while grateful I spend a lot of time just getting lost in the middle of Indian Country.

Next morning, still not chuckling, after a long, hot shower that does little to ease my road weariness and a blue corn pancake breakfast that does, I slip across the Continental Divide, bear east to Chama, then south and east across two mountain ranges, towards home.

⇒ Information
El Malpais National Monument, south of Grants: 1-505-287-3407
El Morro National Monument, east of Zuñi Pueblo:
  1-505-783-4226

Zuñi

    Pueblo of Zuñi Arts and Crafts Center: 1-505-782-5531

    Saturday Guadalupe Mission tours: 1-505-782-4477

Dine' Bikeyah

    Navajo Nation Zoo, Window Rock, Ariz.: Free.

    1-602-871-6573

    Navajo Rug Auction, Crown Point, N.M.: 1-602-786-5302

    Navajo Fish and Wildlife Dept.: 1-602-871-6451 or -52

    Navajo Nation Parks and Recreation: 1-602-871-4941

    ext. 6647

    Navajo Nation Tourism Dept. 1-602- 871-6659

Hubbell Trading Post: Free. Scant services in Ganado.

    1-602-755-3475

Canyon de Chelly National Park: Admission free. Fee for

    guided tour.

    NPS tour information: 1-602-674-5436

Chaco Canyon National Monument: Entry fee.

    1-505-786-7014. Call ahead for road conditions.

Outdoor dramas: Fee.

    Anasazi: *1-800-326-7602*

    Hopi: *1-505-632-2013*

Jicarilla Apache Reservation

    Jicarilla Natural Resources: 1-505-759-3255 or

    Jicarilla Inn: 1-505-759-3663

The Upper Rio Grande

Revived by another home visit and amazed at how much the Aztec kiva has set me thinking again about the Red Road, I embark as if I were, like the Blues Brothers, on some mission from God. Once I thought I kept up this on-the-road pace because I needed the income. The pitiful thing about writers, after all, is they *must* write. They can't, or won't do anything else. And since the circling employer barracudas know the blood of helpless suckerfish when they smell it, independent writers, even many with formidable educations, make less per hour than a car mechanic, plumber or electrician, who can botch their jobs, then walk away from their messes. Not writers. Writers are accountable. Screw up a sink job, only the homeowner knows. Write a mistake, the whole world knows.

Yet, although I miss my family, something else out here in the Great Big Empty also calls, something that demands to be written. Or maybe something that just demands to be found.

By the time I cross the Sangre de Cristos via Pueblo Creek and U.S. Pass to Taos, I've stopped wondering. It's an hour's haul to this trip's ultimate destination, so I relax over some caffeine, if such is not oxymoronic, at my favorite coffeehouse. The hours do zoom by when I'm in Taos: a friend to visit here, a gallery opening there. Finally, crimson late afternoon light reminds me I'm behind schedule.

Costilla

By the time I enter Costilla, just south of the Colorado border, the quarter moon delicately layers yellow light over the pale pink and icy purple, the waning sunset pours over nearby crumbling adobe walls. This must be what that old fraud Carlos Castañeda called "a crack between the worlds." Or a perfect stage setting for some sort of harbinger.

I stop at a pay phone outside a *tiendita* on the Rio Costilla, its bosque banks moistened by recent snowmelt.

Impatient darkness settles over Costilla like widow's lace. I can barely see the phone's punch pad numbers.

I hang up, wait for the line to clear, consider Costilla's history.

Costilla ("rib"), which in 18th-century Spanish also means a long slope along a mountain range, actually was four active, fortified, agriculturally supported colonial placitas strung along the rio. Despite ongoing economic revival efforts, the placitas—de Arriba, del Pelee, del Medio, de Abajo—have been shadows of their former selves for generations. For some reason, I'm spooked, feel as if I'm being watched.

Maybe it's the series of old ruined walls and buildings lurking where once a four-story *torreón* (watchtower), homes and corrals stood.

According to one of several versions of the placitas' founding, its builder, Juan de Jesus Bernál led Taos and Arroyo Hondo settlers here in 1852. At the time, the land was part of the Maxwell Grant. When the Denver and Rio Grande Railway laid tracks through the area late in the last century, the village's future seemed assured. A short-lived gold rush and a Dutch company's failed agricultural development scheme proved disappointing. Eventually cattle ranching and farming replaced the sheep culture around which the placitas had solidified.

In some ways, Costilla's is the story of many New Mexican communities removed from our 20 or so urban centers. They are, in essence, bordertowns. Theirs is a tale of settlement on the edge, far from today's supply lines, hemmed in by encircling wild country. But it's definitely somewhere in terms of Hispanic history: also on the border.

This settlement's story may continue a bit longer due to Santa Fean Helen Doroshaw and her Cottonwood Foundation, which fixed up the old Placita de Arriba and slapped *nouveau* New Mexican turquoise paint on everything that didn't move. The Costilla Valley Livestock Association also developed fishing and hunting areas on their land abutting the Carson National Forest. And Ski Rio, hopefully for good, has thrown off financial problems and is back in operation as New Mexico's northernmost ski resort.

Still trying to get past a busy signal, I walk tight circles around my parked car. One by one the dogs have stopped barking. From the bosque fringing the river, indistinct noises rustle, something large moving closer, then all is quiet.

Suddenly, not 50 yards away in the darkened cottonwoods, the sounds return, so close at hand I jump: Huh HOO-HOO! and the answer, an octave lower: Huh-uh HOO-HOOO!

Two great horned owls are calling each other home.

Then, just beyond the nearest ruins, in the earliest moonlight, a coyote pack whines, whimpers, squeals and barks, then vanishes.

What is going on here?

Never mind. Just a bunch of moonstruck sound doggies laughing at the timid gringo.

I'm not actually frightened. Somehow, I feel as though I've been welcomed back to the Good Red Road.

Nevertheless, like the wanderer in The Band's "Take a Load Off, Fanny," I know it's time to find place where a man can find a bed.

Costilla Bed and Breakfast is booked up in the partially restored southernmost placita, Plaza de Arriba, but the restaurant's cook/waitress assures me that Erlinda, the bartender, rents rooms. Erlinda unglues a middle-aged man from his favorite stool and he silently drives me a half-mile to the clean, motel-like rooms apparently added to someone's home. I don't care. The paneled room is private, quiet and warm, with a spectacular view of the mountains east of Valle Vidal. It has everything I need for a predawn, full-frontal, wildlife-scouting attack on the wilderness. Everything but a phone. I'm glad I've already made my call and don't have to go out again.

Funny, I think, unpacking my toothbrush. I feel no apprehension about the animal choruses back at the grocery. But my room has a deadbolt lock and I'm going to use it. I have a full day of elk scouting to do and I'm not going to be intimidated by up-country spirits.

Valle Vidal

True to form, the chilly dawn breaks early, as it has a habit of doing, no matter the season.

But I'm already on State Road 196, chugging mountainward into the mystic, stalking wildlife, especially the elusive elk of Valle Vidal.

Thinking I'd rise earlier than the elk, I loaded and packed my cameras last night, and carried breakfast and lunch fixings from Costilla's general store.

The only problem: one species rising earlier than this elk stalker is the Hard-working Road Crew, out like eager beavers. Like beavers, that is, who aim multiton rock-hauling trucks that kick up so much dust I can't breathe or see landscape for several minutes after they thundered by. I curse their retreating dust clouds, but when this road's graded, it'll be smooth running from Amalia across the spine of the Sangre de Cristos almost to Cimarrón, so I lighten up.

Besides, since I've pounded this beat on my seat for years now, I appreciate decent roads.

So does the Rio Costilla Livestock Association, one of this economically stressed area's driving forces. The RCLA owns the 79,279-acre Rio Costilla Park, through which I passed on Forest Road 1750 before entering Valle Vidal.

The 10 Latir Lakes, near 12,708-foot Latir Peak, open to fishing after the ice crust melts in late June.

No problem, since I'm headed up the road to Valle Vidal, a 100,000-acre high-country bequest of the Pennzoil Company to the U.S. Forest Service in 1982. I had already visited Pennzoil land at exclusive Vermejo Park, northeast of Vidal and of the "Rock Wall," a vertically upthrust, miles-long palisade in the Cimarrón Range.

Vermejo Park's private and pricey. Valle Vidal's public and free. If I'm lucky, I'll pretty much have the free one to myself.

The Forest Service's map touts Valle Vidal as home to deer, turkey, bear, mountain lion and at least 2,000 trophy elk.

But the monster rock truck dust clouds already have blown my chance to hear one of the big buglers, much less photograph him.

Suddenly, as I creep down a side road, I see something stir in the mixed roadside undergrowth. A stag. Since I hate to pass the buck, I skid to a stop and the mature multi-pointer lifts his head from munching ground cover long enough for us to acknowledge each other. Camera clicking, I wish for more light. Finally, the old boy sniffs and haughtily stalks away. So do I, in the direction of Red River.

Red River

I hit Red River's outskirts looking dusty, hot and disheveled, as usual after extended hours behind the wheel. Why should the townsfolk care? After all, they host an annual bikers' weekend, entertaining thousands of Harley enthusiasts.

By comparison, the friendly townies I'll no doubt encounter will think I'm an IBM salesman.

From a hill above town, I scan the deep, high Sangre de Cristo valley to see if anything has changed since my visit last summer.

At first glance, nothing has. But Red River isn't a stereotypical, sleepy mountain village.

For instance, the huge MolyCorp blemish still scars the mountains northwest of town. Mining companies come and go; their despoliations seem to last forever. Moly's opening again soon, the last I heard. That's good, because mines provide jobs. Especially working mines. I just think we need to clean up what we mess up.

Today, the town's few streets are quiet, still a couple of months before the season, but last summer I'd read a startling sign that sounded a jarring note. It warned that the town's maximum allowed decibel level was 84. That's about the level one of those obnoxious, unmuffled, fat-tired OTR vehicles generates.

This town obviously prides itself on providing almost anything that goes *vroom-vroom-vroom!*

I mean, why else a decibel warning sign?

The answer was obvious when I had cruised busy summertime Main Street. "For rent" signs promised rides for all seasons, every kind of ear-splitting wheeled, fossil-fueled transportation imaginable. Snow-mobiles, jeeps, motorcycles, motor bikes: if it runs on internal combustion and makes lots of jarring noise, Red River retailers will rent it. *¡Ayiii, batos!* there probably would have been a surplus Sherman tank if the merchants could have found one.

There was an era when the only noise near the townsite was the rushing river. But when hopeful miners materialized at the turn of the 19th century, that pristine white noise was driven back to wilderness' edge, all the way to the sumptuous condos now lining the valleys south of town. Even there, unlike the deer and occasional wandering bear that drive urban visitors nuts, the water music rarely emerges, at least not during the tourist seasons.

Red River—named for the Rio Colorado that flows through it— was founded by gold diggers from Elizabethtown around 1870, but wasn't formally laid out until 1894.

Last summer I thought Red River suffered an identity crisis. It wasn't sure if it wanted to be the Southwest's Cowboy Kitsch Capital, some little chalet-ridden burg in Germany, Biker Heaven, or a good ol' place to haul missus and the kids on summer vacation.

The former mining town's business names reflect the season-induced schizophrenia, ranging from Bull O' the Woods (after the nearby high-altitude lake) and Lazy Miner to Edelweiss, Sitzmark and Der Markt.

Those Teutonics gave me a case of *der zeitgeist* blues. No problem. I switched continents to watch Old West gunfighters in front of Frye's Old Town, a fake storefront village with shops, right across the street from the wooden Old World turrets of several ersatz chalets.

Personal noise-related snobbery aside (hey, my ears are sensitive!), this is a great place for kids. Near the ski slopes, the indoor Black Mountain Playhouse sprawls over several acres. Play, in this case for pay, includes pool, miniature golf, foosball, ping-pong, skating, air hockey, video games, a few kiddie rides and dancing.

In summer, The Community House near the town's center hosts a lot of free amusements, such as singalongs and free movies. And the Red River Inn's Mineshaft Theater stages a twice-weekly old-fashioned melodrama.

The Alpine Theater hosts the jingle-jangle of bluegrass and country music two nights a week. Twangy stringed instruments seem appropri-

Faux Western town storefronts appeal to visitors in Red River.

ate in this steep-walled backwoods valley, a favorite venue of singer and *nouveau*-Taoseño Michael Martin Murphey.

Red River's best feature, however, is south of town, where stunning, wildflower-bordered high mountain trails lead to summertime glories like glacial Middlefork Lake. Wheeler Peak's often-snowy 13,161-foot summit is a mere 14-mile round-trip jaunt. I took a break at Pioneer Canyon, behind the ski area, where the Forest Service offers a self-guided tour over, around and through a rough old mining trail. The rangers say the abandoned old mining tunnels are dangerous and cave in without notice. They also advise four-wheel-drive. I heed the warning, instead climbing the trail along Pioneer Creek. About a mile in, numerous old gold and copper mine tunnels yawn, but they're dangerous also, and I stay out.

I'm not putting down the lively, friendly and fun town of Red River. It may have been a primo place for miners, cowboys and kids, but I'm looking for peace and quiet, so I look elsewhere. Since Red River sightseeing isn't why I've ventured through town this time anyhow, I climb through 9,620-foot Bobcat Pass, roll through the Moreno Valley and down to magical Taos.

Taos

Forest-hemmed Taos Canyon can contain only a limited number of summer and year-round homes, and only the lucky few live near splashing Rio de Taos. Knowing that makes me redouble efforts to find live water elsewhere.

I try my luck and wagon's springs, bumping up a rocky forest road to Capulín Canyon, where a mountain park's mica-streaked, slick mud road almost wrecked me years ago. The canyon generates pleasant memories. I'd once clonked much higher up the rutted trail in my '62 Pontiac, contentedly chopped dead-and-down snags for firewood and gazed dreamily over the Rio Grande Valley. That was an extremely romantic winter, I think, pulling off the now-dry dirt road into a spacious glade, spreading a mat and enjoying the thin noon sunlight.

It's nice to relax. I certainly hadn't been able to when I'd first hit Taos 24 years ago, hard on the heels of the hippie horde. In Taos, I quickly learned one of the realities of life in Nirvana: Northern New Mexico version.

Here, where "sense of place" is so pervasive, they pay in mountain scenery *y no mucho mas.* That financial truth, with rare exceptions, applies for Indian, Hispano or gringo.

Millicent Rogers Museum

My first Taos winter, my then-wife, my eldest daughter, then three, and I struggled for survival while I taught at Taos High School. Since the fierce cold was devouring our budget, and scenery buys neither *frijoles* nor firewood except for dead artists or tourism traders, my wife cast about town for a job she assumed would pay commensurate with her B.A. plus 15 graduate hours.

She ended up briefly as a guide at Millicent Rogers Museum, where she was paid less than my teacher's salary.

But she did enjoy one of the museum's fringe benefits. Draped over her tour guide's puffy white blouse and generous Navajo skirt, she wore pounds of turquoise and silver jewelry provided by the museum. That's about as close as we ever came to Millicent Rogers' wealth.

Rogers, a Standard Oil heiress, was born rich and entered Taos that way in 1947. She ventured from the Eastern fashion centers to visit, but happily stayed until her 1953 death.

Her exotic good looks—svelte, abundantly blonde, with almond eyes and a natural *savoir faire*—had made her a sought-after high-fashion model for *Vogue, Bazaar* and other advocates of *haute couture.*

As it has to a fortunate few, Taos reached out and embraced Millicent Rogers.

Returning the compliment, she adapted American Indian dress styles, spreading a casual, yet elegant dress mode later known as "the Santa Fe Look" to the less-enlightened East.

Enamored of the high-desert, small mountain village ambience, and recognizing true quality and beauty when she saw it, Millicent Rogers began collecting the Southwest.

During the '40s, she accumulated a substantial cache of American Indian and Hispanic art: jewelry, textiles, basketry, pottery, paintings, *bultos,* and *retablos.*

The museum houses today an exquisite collection by noted Pueblo pottery revivalists Maria Martinez and her son Popovi Da of San Ildefonso. In the intimate courtyard sits an R.C. Gorman bronze of a

Navajo woman, a three-dimensional rendition of his trademark painted images.

A museum entrance foyer to a small *capilla* (chapel) is draped with Rio Grande-woven rugs and blankets and resounds with melodic Hispanic colonial folk tunes from a concealed source.

The museum attempts a contemporaneous outlook, as demonstrated by its ongoing current exhibits.

When I recently returned to the museum for the first time in years, it was little changed. The only thing: today's Millicent Rogers female staffers no longer dress like Navajos at a social dance.

Kit Carson Home

I remount and drop down to Taos Plaza, stopping for some *burritos y chiles verdes* before visiting with Kit Carson's memory at his old home on Kit Carson Road, near the plaza.

Carson sleeps peacefully now, I assume, as he has for some time in his confining plot near the plaza.

I wonder what he'd think of today's tourist throngs, that illiterate old adventurer, wader-of-icy rivers, chunky Indian-fighting ol' hoss who also had kids by at least one cherished Indian wife. If he knew what a Pandora's Box he opened when he blazed the trails in the 1830s and '40s, opening up the West to waves of U.S. exploitation, would he hang his head?

Of course, Carson, the fur-trapping Scotsman, probably was given neither to contemplation nor guilt. He had mountain man rendezvous' to strut around, generals to lead to California and Navajos to round up. Along the way, in 1843, he married Taoseña Josepha Jaramillo, barely 15.

Señorita Jaramillo, who came closer than anyone to exerting a civilizing influence on Carson, was a daughter of don Francisco Jaramillo and sister-in-law of Gov. Charles Bent, slain at his home a couple of blocks northeast of Carson's in the 1847 Taos Rebellion.

For her, Carson bought a 12-room adobe, much standing near the board-walked portion of Kit Carson Road just off Taos Plaza.

Today a little more than half of the building that was Carson's home is owned by Kit Carson Historic Museums. Three museum rooms are furnished as they might have been during the Carsons' 25-year residence; another concentrates on the archaeological record of Taos and other pueblos; yet another is filled with artifacts pertinent to the history of Taos.

Built in 1825, the old U-shaped home's thick walls still shelter visitors from much outside noise. I stood at the well in the *placita,* imagining the young Josepha as the subject of Jackson Browne's song, "Our Lady of the Well," gazing "across the plains to where the mountains lie so still."

One biographer noted that Carson's check-out after eating a buffalo steak was timed exactly right, just before the buffalo slaughter commenced and the thrusting rails severed the connection between the pre- and post-industrial West.

If Carson haunted Taos today we'd probably find him under a stately tree in the park that bears his name and shelters his grave. Perhaps, having learned to read in his decades in the ethereal realms, he'd be discussing a book with Mabel Dodge Luhan, who also reposes in his park.

And maybe he'd still regale us with tales of wanderlust from some dusty tome he'd just read or a new one he'd written, something Kiplingish like: "Go and look behind the ranges. Something lost behind the ranges. Lost and waiting for you. Go."

Martinez Hacienda

I go, but not far, to see an estate once inhabited by a Carson contemporary, Padre José António Martinez. The hacienda is only a few miles southwest on Ranchitos Road.

Despite its sometimes obvious poverty, New Mexico harbors hidden wealth, both material and spiritual.

The two occasionally blur, synthesize New Mexico-style, into unexpected combinations that produce a third, overriding impression. An example of such synthesis is the Martinez Hacienda, a classic colonial New Mexican *rico's* home.

When I push open the heavy wooden gate to enter past its thick adobe walls, I can all but hear the shouts of yesterday's children as they ran under the long portals and drank from the freestanding well.

And what kids they were!

Severino Martinez, who bought his four-room hacienda in 1804 and expanded it to 21 rooms by the time he died in 1827, wasn't only a prominent merchant in the trade between Taos and Chihuahua, Mexico.

He was the father of the firebrand priest José Martinez, who locked horns with Bishop Jean Baptiste Lamy. The priest's younger brother, Juan Pascual, carried on his father's trade, and both served in Mexico's New Mexican legislature and the first territorial assembly.

Despite its democratic trappings, New Mexico was still a wild place in Padre Martinez's day. For instance, one of the main events of the annual Taos trade fairs were the *rescates,* or ransoming of Indian-enslaved unfortunates.

Due to a fervent wish to avoid slavery for themselves or their servants, the Martinez's rectangular hacienda, as were many in colonial New Mexico, was built so form followed function. That function, first and foremost, was self-defense.

The structure is a monolith of adobe, fronted by two sturdy wooden gates, which with others at the rear are the only passages to the outside world. This architectural fortress reserved its warmth and intimacy for the inside rooms, safely arranged around two placitas.

Some rooms retain their original dirt floors. Their pearl-white interior walls are finished in *tierra blanca,* a rare white micaceous earth found near Taos.

Other rooms, quiet this time of year but for wind whispers and the contented clucks of pigeons on the roof, include the *sala* (formal dining room), a weaving room, a *cocina* (kitchen) with split-aspen ceiling and shepherd's fireplace, a blacksmith's shop, storerooms and a tack room.

At the rear of the second placita, which had melted back to earth before restoration by the Kit Carson Foundation, an exhibit room offers a clue as to the source of Padre Martinez's spiritual strength.

On display are many religious objects—including a wooden statue of Doña Sebastian (Death)—used by the *cofradia de los hermanos de nuestro señor Jesu nazareno* (Penitentes), a group strongly associated with Martinez in life and death.

Padre Martinez (bless 'im) founded New Mexico's first co-ed school, and operated the first printing press, reportedly carted down the Santa Fe Trail by Missouri trader Josiah Gregg. In addition to textbooks and religious documents, in 1834 Martinez began to print *El Crepusculo de Libertád* (The Dawn of Liberty), the area's first newspaper.

His opposition to Lamy's demand for mandatory tithing to finance St. Francis Cathedral's construction in Santa Fe put him at odds with the bishop, who in 1862 told Martinez he'd been excommunicated. The sole record of such action however, was at an Arroyo Hondo church and apparently never forwarded to Rome.

Undaunted, Martinez carried on in the grand old Northern New Mexican tradition, ignoring as much as he could of the nastiness drifting up the Rio Grande from Santa Fe. He continued his ministerial duties, and was buried by his *cofradia,* his religious society, in 1867 at an unknown site.

A granite marker in Kit Carson Park commemorates the Padre's memory, but seems redundant, considering the monumental hacienda. The rambling old ranchito already stands as a testament to the energy, tenacity and sense of purpose that characterized Martinez and most other Hispanic frontiers people on the *rio arriba.*

Blumenschein Home

After nosing around awhile at the Blumenschein studio, my nose tells me things aren't quite right.

The museum attendant's *comadre* complains about the numerous skunks that have emerged from who-knew-where and are infesting houses all along LeDoux Street and Ranchitos Road.

But that isn't all the upsetting news on an otherwise ethereal, cobalt-blue northern New Mexico morning.

There's that nasty business of potentially explosive gasoline fumes that somehow have found their way into the town's sewage system.

Meanwhile, other Taoseños sit idling pickups and four-bys on Paseo del Pueblo Sur, drumming their fingers and shooting hateful glances at the long line of traffic. Even with ski season over and summer tourism months ahead, it crawls from the plaza stoplight to the old Jack Denver Motel grounds.

They all, I suppose, are paying the sacrificial cost of living in Taos.

Taos, beautiful as it is, often has demanded a sacrifice for occupying its hallowed space.

In the case of Ernest Blumenschein, it was sore shoulder muscles and blistered feet.

Blumenschein and fellow Easterner Bert Phillips had sketched and painted their way through the muddy southern Rockies as far as Questa when, on Sept. 3, 1898, as Blumenschein noted in his journal, "At the top of a foothill at the edge of a canyon on a narrow curve, we slid into a deep rut and the wagon suddenly sat down. One rear wheel collapsed and there we were balancing with our precarious load at an angle of 45 degrees."

Blumenschein lost a coin toss, and carrying the heavy wheel like an industrial-age Christ ascending his Golgotha, walked the 30 or more miles to the heavenly town of Taos for a replacement.

Of the trek through canyon, mesa and unbounded skyscapes, he recalled, "I was receiving, under rather painful circumstances, the first great unforgettable inspiration of my life."

After success in Taos, Blumenschein met Mary Greene, critically acclaimed for her shows in the prestigious Salon de Automne in Paris. Despite her mother's aversion to the upstart American, Mary and Ernest married and set up joint studios in New York, Paris and Taos.

They supported themselves through illustrating magazines and books for famous authors such as Booth Tarkington, Willa Cather and Jack London.

Mary, who smiles like a full-figured Meryl Streep from a museum photograph, painted happily until Ernest's ego apparently stepped in. Suddenly, she stopped. She studied silversmithing in New York, and never again lifted brush to canvas.

When asked why she didn't join the Taos Society of Artists, she curtly replied, "One member of this family is enough."

As I browse through the old (1797), 12-room adobe home the couple bought piecemeal from fellow TSA member Buck Dunton and others, I feel the loss. My nose had been right; something here stinks.

I view the paintings again. Ernest's works—at least the few oils on exhibit—favor massive forms wrought from a dark, somber palette. He even extrapolates the style and colors to a painting of a big-city railyard, where he stroked desert tones straight from his Taos palette onto mountainous buildings and mesa-like boxcars. Mary's work, on the other hand, reflects a glowing, neo-Tiffany influence: broad, well-defined outlines; delicate, but bright charcoal pastels; saturated primary colors and hues; accessible, if sometimes romanticized, human models.

I may not know art, but I know what Art likes: Mary, and Mary's work.

Ranchos de Taos

Driving out of Taos to Ranchos de Taos, I'm reminded of a reincarnation thing I tumbled into in the early '70s. It goes like this: A few miles east of Ranchos is Talpa ("knob"), which straddles a ridge overlooking the Rio Chiquito, water source for the apple orchards and chile, corn and alfalfa fields that blanket the valley below.

On the right, departing Ranchos on the way to Fort Burgwin, runs Lower Talpa Road. It's a narrow recently paved road between Talpa ridge and Ranchos that wanders past pastoral scenes many artists have romanticized. It ends near Ranchos Plaza, site of the most idealized, much-painted and photographed San Francisco de Asís Church, one of the oldest in America dedicated to St. Francis.

Everybody knows the one: Georgia O'Keeffe did it; Ansel Adams did it; the birds do it, the bees do it. It's popular.

Built between 1813 and 1815 under Franciscan friar Jose Benito Pereyro's direction, it's still an active asset to the surrounding community, with an annual feast day the first week in October. Although the church's plaza has birthed gift shops and galleries, it still is reminiscent of Santa Fe before it went on the market to the highest bidders.

Ranchos was founded mainly as a home for *genízaros,* Christianized Indians who served the Hispanic colonials.

Ransomed genízaros here didn't always find safety, however. Navajos, Utes and Comanches routinely raided Taos Valley's ranchitos until about 1760. On their final foray, the marauders captured 50 Taoseños, mostly women and children. Soon afterward, Spanish soldiers in hot pursuit massacred 400 Indian raiders.

Tough times, little remembered in this age of reconciliation.

At least one Ranchos-area resident remembers, however.

He is former state representative, Francisco "El Comanche" Gonzales, Talpa-bred and University of California-educated. I roll past his home adobe compound on Lower Talpa Road. It's hard to miss the casita: "El Comanche" is emblazoned on the adobe wall.

Some years ago, Gonzales, whose ancestors were *genízaros* compliments of the Comanches, organized a well-regarded troupe that specializes in Comanche dances.

He follows an old tradition. For many years, a realistic folk pageant called "Los Comanches," which recounted the defeat of the Comanche leader Cuerno Verde ("Green Horn"), was staged near Taos and all around Northern New Mexico.

At the time of my visit into the World of the Reincarnated, however, I was renting part of what is now Gonzales' compound from his father, Nelson, a gentle, kind man who taught for many years at Talpa Elementary.

My then-wife and I, still under the Woodstock influence and bored on a lovely autumn Sunday afternoon, picked up two University of Michigan hitchhikers near Taos Plaza. Things were safer in those days, it seemed.

For some reason, the young woman hitcher and my partner started fiddling with our Ouija board. I didn't object. I should have.

The board's first message: "FLEE. TANKS WILL COME. WALLS WILL CRUMBLE."

A bit unsettling, so we shelved the board. But the next morning, the women were back at it. This time the disembodied "spirit" sending the message identified itself and asked us to light a candle for "him" so he could advance from purgatory into heaven. Fine for him; not too fine for me.

Obediently, we visited San Francisco de Asís Church at Ranchos Plaza twice in the next two days, launching a series of events that ended up with me cast down from the heaven of Ranchos to the purgatory of the East Coast.

The famous San Francisco de Asís church in Ranchos de Taos under visitor scrutiny.

Shaken, the hitchers struck for the relative safety of the Midwest. Soon, so did my ex, claiming the house was haunted and the whole region, not to mention me, was just too weird. This from a woman born and raised in Ohio.

Picurís Pueblo

Before leaving the Taos area, which I always postpone as long as possible, I visit the home of some present-day Anasazi descendants: Picurís Pueblo, once known as San Lorenzo.

But first, on the way on State Road 518, I pass Pot Creek Cultural Site, where Picurís ancestors once lived.

Picurís, the ancient home of Tiwa-speaking American Indians, is tucked away off State Road 75 near Peñasco in a secluded declivity the tribal council named Hidden Valley. The pueblo is nestled along the north bank of Rio Pueblo, which feeds trout-stocked TuTah Lake and Puu-Na Pond.

The Picurís, now numbering about 270, moved to their present homes about 800 years ago, splitting off from Pot Creek, a ruined pueblo once home to 3,000 people. Parts of that three-to-four-story structure, including a kiva and a pueblo home, are being restored by Taos and Picurís pueblos in the Carson National Forest.

The Pot Creek people used ditches and check dams to irrigate fields of corn, beans and squash, tilling their fertile soil with juniper digging sticks, stone axes and wooden shovels.

The Picurís, as do all Pueblos, still conduct their religious ceremonies in kivas, much as they did at Pot Creek. The Roundhouse, an above-ground kiva built around 1200 A.D., still stands on a high knoll above the pueblo, but it's not used.

In Picurís, I begin at the visitor center at Hidden Valley restaurant, which features native food like blue corn tortillas and a view of TuTah Lake.

In the same building, a small museum houses artifacts such as ancient black on grey and black on white vessels from Pot Creek. Juan de Oñate named the pueblo from the Keresan Indian word *pikuría,* (those who paint.) Today the pueblo's noted for its micaceous pottery, bronze-toned, sparkling pots made from clay found in Tres Ritos Hills north of the village.

The Picurís are thought to be also of Kiowa blood. Both Picurís and

Taos certainly have historic and prehistoric trading ties to the plains. When things got hot for the San Lorenzans in 1696 after the Spanish re-invasion, many packed up and went to live for a number of years with their Cuartelejo Apache friends on the Great Plains. When they finally were repatriated in 1706 by Juan de Ulibarrí, they told the Spaniard the Apaches had made them work twice as hard as they had at home.

Pueblo tours lead past remains of Picurís' early churches and the church in use today. The old pueblo, some small family kivas, and artists' homes and studios, are open to the public. Visitors can buy pottery, paintings, weavings, textiles and leather goods directly from the artists, although I don't today.

Truchas

From Picurís, I proceed south along State Road 76, the colonial village tour the promoters call "The High Road to Taos."

A real pioneer village, Truchas, perches on a mountainside upmountain from Chimayo. It's a major crafts center and jumping-off point for several back-country jaunts.

I turn left into the village, towards Truchas Mountain, which the Tewa called "Rock Horn Mountain." Truchas Creek was "Crooked Chin Place Arroyo." The Spanish thought Truchas, or "trout," was more appropriate for the area.

For picnicking possibilities later, I check out Tafoya's General Store. Not far on the left, across from Holy Rosary Mission, stands the three-room, wooden-floored weaving shop Alfredo Córdova, now in his late 70s, finished in 1971. The Córdovas, descendants of many generations of weavers, participated in the Smithsonian Institution's American Folklife Festival during the Bicentennial.

I talk with Alfredo's son, Harry, now in his late 40s, who returned from business courses in Albuquerque to organize his family's enterprise. He's always happy to discuss his scores of yarn colors and help design a personalized blanket or rug.

Later, I shop a half-dozen other handicraft outlets, and observe two tienditas and a bed and breakfast in the mile to the east before the street becomes Forest Road 639, which leads to Trampas Canyon campground. At pavement's end, the dirt road ahead disappears into the overwhelming beauty of rolling, verdant hills backed by soaring granite spires. One of those is 13,102-foot Truchas Peak, the state's second-highest.

Santa Cruz

Turning around, I coast carefully through Truchas and down the State Road 76 roller coaster to Santa Cruz, just outside Española, for a tale of three plazas.

The first, San Gabriel, is across the Rio Grande from Santa Cruz. It slumbers in ruin beneath the sprawling roots of an apple orchard on Indian land near San Juan Pueblo. The second, Santa Cruz, is a vital placita still used by real people. The third, Santa Fe, is a touristy, ersatz, overpriced rectangle that retains little of its Spanish colonial heart.

In 1598, when Juan de Oñate's colonists stumbled into the Indian settlement of Ohke, they renamed it San Juan de los Caballeros. Oñate soon moved to the west bank of the Rio Grande, establishing the first

Santa Cruz Church faces a plaza that survived the 20th century's commercial onslaught better than did Santa Fe's.

Hispanic plaza in New Mexico at Yunque-Yunque, an abandoned pueblo Oñate renamed San Gabriel, marked today only by weeds and a stone cross near State Road 74.

San Gabriel languished while Oñate was off fighting the Acomas, and many of its colonists, soldiers and priests deserted.

In 1610, most remaining Oñate colonists moved lock, stock and *carreta* to the plaza the new governor, don Pedro de Peralta, had laid out at Santa Fe. Some resettled in Santa Cruz, along the Santa Cruz River's south bank, until the Pueblo Revolt dislodged them.

In 1695, after the Reconquest, the new Spanish governor ousted some San Cristobal and San Lazaro Towas who had re-established at Santa Cruz. He called it Villa Nueva de Santa Cruz de los Españoles Mexicanos del Rey Nuestro Señor Carlos Segundo. A later settlement nearby took only one of the names and became known as Española.

The new Santa Cruzans included 60 families from Zacatecas, Mexico. Most were happy when the entire town was moved to the river's higher north bank. There in 1733, they built the Spanish mission church that dominates today's Santa Cruz Plaza.

So impressive are the church's appointments that one travel guide calls its interior "a treasury of Mexican art." The exquisitely restored altar screen is adorned with Our Lady of Sorrows, Our Lady of Guadalupe, and a host of saints. A *nicho* in the south nave wall shelters a wooden Christ lying in the tomb. The Capilla de San Francisco houses a St. Francis *santo* carved in the 17th century.

Santa Cruzeños spread out to settle Chimayo, Córdova, and the area west of the Rio Grande later known as Española. Santa Cruz and its plaza gained importance, taking advantage of its location on the Camino Real and a newer road until it was bypassed by today's paved highways.

Why did San Gabriel's plaza crumble back into earth, Santa Cruz's continue as a religious and educational center and Santa Fe's develop into a world-class tourist trap? Here's my theory:

In San Gabriel, the people abandoned their church and plaza. In Santa Fe, the church was cut off from the plaza when St. Francis Cathedral was constructed and other, Anglo-inspired buildings filled up the space between San Francisco Street and Palace Avenue. In Santa Cruz, the people rallied around their church, registered it as both a state and national historical site, and never re-commercialized the plaza once business moved west to Española.

Looking at Santa Fe's growth-related problems today, I'd consider what happened in Santa Cruz as all to the good.

⇒ Information
Millicent Rogers Museum, Taos: 1-505-758-2462
Carson Historic Museums, Taos: (Carson Home, Martinez
Hacienda, Blumenschein Home and Studio.)
Fees. 1-505-758-0505
Pot Creek Cultural Site, Pot Creek: 1-505-587-2255
Picurís Pueblo, Picurís: Free entry. Tour fee. 1-505-587-2519
or 587-2957
Red River: 1-800-348-6444
Española/Santa Cruz: 1-505-753-2831

The Chama

At Española I cross the Rio Grande and parallel the Chama River about 30 miles northwest on U.S. 84 to the Chama Valley, intent on serpent hunting.

Rio Chama

Back on the Red Road now, I recall the Pecos snake stories I've heard that remind me of another legendary New Mexico snake.

This one is real, however, and I can't pass his den without paying respects.

Cuentos persisted for centuries in the Chama River Valley about *el vivarón,* a serpent that ambushed anyone entering the wrong canyon. The legend endured until paleontologists dug up so many dinosaur bones on Ghost Ranch land that the property was listed as a National Natural Landmark in 1976. Scientists thought the snake and lizard-like fossil they unearthed laid the vivarón legend to rest.

I think they were wrong.

The vivarón myth, and perhaps the Pecos tale, sprang from a more contemporary critter.

The argument for my contention lives at the Ghost Ranch Living Museum, just north of the Ghost Ranch Convention Center. The museum includes the Gateway to the Past exhibit, which documents the history and lives of today's Chama Valley people.

My younger daughter and I once explored the museum's small outdoor zoo.

The miniature Beaver National Forest at the visitor center was flashing its full autumn aspect, with its tiny "river" flowing into an aspen-bordered artificial pond where a real beaver lives. A nearby building housed beaver-related exhibits, as well as glass-fronted homes for some reptiles, the most impressive of which was a rattlesnake.

I mean R*A*T*T*L*E*S*N*A*K*E! That sucker was 10 or 12 feet long and thicker than my thigh. When he fixed his beady little eyes on us, my daughter froze like a rabbit. Just didn't move for a couple of minutes. I wondered if The Serpent used the same hypnotic technique to snare that *gabacho* legend-writer on the Pecos, or those Hispanic *cuenteros*.

At any rate, while we picnicked later in the Chama River canyon, I thought how the rattler's entrancing eye had revealed a sinuous thread binding the voracious serpent of the Pecos Valley to the vivarón of the Chama Valley, thus binding legend to reality.

Christ in the Desert Monastery

Today I bypass the museum by a mile or so and shake along the 13 miles of dusty, at places steep Forest Road 151 to Christ in the Desert Monastery.

This road, not on the state map, gets treacherous, warns the monks' brochure. Believe it.

On my way in to the monastery, I note a long mesa on the right, Mesa de Las Viejas. On its western slope, the Santa Fe and Carson national forests' boundaries meet. On its far east side is Echo Amphitheater, a natural concavity once taken over by Reies Lopez Tijerina's land grant activists. Along the river on the left, bordering the Chama Wilderness, are several rafting launch sites.

Despite its near-wilderness location, the monastery is not a recreation, but a re-creation site.

Founded in 1964, the monastery in which I'll pause for a few days houses a handful of Benedictine monks who live there year-round. The brothers live in seclusion, without red meat, public conversations or electricity, but with obligatory physical labor. It is not an easy existence.

The monastery's glorious center is the rock-buttressed, acoustically live chapel, in which the monks praise God in *a capella* psalms seven times a day, beginning with vigils at 4 a.m.

San Francisco de Asís guards the guesthouse courtyard at Christ in the Desert Monastery on the Chama River.

I wake at 3:57 a.m., missing vigils, but I make the 6 a.m. lauds and Eucharist. While I can't take Catholic communion, being non-Catholic and all, I'm blessed by the special glow of the new day creeping over the stark buff, tan and green cliffs visible through windows high in the chapel walls.

At later services, tourists continually buzz in, stare, retreat. The monastery is not exactly set up to receive casual visitors.

I've been assured a cot with rough wool blankets only because I wrote far in advance and received a confirmation letter from the guestmaster. The room in the rustic adobe guesthouse was Spartan—no electricity, a wood stove for heat—but it opens to a long interior portal bordering a small garden. I peer out my only window at the shadowy wooden St. Francis carving in the graveled placita, gleaming white in the moonlight, a white that recently could have been snow. Since the guesthouse is a cold quarter-mile walk from the chapel, the better to enforce the Benedictine rule of silence, I think perhaps I'll confine my future visits to warmer weather.

Of course, snow, a minor nuisance to me, is a major problem to the monks, who must pick up mail in Abiquiu about twice a week and otherwise are connected with the seemingly remote outside by a radio telephone, used mostly in emergencies.

A visit to the monastery is not some sort of seeker's trip to a spiritual Disneyland. After the initial check in, nobody takes my hand to guide me through the services, or tells me where the daily work crews meet, or advises me about the dinner menu.

I'm flying solo here, led only by intuition, a sense of responsibility and self-knowledge about just how lost I really am.

Poshuouinge Pueblo Ruin

Somewhat subdued, but optimistic after my retreat, I take U.S. 84 back towards Española to visit an old Chama-side pueblo.

Reading the few extant reference works on the subject, I had often wondered where the early Tewas wandered after leaving their mythical emergence place under San Luís Lake in today's southern Colorado.

Apparently various Tewa bands migrated south from Colorado to the Rio Ojo Caliente and Rio Chama valleys, where they built pueblos. Some remained in those pueblos until Europeans arrived in the 16th century. By the time Oñate rode in, however, most already had settled in their present villages along the Rio Grande.

The transition pueblos today are uninhabited, some so decayed I've been hard-pressed to recognize those I've visited as "ruins." Once bordering terraced fields and encompassing kivas, they dominated dozens of mesa-top sites, all near live water sources.

It's a good time to go ruins-hopping, here in the spring of the Tewa ceremonial year. The dark "sky looms," rainstorms resembling cloth, have appeared again, and I avoid the persistent winds by arriving when early morning light best reveals mounds hinting of vanished rooms, plazas, kivas and fields.

To understand the scope of prehistoric population patterns in the Rio Chama's drainage, I'd earlier visited the Gateway to the Past exhibit at Ghost Ranch Visitor Center. I learned of vanished Tewa pueblos such as Rio Oso, Kat or Leafwater, Hupobi, Yunque and others now but weathered memories.

The exhibit included maps, cultural interpretations from Hispanic and Indian viewpoints and an interactive computer program narrated by Santa Fe Indian School students.

I was especially struck by a quote by Popovi Da of San Ildefonso: "... there is another matter that disturbs me: the way we are treated as academic curiosities. You have written too many books about us without having the experience of feeling us."

Perhaps one way to experience the Tewa is to visit the ancestral sites.

Some of those are on private, some on public land. I hike a short, steep trail into one of them now, Poshuouinge, just south of Abiquiu, on U.S. Forest Service land.

The Forest Service acquired Poshuouinge's 23-acre mesa-top site long after its original 1919 survey and excavation by pioneer archaeologists. Early work revealed two plazas, bordered by room blocks of at least two stories, with 500-700 first-floor rooms. Still visible are a single kiva and a watch tower possibly used by early Abiquiu settlers to scan the Chama valley.

Abandoned around 1500 A.D., Poshuouinge has suffered the indignity of being intersected by power lines.

That probably won't happen again, at least at this pueblo. When the Forest Service took over, it removed a phone line and hopes to relocate the power lines that slice through the view of the twisting Rio Chama below

The Forest Service has become so sensitized to Indian voices, it might never dig at the site again.

"We're moving away from excavation to interpretations" Mike Bremer, of the U.S. Forest Service's Heritage Resource staff, had told me.

Bremer, an archaeologist, works in the Forest Service's Española district, which includes many of the now-abandoned Tewa pueblos.

His work has shown him that while the European *entradas* physically changed Tewa lives, they didn't touch the way Tewas interpret their own existence.

"Among the Pueblos, there's no concept of prehistory," said Bremer. "It's all part of the story, their story."

Elena Ortiz of San Juan, who with her brother Nico runs Native American Tours, once told me something similar. On their tours, visitors often ask where the Indian people who occupied pueblos such as Puyé and Tsankawi went.

"I tell them 'We didn't go, we became,' " she said.

When walking through ancient rooms and plazas, I always remember: pueblo ruins are the physically, but not necessarily spiritually abandoned homes of a very real people who live among us and among whom we live.

Not everybody thinks that way, however. As I start to leave the hillside trail above the pueblo's mesa, I spot two seedy men below. They're pothunters, checking for loot, even for pottery sherds. I avoid them by detouring down the hill's far side. I would wish them bad luck, but my medicine man friends assure me such wishes only backfire. I'll call them in to the Forest Service as soon as I can, but by then, they'll be gone.

⇒ Information
Ghost Ranch Living Museum and Gateway to the Past:
  Donation asked. 1-505-685-4312
Christ in the Desert: Fee. No phone
Poshuouinge Ruins: No fee. 1-505-685-4312

The Middle Rio Grande

The Rio Grande's persistent calls hook me again, and I answer with two visits. Santa Clara Canyon and Los Alamos National Laboratories, two sites a few miles from each other, are imbued with contrasting histories and frames of world reference millennia apart. One is rooted in centuries-old traditions; the other dedicated to destroying them.

Puyé Cliff Dwellings

The Tewa-speaking Santa Clarans, like many Pueblos, are tied to ancient Mesoamerican cultures in many ways we do not yet fully appreciate.

I inch up State Road 5 towards Puyé Cliff Dwellings and the searing memory of a Quetzalcoátl encounter that almost killed me streaks across my mind. If Chaco returned me to the Red Road, Puyé set me on that road years ago.

Puyé, a buff-and-tan mesa on the Pajarito Plateau four miles southwest of Santa Clara Pueblo, which owns it, seems a tranquil place for such encounters. Its sheer face, like others in the vicinity, is riddled with cliff dwellings, its top blanketed by ruins of an ancient village. Among the stones, archaeologists found abundant glazed pottery adorned by depictions of Avanyu, the (Yikes!) plumed serpent, guardian of streams and springs. Legend says Avanyu threw himself across the sky, leaving his trail in the Milky Way.

And he threw himself at me on my birthday, July 26, 1981, atop Puyé Mesa.

188

One of Santa Clara Canyon's fine fishing ponds.

I arrived at the annual ceremonials that day around 3 p.m., accompanied by two young women and a guy, friends I'd met only a few hours before at a Santa Fe community church. By then, Santa Clarans already had been dancing for hours under increasingly threatening skies. A vicious gust rocked us as we entered the plaza. I wandered among food and souvenir booths as owners scurried to secure their wares as the wind howled louder than the drums. Soon a grumbling, jet-black thunderhead boiled up over Santa Clara Peak to the west.

Intending to descend to the cliff dwellings below, we were standing on the mesa's south edge when lightning struck repeatedly a few miles up Santa Clara Canyon. It swiftly walked our way as we watched, fascinated as mongooses in a cobra's glare, holding hands to keep from being blown off the mesa. Behind us, the drums continued. Lightning stalked down the canyon sides like the mythological Navajo Warrior Twins.

About the time I opened my mouth to say "Let's get out of here!" an eerie light, flapping like a sheer blue-white bedsheet hung out in a breeze, rippled before us, apparently passing through us. The hair on my companions' arms bristled, but not on mine, I suppose because my rubber zoris grounded us. We stood in a line, holding hands—woman, man, woman, man—facing south. I squatted just as the bolt struck, and my companions (whom I've not seen since that day), toppled backwards to earth. We weren't hurt, maybe because of my lucky zoris. Others weren't so fortunate.

The bolt's passage produced a tearing blast that shattered the air behind us, and since lightning continued to streak nearby, we raced for my car, where we sat watching an ambulance wail up the dirt mesa road.

Later we learned that two women, a Santa Claran and a Españolan, were killed by the energy that surged through us. Santa Clara leaders closed the ceremonies for several years, although they now are reopened.

A Ute-Picurís medicine man later told me such an event marked the christening, so to speak, of a medicine person, woman or man. I don't know. I was glad just to have survived. But for me, the visit to Puyé marked the beginning of a new year and a new way of life.

Los Alamos

After the solitude and otherworldliness of Santa Clara's real estate, the next little jaunt—up to Los Alamos—also haunts me, but for different reasons.

The folks on The Hill bill their self-guided tour as an eight-century "walk from the Stone Age to the Atomic Age," but I make it in about two hours.

I start at the Historical Museum near Ashley Pond, which should be called Ashley Pond Pond. It was named after Ashley Pond, who ran Los Alamos Ranch School from 1917 until Robert Oppenheimer and other Manhattan Project officials decided the then-isolated mesa would be a dandy place to smash atoms.

Although many of the project's "hot" materials were stored around the pond, the only discomforts I encounter are mosquitos and an aggressive mastiff determined to bite anyone near him.

Since the pond once was ringed by physics labs and radioactive materials storage areas, maybe the mutt has been drinking some weird water. But I don't know. He doesn't have two heads or glow. (Obligatory Los Alamos joke, there, friends. No offense.)

But seriously, to put it all into some sort of perspective, the Historical Museum had mounted an excellent exhibit that begins with Paleo-Indians, moves to the Anasazi, then to historical Indians. Exhibits also recreate the strenuous, challenging life at the boys' school and in early Los Alamos, where the only constants seemed to be secrecy, isolation and mud. There's even a replica of the base post office, once known to the outside world, as was the entire city of Los Alamos, as "Box 1663, Santa Fe, N.M."

On one side of the museum is the Ranch School's Fuller Lodge, a two-story, chinked-pine-log structure constructed in 1928 under the supervision of noted architect John Gaw Meem. The building still serves as a community meeting place, housing county offices, the chamber of commerce and an art center.

Behind the museum is the Ranch School's power house, used as a honeymoon cottage by the lab's explosives expert, George Kistiakowsky. Nearby, down shady lanes, are the homes known as "Bathtub Row" because they were the only dwellings in town with tubs. Oppenheimer, the project director, lived in one of these cottages, about a three-minute walk from Ashley Pond and its encircling complex of two-story wooden barracks, where scientists assembled the world's first nuclear weapon.

A few paces from Oppie's comfortable bungalow are Tewa Indian village ruins that date back to 1225 A.D., and a cabin built on a neighboring mesa by the homesteading Romero family about 1913, but relocated here in 1984.

Next I enter a landscaped, level promenade boxed by long, low buildings that resemble the flat-roofed shopping centers of the early '60s. It was built in 1949 as the community center.

At Bradbury Museum, well-informed docents help visitors understand anything they don't get from viewing the masterfully executed exhibits. A decent bookstore next door helps fill in any gaps.

One jarring note: in Bradbury, I hear a hysterical woman comment bitterly that the Japanese "deserved" to be nuked because their soldiers committed so many rapes.

Excuse me?

My thoughts: The first casualty of war is truth. It's extremely hard to differentiate wartime propaganda from truth. But even if Whining Woman's paranoia is fact-based, nobody is exempt from war's wrath when it descends. Nobody, women and children included.

Although still deeply entrenched in its privileged, snooty, bunker mentality, Los Alamos National Laboratories says it's struggling to redefine itself as nuclear science shifts gears to accommodate new world realities. Whatever, my guess is that the Lab's primary mission always will involve nuclear or other advanced weaponry.

But I think even the most diehard Hilltop techie would agree that our brief shining moment of nuclear technological triumph also may have dimmed American senses of proportion, priority, decency and morality.

Jémez Valley

Beyond Los Alamos, over the mountain and past Valle Grande on narrow, steep State Road 4 is a valley playground that almost helps me forget the Nuke City. I hope its hot springs also will help me forget how long I've been on the road.

Now, between the Season of the Ski and the Season of the Smog-sick Californians is a perfect time to check out the relatively quiet, thickly forested Jémez Valley.

The 20-mile-long vale has it all: scenic splendor, history and plenty of isolated, but easily accessible natural wonders. The only problem is where to start.

I start at the top and flow down the valley with the Jémez River.

The highway clears the open sweep of Valle Grande Caldera and dips west into ponderosa forest. About 10 miles after entering the woods,

I see the small Forest Service sign that marks the short, paved road to Jémez Falls.

For some reason, the Jémez River's upper reaches aren't well-documented in our local tour literature, so I have to snoop to learn a couple of its secrets.

First, here at the well-maintained falls picnic area, the gentler Valle Grande slopes give way to the gorges that mark the infant Jémez River's passage. A short hike through aromatic ponderosa groves leads to Jémez Falls, a roaring cataract even in the dry season.

Second, the ridge-scaling trail west from the picnic area towards Battleship Rock in about three to four miles reaches a secluded hot spring, one of many along the Jémez. I pass for today.

Visitors not crazy about hiking the back country can find plenty of hot action in the Jémez Valley by returning to State Road 4 and driving west. Before long, the road turns south into the Jémez Valley proper.

A few miles south of La Cueva, I look for vehicles parked at an unmarked area on the river side of the road. Locking my wagon, I teeter across a log spanning the rushing river. Up the mountain to the east is Spence Hot Springs, where a series of hot bubblers trickle into pools, then fall to the cooling river far below.

Favored by hardy tourist and jaded native alike, Spence Springs are but a warm-up compared to what awaits down-river.

Downstream from Spence, warm springs cross under the highway to enter the river at Soda Dam, a massive calcium carbonate deposit laid down by other hot springs just north of the "dam."

Also north of the dam is Jémez Cave, first used by Paleo-Indian big game hunters several thousand years ago.

More recently, relatively speaking, the Basket Makers, who were hunter-gatherers and early farmers, settled in the area. By 600 A.D., newcomers from the north and west entered the valley, building pit houses, then above-ground settlements that evolved into communities the Spanish called pueblos.

Around 1150 A.D., an extended drought drove people from Chaco Canyon, Mesa Verde and the area around today's Cuba, N.M. to the Jémez Valley, where they mixed with the natives. We know the resultant civilization as the Jémez, their Towa word for "people." Towa, reportedly spoken by the Pecoseños and others, is related to Tewa and Tiwa.

Giusewa Pueblo Ruin (Jémez State Monument)

At first, Jemezeños lived on the surrounding mesa tops, where archaeologists have unearthed at least 50 prehistoric sites, including ruins twice as large as Chaco's Pueblo Bonito.

About 500 years ago, a large group moved down to a flat rock shelf above a hot springs, naming the pueblo they built Giusewa ("at the hot place").

There, just north of the village today known as Jémez Springs, the Spanish found them and did what the Spanish did best: built an imposing mission church and won converts for the European way of cross and sword. Not everybody at Giusewa was happy about this, but that's a later story.

Today's Jémez Pueblo stands a few more miles down the road. The ruins of the older pueblo and the first church, as well as its successor, which was built around the first, make up today's Jémez State Monument. After examining the monument museum's exhibits, I climb the gravel path to the church ruins.

The 17th-century San Jose de los Jémez mission is remarkable for its intact eight-foot-thick walls and its unique octagonal tower. The pueblo, however, which once extended west all the way across the trail that later became State Road 4, is now but a few collapsed, cactus-covered mounds.

Earlier in this century, the pueblo and church were excavated sloppily by archaeologists learning their trade on-the-job. Luckily, a more recent state Monuments Department stabilization saved one of the pueblo's three kivas. The other two are visible to the observant.

Jémez Springs

Today, geothermally active Jémez Valley, guarded at its southern mouth by Jémez Pueblo, tolerates soon-to-be extinct Californios, New Agers and Los Alamos layabouts. I've arrived in the valley in late afternoon, fatigued and mad at the world. I plunge into a brain-befuddling hot springs at Spence, watched by an old Indian man in one of the higher pools. I cool off, dress and cruise south along the Jémez to Cañones, searching for two of the state's three highway tunnels. Yeehaw!

A few miles above the "new" Jémez Pueblo, I turn northwest on narrow State Road 485 toward Cañones.

Before long, I enter one of our spectacularly deep, grotesque canyons, with unlikely red-rock sandstone forms reminiscent of Navajo country, steep cliffs and few turnarounds.

I watch *zopilotes* ride the chilly thermals over Rio Guadalupe until it's time to return to the Jémez and cut back up-canyon to Jémez Springs.

Maybe the 154° to 186° F. water at Jémez Springs is so intense it cools off everybody's intolerances. The heat, especially as it's my second soak of the day, sure helps me chill.

The springs spout gallons of mineral-laden waters containing arsenic, acid carbonate, potassium, sodium, lithium (won't that calm me down?) and other friends from the Periodic Tables.

There's nothing left above ground of the part of the pueblo that once ran down to the river, but not far south is a low, stone bathhouse built between 1870 and 1878. This is definitely not a ruin, but a luxurious, renovated Territorial setting in which I cheerfully plunge for an

Jémez Springs Bathouse shelters simmering hot springs.

hour in a deep, private, scalding, spring-fed indoors bathtub. For a few more dinero, I luxure in a full-body massage by one of Jémez Springs' seven or so licensed massage therapists. One is enough.

She tells me intrepid early Anglo settlers first enclosed the springs after they heard a deafening roar and found that one of the outlets had spouted like a boiling geyser.

Water can't enter the tubs after the spigot's turned off, so there's little danger, but I'm glad I learned about the eruption *after* my soak.

I towel my water-wrinkled skin and turn towards home, ready for a well-deserved break before I tackle the Rio Grande's better-known urban areas.

⇒ Information
Puyé Cliffs: Fee. 1-505-753-7326.
Santa Clara Canyon: Fee. 1-505-753-7326
Jémez State Monument: Fee. 1-505-829-3530
Jémez Springs Bathhouse: Fee. 1-505-829-3303

The Central Cities

I scramble along the Gallinas River's steep granite banks near my Baca House home, wondering this July morning why I'd ever want to leave this natural paradise for the Santa Fe Hustle. Cattails swing with the weight of melodious red-winged blackbirds; wood ducks paddle in a placid river-fed pool far below my stone garden wall. Moisture saturates the warm breeze, hinting at the coming monsoon rains. Maybe I can avoid a visit to Santa Fe by just envisioning it while I relax in my streamside retreat. I sit on an exposed boulder to give it a try.

Santa Fe

Despite the written barbs I frequently hurl in its direction, I've found myself inexorably drawn to the state capital over the years. The old Spanish and Mexican colonial town and later zippy/hippie cult center has been replaced by an ever-expanding wall of fake adobe and a permanent big city bustle. The ringing mountains have taken major real estate hits, and the CitDif increasingly looks like a stockade under siege in the War of Economic Imperialism.

No, that's not my editorial for *Mother Jones* mag; it's an informed opinion offered after observing and sometimes participating in the life of Santa Fe for three decades.

Those decades have not been without their ups and downs. All I can summarize from my experience is that Santa Fe's capable of producing extreme emotional ambivalence in the hearts of those who love her.

Sometimes it's rotten living in the City Difficult; other times the contentious old adobe mudpile doesn't look so bad.

A couple of years ago, wrapped in one of my warm Santa Fe Glow periods, I strolled around the humming old streets and rediscovered a very familiar, deceptively stable landmark right on the Plaza: the Palace of the Governors.

Here's the story:

In 1974-75, "Dedie" Snow, a state archaeologist, excavated the palace's west end. She reviewed her findings and added fresh research results in *La Crónica de Nuevo México*.

Her article supports one of my favorite Santa Fe saws: despite our treasured notions about the historic significance of every single adobe brick in town, nothing here is what it seems. The town is a chimera, a fleeting flash against a backdrop of desert to which it someday will return. Whatever, palace aficionados can mine their own lode of lore.

For instance: Heard the one about the invincible don Diego de Vargas?

After suppressing the Indian revolt, the brave and indefatigable Vargas saddled up and headed south, where he died of an unknown disease while chasing Apaches near the Sandia Mountains. His body reportedly was buried under the altar of the *capilla* at the Palace's east end. The little chapel doesn't exist any more; it was torn down, perhaps to make room for "progress" in the form of the paved Palace Avenue-Washington intersection. I wonder what the dashing old don would think if he knew tons of metal and many feet tromp over his head daily?

But back to my story.

At the urgings of Museum Director Edgar Lee Hewett and under the hand of Jesse Nusbaum, the present Palace was restored between 1909 and 1913, supposedly to its original appearance.

Not so, said Snow.

Today's palace, she said, in no way resembles the 17th- and 18th-century predecessors.

Aha! Historic integrity, huh?

I verified her assertions by perusing pre-restoration photos. Immediately before "restoration," the Palace sported a Territorial, gingerbread-trimmed wood balustrade along the portal's front and sides. At least four electric light or telephone poles sat smack up against the portal. Nary a *viga* protruded from the interior, and the iron-barred windows were rectangular, topped with wood pediments.

That's not all.

Recent research indicates that during the 17th and early 18th centuries, portions of the Palace were two stories high. And during the early 18th century, the Palace's south facade had a second-story balcony with a window overlooking the Plaza.

Snow based her statements on the 1974 dig, when archaeologists found a massive cobblestone foundation, more than three feet wide and set in mud mortar, beneath the present Palace floor. The foundation was Spanish-built, possibly as early as the 1640s.

The foundation's width, Snow said, indicates it could have supported a structure up to 30 feet high.

The foundation, visible today through a trapdoor in the Palace of the Governor's floor, bears no relationship to the present building, Snow maintained.

She cited two pieces of evidence. One, a 1716 inspection report, included a coachroom with "two rooms, one above and one below, of adobes" in the courtyard.

Also a 1720 court deposition related the adventures of a true "second-story man," Ysidro Sanchez, who entered the Palace through a second-story balcony window twice in two nights to rob Palace storerooms.

How did the building lose its upstairs?

Snow assumed it was because there was no oral tradition concerning the second story, and because by the time American observers such as cranky Josiah Gregg arrived, the second floor was gone.

The Palace was made over to provide space for the then-new Museum of New Mexico and "most importantly, to produce a monument to the Spanish civilization," she said.

Restoration probably wouldn't have included the second story anyhow, partly because the project was under-funded.

Nor would a two-story building have projected the revisionist image history manipulators Hewett and Nusbaum wanted to convey, Snow said.

Speaking of historical accuracy: I grumble about "newcomers," almost as if I weren't one.

I don't mean to sound as if I'm suffering from Site Seniority Syndrome. We need to keep in perspective this newcomer thing that pervades Santa Fe politics and society.

After all, everybody here washed up on our cottonwood-shaded banks from somewhere else. Pueblos migrated from Anasaziville (and perhaps Mesoamerica before that), while Apaches and Navajos arrived from way up north. Hispanos came by way of Spain to Tenochtitlán (Mexico City) and other ancient Mesoamerican villas. A recent wave washed in from all parts of Europe and Africa. Lately, a backwash of West Coasters has surfaced here.

Each wave, regardless of how it initially acculturates, has contributed something valuable to our unique society.

While many times our tourism efforts concentrate on the Indian and Hispanic cultures visitors find exotic, the largely neglected Swiss and German settlers who arrived during Territorial times also made enduring contributions.

Take, for example, the Bandeliers.

Adolph Bandelier, the Swiss-born scholar for whom the Frijoles Canyon national monument is named, documented the area's ancient Indian cultures, discriminating between historic and prehistoric Indian traditions.

He completed his novel, *The Delight Makers,* while he and his first wife, Josephine, lived in the house they rented from John Schumann. Schumann, who arrived here from Saxony, Germany in the 1860s ran a Plaza bootery.

When Josephine's health failed in 1891, the family moved to a Canyon Road residence later named *El Zaguan,* where a garden Bandelier planted still grows.

In 1892, the Bandeliers began a South American journey during which Josephine died. Bandelier died in 1914 while researching the Spanish archives, never returning to New Mexico.

But the "Bandelier House" didn't pass out of the family.

Before he moved to Santa Fe, Adolph's American-born second cousin, Elizabeth, lived with the childless Bandeliers in Highland, Ill., where she married American-born Henry Kaune, whose parents were from Hanover and Saxony, Germany. The Kaunes moved to Santa Fe in 1887 for Henry's health and to be with the Bandeliers.

After the Bandeliers left Santa Fe, the Kaunes leased their former home on DeVargas Street, buying it from the Schumann estate in 1919. The house was occupied by family members until 1982.

The Kaune name is associated with two specialty grocery stores and an elementary school in Santa Fe.

Henry Kaune opened a grocery on the Plaza in 1896. His business steadily grew, as did his civic reputation.

He was a city councilor, chamber of commerce treasurer for 30 years and a charter member and director of the Kiwanis Club. Through Kiwanis, he supervised the planting of the spectacular cottonwoods that today lend a campus-like atmosphere to East Alameda.

Kaune was 78 when he died in the Bandelier-Kaune house in 1933. His wife, equally prominent for her civic works, lived there until her 1954 death at 93.

Two of their seven children lived on the property all their lives. Alfred, a county commission chair and city school board president after whom Kaune School was named, died in 1971. Charles, who lived for a while in a log cabin on land now crossed by the relatively new Paseo del Peralta, pursued the company's business until his 1974 death.

Not a bad record for a bunch of newcomers whose descendants still figure high on any list of Santa Fe's prestigious families.

***

For every bulwark family grounded in civic responsibility, however, Santa Fe seems to produce or attract someone more interested in constructing a fantasy life here. Sometimes that works to my advantage.

Carretas at Rancho de Las Golondrinas near Santa Fe.

During the seven years I worked in Santa Fe, when the weather was too cold to travel, I substituted a video of a movie made in New Mexico. (Summer production, please, exuding warmth, its stars sweating, brilliant sky burning permanent squints into their eyes.)

New Mexico movies? Dissolve to flashback: my first Plaza cruise, 1971. This pueblo's architecture made me feel like I'd dropped in on the Williamsburg of the West. And evergreen smells blowing cool from the Sangres returned me to the mountain temples around the ancient city of Kyoto, Japan.

Santa Fe socked me with its scenery and ambience. Light was right. Neon landscape sort of vibrating, pulsing, humming. But something sounded a jarring note. It was the people: Cowboy clones or frontier freaks; costumed in ersatz Indian feathers, fur trapper hats, and gambler vests.

Just back from Pacific duty, I knew the score. I'd been to Old Tucson, Tijuana and Toronto, visited China, Japan, the Philippine and Hawaiian islands. I knew phonies when I saw them. I decided everybody in town looked like a movie extra. Of course, the extra was me; another *gabacho huero*, another ugly outsider, ambling into a multicultural, world-class tourist trap in the making.

Over the years the town has enhanced its movie-set quality, now resembling a studio theme park, a frontier facade where everybody works, but nobody sleeps.

But truth can be stranger than fission. Recently, I realized that 1971 Plaza crowd actually *was* involved in a flick.

The state Film Commission has produced "Shot in New Mexico," Casey St. Charnez' list of the 200 or so productions filmed here from 1898 to 1994.

And lo, in 1971 in and around Santa Fe, several major studios were making movies, mostly Westerns.

John Wayne, even, was shooting Warner Brothers' "The Cowboys" at San Cristobal Ranch near Galisteo and at Chama; Lee Marvin and Paul Newman were filming "Pocket Money" for First Artists in Santa Fe and Truchas. Bo Grimes was working in Fox's "The Culpepper Cattle Co." in Santa Fe. "Greaser's Palace," a comic Christian allegory set in the West, was filming in Santa Fe and at Camel Rock. James Coburn was making "The Honkers" in Carlsbad. The state was crawling with movie types, so what I took at first to be representative Santa Feans may well have been extras or movie star-types. Or not. What a town.

El Rancho de las Golondrinas

When early summer visitors drift in and Santa Feans don't have time to treat them to the Grand Northern New Mexico Tour, the natives and semi-natives don't despair.

There's an alternative jaunt visitors can undertake alone, and it's close at hand.

El Rancho de las Golondrinas, the restored and reconstructed Spanish colonial rancheria near La Ciénega, is so close to home many Santa Feans take it for granted.

They shouldn't.

Living history is folded into the ranch's 200 wooded acres like *metate* limestone in corn meal. And Golondrinas rewards both neophyte and repeat Santa Fephiles with a glimpse of a sustainable, 300-year-old rural way of life.

Whether I'm attending a theme event, such as the spring festival, or visit on a quiet weekday, Golondrinas tempts me to spend too much time examining historically accurate exhibits and crafts demonstrations lined up its dirt paths, far from automobiles. The trails up and down arroyos and along the meandering, cottonwood-lined streams help visitors capture the feel of Santa Fe's earliest days as a Spanish territorial capital.

If the colonial mountain hacienda and village didn't exist in the idealized form presented at Golondrinas Land, they should have.

Not that the composite village is plastic; certainly not. It's real adobe, stone and wood, with a fortified 18th-century placita house compound complete with a defensive torreón. I ambled about a bit more and revisited a 19th-century home and its logistically important outbuildings.

I've promenaded the Golondrinas grounds so often I've almost memorized the structural inventory: molasses mill, threshing ground, four primitive water mills, blacksmith shop, wheelwright, winery, vineyards.

On a slope with its own *calvario* (calvary hill), the rebuilt Sierra Village testifies to the deep Penitente faith that sustained early settlers. Here, without trespassing on private sacred land, I also visited a *morada* (church), *descanso* (resting place on the way to the cemetery), *campo santo* (cemetery) and *oratorio* (chapel).

Owned for a couple of centuries by New Mexico's all-pervasive Baca family, Golondrinas was a day's horseback ride south of Santa Fe.

As a *paraje,* or resting place, it was the final stop before Santa Fe for those making the dusty journey north from Chihuahua.

In 1932, the Curtin-Paloheimo family bought the land, then spent many years finding and relocating buildings and other implementata from Ratón, Truchas, Mora, Talpa, Sapelló and other villages.

During the various seasonal festivals, looms clack, blacksmiths clang and clank, dye bubbles in black caldrons. Once I thought I heard the melodic strains of the ever-popular Guadalupitan "Las Mañanitas."

Or maybe I did, considering the on-going air of revelry and fiesta that permeated the heavy summer air.

There it was again: a scratchy fiddle and a guitar, transmitting ripples of folk tunes across the rancho's valleys.

Preserved "living history" villages such as Golondrinas go far to help explain Northern New Mexico's culture to visitors and residents alike, and traditional music is critical to an accurate historical interpretation.

***

Speaking of living history, I once heard New Mexico musicologist Enrique Lamadrid lecture.

"The role of the artist or of music," Lamadrid said, "is to clarify communications between the heart and the face, which is a symbol of what you can see of the artist."

New Mexico's folk music even reflects a revolution in cultural self-perception.

Lamadrid played tapes of centuries-old ballads from Spain, an *ave maria* which had been sung by Columbus' sailors, and a buffalo dance song sung in Spanish by the Tesuque Pueblo Tewa.

A series of *inditas* included the lighthearted "El Indio Manuel" about the Navajo leader, Manuelito. Tragedies told of "El Indio Victorio," the unlucky Apache leader, Victorio and "La Cautiva Marcelina," a Spanish woman captured by Comanches.

"The sounds of Spain are all around us," he said. But other sounds are also present in New Mexico's rich cultural heritage, sounds just beginning to emerge from behind a cultural cloak.

The nuances of "The New Mexico Sound" depend on the region in which the music evolved. In the north, it's the combination of fiddle, guitar, and sometimes Indian drums. Further south, below El Paso, exit fiddle, enter the accordion.

Another distinctly New Mexico art form, *los matachines*, is performed by *los matachins*, dancers who represent "a spiritual coming together of Hispanic and Indian values; like a morality play of the coming of the new, mixed culture," Lamadrid said.

Introduced into Mexico by settlers, the matachines were "modified by the clergy to include aspects of Aztec rituals and the clash of Spanish and Mexican Indian cultures," according to Rubén Cobos, in his *A Dictionary of New Mexico and Southern Colorado Spanish.*

Hmmm. There's that sneaky syncretism again.

Matachines are danced from south of El Paso to Northern New Mexico. As noted, southern dances are accompanied by accordions; northern dances by fiddle and guitar.

The Maximilian tragedy in Mexico was a political fiasco, but a musical success, he said.

"Before the French, all the dances were done with drums and the raspy *chitmias*," Lamadrid said. "People were glad to hear the new band music, and European waltzes and polkas were the craze. The waltz was the *lambada* of the 19th century. All the grandmothers were scandalized that people would dance so close together."

For an example, he played "La Varcelona," perhaps better known to Anglos as "Put Your Little Foot Right In."

He also played several *corridas:* from "Adelita," the popular marching song of the Revolutionary Villistas, to "Los Contrabandistas," a celebration of whisky smugglers crossing the border during Prohibition.

"Corridas often have a border crossing theme, and see borders as lines that exist to maintain political or economic inequalities," Lamadrid said. "Today's corridas are about drug runners. Every time a *narcotraficante* gets arrested, there's a new corrida.

"New Mexico's folk culture is not just in the north. We are surrounded by it in the south as well.

"For instance, the Mesilla Valley has for years been a cradle for *norteño* culture. This valley is a cultural corridor, and culture has flowed back and forth in thick waves ever since the people settled down south," he said.

The most recent wave of Mexican culture to surge up the Rio Grande Valley was *música ranchera:* Tejano or Mexican country music, he said.

"People listen to this music like they listen to music coming out of Nashville; they love it. And like the Nashville sound, this music is a combination of the commercial and folk music," he said.

Lamadrid credits José Alfredo Jimenez, whom he compared to Hank Williams, with popularizing the ranchera sound.

"You can't tell the people what to like. We're coming back to the old traditions, with so many facets to it," he said.

Then he played "Volver," by Bernie Romero of San Antonio, N.M. Los Lobos played the widely popular song during their 1994 Las Vegas, N.M. concert. The audience went wild, dancing and singing along.

"To fly," sang Romero in Spanish, "pay attention to your heart."

I pulled the iron garden gate shut behind me, determined, now I had lodged the melody in my mind, to find a Los Lobos tape for my short hop from the Gallinas to a few old villages near Santa Fe.

Galisteo

A handful of colonial villages struggle for existence near Santa Fe, having escaped Las Golondrinas' fate of mutating into a museum. Some have upscaled, others hang on for dear life, but somehow survive.

In fact, so imbedded is New Mexico's dry soil with lost villages, it's possible here to walk unaware over entire vanished civilizations.

For example, Santa Fe in pre-Hispanic times apparently was a pueblo site, but who knows where the drums reverberated in the kivas of yesterday?

The Santa Fe area also is saturated with pueblo ruins, but many are on private property and inaccessible without an *entré*.

Many such sites are near Galisteo, itself situated near many ancient, now-vanished Tanoan (Tewa) Indian towns.

Using my imagination and a little more gasoline, last year I took a tour that helped me appreciate our own civilization's brief and probably transitory tenure in this ancient land.

I drove south past Lamy on U.S. 285, turning right onto State Road 41. I immediately pulled over on the paved apron, parked and contemplated the rugged mesa and butte country that protrudes south and west.

That seemingly inhospitable landscape sequesters many springs, precious water that meant life to at least nine Galisteo Basin pueblos. Indians who lived here spoke the Tewa dialect of Tanoan, which also includes Tiwa and Towa dialects. They occupied five pueblos by the time the Spanish arrived. One of those, also known as Galisteo Pueblo, today but a ruin, appears on maps as Pueblo de los Tanos.

All the ruins are on private land, but the pueblo was about two miles southwest, about a mile-and-a-half northeast of today's Galisteo village.

Galisteo apparently means a resident of the Spanish province of Galicia, but the Spanish seemed to have had a hard time agreeing on a name for the original pueblo. It was called San Lucas by Castaño de Sosa in 1591, renamed Santa Ana by Oñate in 1598. .

Between 1617 and 1629, the pueblo was home to Santa Cruz de Galisteo mission, one of the struggling province's 10 churches.

During the Pueblo Revolt, the Indians killed the priests and lived in Santa Fe until Vargas booted them out in 1692. Gov. Cuervo y Valdez re-established the pueblo in 1706, with 90 Tewas in residence. By 1790, more than 350 Tewas lived there, but decimated by smallpox and Comanches, the survivors moved to Santa Cruz de la Cañada, which I visited earlier.

But while the Galisteo Tewas may have disagreed with the Spanish about many things before the revolt, half a century afterwards, violent new winds blew in from the Plains in the form of the hard-riding, in-yer-face Comanches. Shades of the Huns at the Gates of the Roman Empire!

Tepee rings and oral history testify to an era of cooperation between Mescalero Apaches and Pueblos, who banded together with the Spanish against the Comanches. It was a Mescalero medicine man, in fact, who first showed me the location of San Cristobal ruins on private property east of Galisteo.

Driving through Galisteo village, I turned right at the church and took the washboard road back to Santa Fe. Just past the State Road 14 intersection, I descended a piñon ridge that once sheltered San Marcos Pueblo, another Tanoan-speaking center. Those people merged with Keresan-speaking Santo Domingo after the revolt.

The oft-mentioned Avanyu, the snake which in disgust abandoned Pecos Pueblo, also was known to some Galisteo Indians. They followed the departing serpent down Galisteo Creek to the Rio Grande to join their relatives at Santo Domingo. Another source says they fled to Santo Domingo between 1782 and 1794 to escape Comanche attacks.

Cerrillos

In the centuries surrounding the massive Indian relocations and Spanish and gringo invasions, mining thrived in Santa Fe County.

What with all the controversy surrounding mining south of Santa Fe, a side trip I took earlier to Cerrillos helps relate the history of extractive industries here to real-world geography.

The Santa Fe area's love affair with mineral extraction is a long one. In the old days, when minerals meant more than mountain scenery to Santa Fe, even Thomas Edison tried his hand at gold digging near Golden.

Archaeologists think Chacoans traded turquoise for Aztec macaw feathers and copper bells. Some, but not necessarily all of Chaco's blue gold was dug from pits near present-day Cerrillos, which were mined from 1200 to 1000 B.C. and again from 1350 to 1680 A.D., long after Chaco was deserted.

Mount Chalchihuitl or Turquoise Hill, two-and-a-half miles north of Cerrillos, was the site of an ancient 200-foot deep pit ringed by 100,000 tons of waste rock. Geologist William P. Blake, who located the pit in 1858, called it "the site of the most extensive prehistoric mining operations on the North American continent."

Long before the Spanish came and up until the Pueblo Revolt, Pueblo Indians were using stone hammers to punch turquoise from the mineral-laden ledges of the Cerrillos Hills.

Miners rest in this Cerrillos graveyard not far from the old mines.

Later, enough turquoise was found to interest the Tiffany jewelry people, who operated a mine of the same name in the area for years.

Today the turquoise-rich area is mined mostly for gravel, although a few hard-core business people continue to extract turquoise from slivers found around the old mines. Their sites are almost impossible to find, however, and visitors really aren't welcome there.

To get a feel for the mining life, I drove to Cerrillos, took the first right turn in the village and crossed the railroad tracks. On the maps, the old mines are north in this direction, but you couldn't prove it by me.

Shortly, I cleared the village and crossed a cattle guard. Dirt roads forked left and right. The left-hand road passed to the left of one of the village cemeteries and forked again; the left fork returned to Cerrillos. The right fork continued through mud and ice to a gravel pit. This way, mammoth mining trucks that zipped along the narrow canyon road seemed happy to wipe out intruders.

Back at the cattle guard, I took the right dirt fork a mile or so to a dead end at a water tank marked El Vado de Cerrillos. Along both roads I saw a couple of greenish turquoise-colored slopes on the left, but they might have been copper for all I know.

In fact, the only thing I had seen vaguely resembling turquoise was due to the unseasonably warm weather: in the canyons, hundreds of brightly colored bluebirds swirled ahead of my wagon, a nice compensation for not finding the mines.

Petroglyph National Monument

Yesterday, I had driven my wagon to Albuquerque for maintenance after all the miles I'd added to its odometer.

I arranged for other transportation while the Silver Streak was drydocked, and drove to Petroglyph National Monument west of the city.

Before there was a Santa Fe Style (now *outre,* the East Coast trend mavens tell us), there was a Rio Grande Style.

It shows up at thousands of sites state-wide. One of the more accessible is development-besieged Petroglyph Monument, a tribute to long-dead artists who practiced Rio Style, pecking or carving their art into rocks. Their descendants, today's Pueblo people, not only continue the traditions, but can help explain the art's religious significance.

Rio Grande Style, probably not defined in the latest trade journals, includes such rock art all-stars as: Flute-playing Kokopelli, the ubiquitous feathered serpents, and masked and unmasked dancers with arms raised.

I walked all three self-guided trails in less than an hour total. The Mesa Point trail is for the hardier, while the Cliff Base trail was shorter and easier, and the Macaw trail was a piece of cake.

On each trail I was engaged by a fantastic mix of rock art at the most easily accessible site west of Bandelier National Monument.

Two paved pull-off areas provide vistas of "embayments," the curving canyons that shelter the petroglyphs. The panorama from the windy escarpment down to the embayments reminded me of Hawaiian seaside lava-scapes.

As I walked among the petroglyphs at the national monument's Boca Negra Canyon, I noted a few enclosed figures, to me but designs. To me, also these were windows opening on to space and time and a view of the Red Road.

The windows yawn widely all over the monument, part of a microcosm where a 17-mile-long basalt ridge has crumbled into thousands of black rocks, handy blackboards where Puebloan ancestors etched more than 15,000 figures and designs.

Although a few of the monument's petroglyphs might be up to 3,000 years old, most of the earliest date between 800 B.C. and 400 A.D. That's when the valley's people were beginning to hunt and gather less and farm more, settling in increasingly larger, permanent, protected adobe villages, a whole millennium away from any contact with Europeans.

Once that contact came, it threatened more than petroglyphs; it almost exterminated the people who created them.

Both the Pueblos and their art survived. But it's funny how, here in the land of the free, American officialdom has had so much trouble recognizing the legitimacy of religions other than those practiced by Judeo-Christian cultures.

For instance, American Indian tribes couldn't practice their religions legally—including the widespread Plains Indian Sun Dance—until the American Indian Freedom of Religion Act of 1978.

Maybe that explains why, even with relentless development pressures on the fragile environment that shelters the petroglyphs, it took the U.S. Congress until 1990 to protect the site.

⇒ Information
Santa Fe: 1-505-984-6760
Rancho de las Golondrinas: Fee. 1-505-471-2261
Albuquerque: 1-505-243-3696
Petroglyph National Monument: Fee. 1-505-768-3316

Epilogue

Treeless Boca Negra was noticeably hot, and I ran for the cool cover of my mountain valley home, cutting through Tijeras Canyon to ride the back highways east, then north.

The hypnotic plains beyond Cedar Crest bored me into trying to summarize my year's journey. I had come full circle now, east to south to west to north, on the way stirring up powerful memories that set me back on the Red Road. And I hoped my travel photos would yield a composite picture of New Mexico: physical and spiritual.

Still, I hadn't resolved a major question. Did New Mexico's older cultures simply get lost when overrun by the successive Invader of the Decade? Despite the veneer of "civilization" coating border fortresses like Las Cruces and Albuquerque, I think not.

I've fumbled with my notes for days now under the elms, watching the antics of a family of magpies, expecting a Muse to scramble up the weedy river bank to inspire me. Today, I decide I've waited long enough. Besides, I need fresh air to help slough the grime that always coats my skin after an Albuquerque trip. I take a break, crossing the wooded range west of town, returning to Gallinas Canyon, where I had dallied before embarking on this journey, now four seasons old.

From my cliffside vantage point, the river snaking below seems to burrow through the heart of the country. Not far downstream, it slips past several Guadalupean chapels. Of course. Epiphany! That's it: the ultimate synthesis, the yet-emerging New Mexico icon, might resemble a modified physician's symbol, the caduceus. Except in New Mexico, the symbol is a snake and a cross.

A Guadalupe chapel in a canyon near Las Vegas, N.M.

The winged serpent that so infuses New Mexican culture never actually died, just transmuted. Instead, as the park ranger at Abó tried to explain, the serpent, like other Indian beliefs, was syncretized, layered with Catholic forms, but retained its original intent.

Consider: The worship of Guadalupe, the spiritual essence of colonial Spain in this hemisphere, and much more, is embodied not directly in the serpent, but in the story of Juan Diego. To this Christianized Aztec appeared, 10 years after the Conquest, a lovely young woman on a lonely, bare hilltop north of today's Mexico City. Her image also appeared on his cloak or *tilma*, soon after.

The many remnant Aztecs, who earlier had built a temple on the site, knew Diego's apparition as Coatlayupaut, "she who crushed the serpent."

Her demurely smiling image graces votive candle holders, t-shirts and retablos. Her turquoise veil is embossed with stars and circled by rays signifying the sun. And in her miraculous portrait, she steps on a crescent moon, an Aztec symbol for Quetzalcoátl, the winged serpent.

To Aztecs, Spanish, and their Mexican and Mexican-American descendants, Guadalupe embodied and embodies the final conquest of the ancient, bloody, pagan religion, personified, although perhaps not accurately, by Quetzalcoátl, Lord of the Dawn, the Morning Star.

As her devotees spread, so did her image, adorning *capilla* walls all over Spain's former empire. A New Mexico county, a river, a mountain range, and several settlements are named for her. As Spain's American empire of cross and sword pushed forward, her faith was carried Kokopelli-like by the Tlaxcalan Indians, those staunch Aztec-hating Spanish allies who later settled in New Mexico in such places as Santa Fe's Barrio Analco and at San Miguel del Vado.

When the first hopeful settlers trudged north with Oñate, they carried paintings of Guadalupe. She became "Our Lady of the Highway" for those tireless pioneers.

On Dec. 11, in many villages such as Tortugas, vespers are held for her, usually followed by a procession and a bonfire. A solemn mass is celebrated Dec. 12, the same day many pueblos honor her with dances: matachines, buffalo, butterfly, eagle and bow and arrow.

Somewhere near all New Mexicans there's an image of Guadalupe, but like Juan Diego's sacred tilma image, it's not always evident. To find her, seekers must hike beyond the obvious mountains, into the spaces between things, into the realms where we have relegated our archaic dreams and nightmares, enduring images that nevertheless are as real as faith.

Peregrinos, pilgrims hoping to encounter Guadalupe's image and grace, probably have known this simple truth for centuries: in New Mexico, one of the best ways to find yourself is to get lost.

The End

Bibliography

Adams, E. 1991. *The origin and development of the pueblo katsina cult.* Tucson: University of Arizona Press.

Adams, E. & Chavez, Fr. A. 1956. Trans. of Fr. Francisco A. Dominguez. *The missions of New Mexico, 1776.* Albuquerque: University of New Mexico Press.

Akens, J. 1987. *Ute Mountain Tribal Park: The other Mesa Verde.* Moab, UT: Four Corners Publications.

Anaya, R. 1987. *Lord of the dawn: The legend of Quetzalcoátl.* Albuquerque: University of New Mexico Press.

_____. 1984, 1994. *The legend of La Llorona: a novella.* Berkeley, CA.: TQS Publications.

Anderson, A., Berdan, F. & Lockhart, J. 1976. *Beyond the Codices: The Nahua view of colonial Mexico.* Berkeley: University of California Press.

Anderson, D. & B. 1981. *Chaco Canyon: Center of a culture.* Tucson: Southwest Parks and Monuments Association.

Aragon, R. 1980. *Legend of La Llorona.* Las Vegas, NM: Premier Publishing House of the Southwest.

Aranda, C. 1977. *New Mexico folklore from the Spanish.* Las Vegas, NM: Privately published.

_____. 1977. *Dichos: Proverbs and sayings from the Spanish.* Santa Fe: Sunstone Press.

Arellano, A. & Vigil, J. 1985. *Las Vegas Grandes on the Gallinas: 1835-1985.* Las Vegas, NM: Editorial Teleraña.

Arnberger, L. 1982. *Flowers of the Southwest mountains.* Tucson: Southwest Parks and Monuments Association.

Athearn, F. 1992. *A forgotten kingdom: The Spanish frontier in Colorado and New Mexico, 1540-1821.* Denver: U.S. Department of the Interior, Bureau of Land Management.

Ball, E. 1969. *Ma'am Jones of the Pecos.* Tucson: University of Arizona Press.

215

Bannon, J. F. 1963, 1974. *The Spanish borderlands frontier, 1513-1821.* New York: Holt, Rinehart and Winston. Albuquerque: University of New Mexico Press.

Beckett, P. & Corbett, T. 1992. *The Manso Indians.* Monograph 9. Las Cruces: COAS.

_____. 1990. *Tortugas.* Monograph 8. Las Cruces: COAS.

Bolton, H. 1921. *The Spanish borderlands: A chronicle of old Florida and the Southwest.* Chronicles of America Series, XXIII. Allen Johnson, Ed. New Haven: Yale University Press.

Bowers, E. 1987. *One hundred roadside wildflowers of Southwest woodlands.* Tucson: Southwest Parks and Monuments Association.

Bryan, H. 1991. *Robbers, rogues and ruffians.* Santa Fe: Clear Light Publishers.

_____. 1988. *Wildest of the wild west.* Santa Fe: Clear Light Publishers.

_____. 1986. *Tours for all seasons.* Albuquerque: The Albuquerque Tribune.

Bullock, A. 1978. *The squaw tree: Ghosts, mysteries and miracles of New Mexico.* Santa Fe: The Lightning Tree.

Burdett, W.H., Dir. 1993. *The Roads of New Mexico.* Fredericksburg, TX.: Shearer Publishing.

Campos, A. Ed. 1977. *Mexican folk tales.* Tucson: University of Arizona Press.

C de Baca, E.. 1992. *Los Hermanos de la Luz or Brothers of Light.* Privately published.

_____. 1991. *La bruja Maruja and two other witch stories.* Privately published.

_____. 1986. *Ghost Stories.* Privately published.

_____. 1985. *Folk tales of New Mexico.* Privately published.

_____. 1984. *Legends of a hermit.* Privately published.

_____. N.d. *Christmas in New Mexico.* Privately published.

Cabeza de Baca, F. 1954. *We fed them cactus.* Albuquerque: University of New Mexico Press.

Cabeza de Vaca, A. N. 1961 *Adventures in the unknown interior.* La Relación. C. Covey, Trans. New York: Macmillan.

Carson, K. M. Q., Ed. 1966. *Kit Carson's Autobiography.* Lincoln: University of Nebraska Press.

Chadwick, N. 1989. *Celtic Britain.* North Hollywood, CA: Newcastle Publishing.

Chilton, L., et al. 1984. *New Mexico: A new guide to the colorful state.* Albuquerque: University of New Mexico Press.

Chronic, H. 1987. *Roadside geology of New Mexico.* Missoula, MT: Mountain Press.

Cobos, R. 1985. *Refranes: Southwestern Spanish proverbs.* Santa Fe: Museum of New Mexico Press.

Bibliography

_____. 1983. *A dictionary of New Mexico and Southern Colorado Spanish.* Santa Fe: Museum of New Mexico Press.

Cohn, P. 1991. *Trail guide: Pecos Wilderness.* Albuquerque: Southwest Natural and Cultural Heritage Association.

Coronado Cuarto Centennial Commission. 1940, 1989. *New Mexico: A guide to the colorful state.* Tucson: University of Arizona Press.

Davies, N. 1980. *The Toltec heritage: From the fall of Tula to the Rise of Tenochtitlán.* Norman: University of Oklahoma Press.

_____. 1973, 1980. *The Aztecs: A history.* Norman: University of Oklahoma Press.

Delgado, D. 1990. *Historical markers in New Mexico.* Santa Fe: Ancient City Press.

Denevan, W. M. Ed.. 1976. *The native population of the Americas in 1492.* Madison: University of Wisconsin Press.

Dorian, N. 1981. *Language death: The life cycle of a Scottish Gaelic dialect.* Philadelphia: University of Pennsylvania Press.

Drinnon, R. 1972. *White savage: The case of John Dunn Hunter.* New York: Schocken.

Dutton, B. 1983. *American Indians of the Southwest.* Albuquerque: University of New Mexico Press.

Espinoza, A.M. 1985. J. M. Espinoza, Ed. *The folklore of Spain in the American Southwest: Traditional Spanish folk literature in northern New Mexico and southern Colorado.* Norman: University of Oklahoma Press.

Fehrenbach, T. 1973. *Fire and blood: A bold and definitive modern chronicle of Mexico.* New York: Macmillan.

Flint R. & Flint, S. 1989. *Chacoesque: A guide to Great Pueblo architecture outside Chaco Canyon.* Albuquerque: Century.

_____. 1987. *A pocket guide to Chaco Canyon architecture.* Albuquerque: Century.

Forrest, S. 1989. *The preservation of the village: New Mexico's Hispanics in the New Deal.* Albuquerque: University of New Mexico Press.

Garcia, N. 1987. *Recuerdos de los viejitos: Tales of the Rio Puerco.* Albuquerque: University of New Mexico Press.

Giese, D. 1976. *Forts of New Mexico: Echoes of the bugle.* Albuquerque: Phelps Dodge Corporation.

_____. Ed. 1967, 1993. *My life with the Army in the West: Memoirs of James E. Farmer.* Santa Fe: Stagecoach Press.

Gregg, J. 1844, 1933. *Commerce of the prairies: The journal of a Santa Fe trader.* Dallas: Southwest Press.

Guild, T. & Carter, H. 1984. *Kit Carson: A pattern for heroes.* Lincoln: University of Nebraska Press.

Harrington, J. P., M. Weigle, Ed. 1989. *Indian tales from Picurís Pueblo.* Santa Fe: Ancient City Press.

Bibliography

Hayes, J. 1987. *La Llorona: The weeping woman.* El Paso: Cinco Puntos.

Hodgkinson, H. 1990. *The demographics of American Indians: One percent of the people; fifty percent of the diversity.* Washington, D.C.: Institute for Educational Leadership, Inc., Center for Demographic Policy.

Hoover, H. 1958. *Tales from the Bloated Goat: Early days in Mogollón.* El Paso: Texas Western Press.

Horgan, P. 1984. *Great river: The Rio Grande in American history.* Austin: Texas Monthly Press.

_____. 1982. *Conquistadores in North American history.* El Paso: Texas Western Press.

_____. 1941. *Josiah Gregg and his vision of the early West.* New York: Farrar, Straus & Giroux.

Jennings, J.D. Ed. 1978. *Ancient Native Americans.* San Francisco: W.H. Freeman & Co.

John, E. 1975. *Storms brewed in other men's worlds: The confrontation of Indians, Spanish and French in the Southwest, 1540-1795.* College Station: Texas A & M Press.

Jones, O. 1966. *Pueblo warriors and Spanish conquest.* Norman: University of Oklahoma Press.

Keen, B. 1971. *The Aztec image in Western thought.* New Brunswick, NJ: Rutgers University Press.

Keleher, W. 1957, 1982. *Violence in Lincoln County, 1869-1881.* Albuquerque: University of New Mexico Press.

Kenner, C. 1969, 1994. *The Comanchero frontier: A history of New Mexico-Plains Indian relations.* Norman: University of Oklahoma Press.

Kessell, J. 1979. *Kiva, cross and crown.* Washington, D.C.: U.S. Department of the Interior, National Park Service.

Kimbler, F. and Narsavage, R. 1981. *New Mexico rocks and minerals.* Santa Fe: Sunstone Press.

Kraul, E. and Beatty, J. Eds. 1988. *The weeping woman: Encounters with La Llorona.* Santa Fe: The Word Process.

LaFarge, O. 1994. *Behind the Mountains.* North Hollywood, CA: Charles Publishing.

Lister, F. and Lister R. 1966. *Chihuahua, storehouse of storms.* Albuquerque: University of New Mexico Press.

Lummis, C. F. 1952. *The land of poco tiempo.* Albuquerque: University of New Mexico Press.

MacCarter, J. 1994. *New Mexico wildlife viewing guide.* Helena, MT: Falcon Press.

MacDonald, E. & Arrington, J. 1970. *The San Juan Basin: My kingdom was a county.* Denver: Mido Printing.

McFarland, F. 1967. *Forever frontier: The Gila cliff dwellings.* Albuquerque: University of New Mexico Press.

McKenna, J. 1963. *Black Range tales*. Glorieta, NM: Rio Grande Press.

Maestas, J. & Anaya, R. 1980. *Cuentos: Tales from the Hispanic Southwest*. Santa Fe: Museum of New Mexico Press.

Martin, L. 1993. *Mesa Verde: The story behind the scenery*. Las Vegas, NV: KC Publications.

Martinez, O. 1988. *Troublesome border*. Tucson: University of Arizona Press.

Matthiessen, P. 1984. *Indian country*. New York: Viking.

_____. 1983. *In the spirit of Crazy Horse*. New York: Viking.

Mercurio, G. & Maxymilian, L. 1994. *The guide to trading posts and pueblos*. Cortez, CO: Lonewolf Publishing.

Metz, L. 1990. *Border: The U.S.-Mexican line*. El Paso: Mangan Books.

_____. 1981. *Pat Garrett: The story of a Western lawman*. Norman: University of Oklahoma Press.

Murray, J. 1988. *The Gila wilderness: A hiking guide*. Albuquerque: University of New Mexico Press.

Noble, D. 1994. *Pueblos, villages, forts and trails*. Albuquerque: University of New Mexico Press.

_____. 1981. *Ancient ruins of the Southwest*. Flagstaff: Northland Publishing.

Nostrand, Richard L. 1992. *The Hispano homeland*. Norman: University of Oklahoma Press.

Oliva, L. 1967. *Soldiers on the Santa Fe Trail*. Norman: University of Oklahoma Press.

Ortiz, A. 1969. *The Tewa world: Space, time, being and becoming in a Pueblo society*. Chicago: University of Chicago Press.

Parent, L. 1994. *New Mexico scenic drives*. Helena, MT: Falcon Press.

_____. 1992. *Gila Cliff Dwellings National Monument*. Tucson: Southwest Parks and Monuments Association.

_____. 1991. *The hiker's guide to New Mexico*. Helena, MT: Falcon Press.

Pearce, T. *1965. New Mexico place names*. Albuquerque: University of New Mexico Press.

Perrigo, L. 1986. *It happened here: Incidents in Las Vegas, N.M.* Las Vegas, N.M.: Las Vegas-San Miguel Chamber of Commerce.

_____. 1982. *Gateway to Glorieta: A history of Las Vegas, New Mexico*. Boulder: Pruett.

Rees, A. & Rees, B. 1961. *Celtic heritage: Ancient tradition in Ireland and Wales*. New York: Thames and Hudson.

Rice, T. 1957. *The Sythians*. New York: Frederick Praeger.

Robertson, J. 1967. *Pagan Christs*. New York: University Books.

Sando, J. 1992. *Pueblo nations: Eight centuries of Pueblo Indian history*. Santa Fe: Clear Light Publishers.

Simmons, M. 1967. *Border Comanches: Seven Spanish colonial documents, 1785-1819*. Santa Fe: Stagecoach Press.

Sonnichsen, C. 1960. *Tularosa: Last of the frontier West.* New York: Devin-Adair Co.

_____. 1958. *The Mescalero Apaches.* Norman: University of Oklahoma Press.

Soutstelle, J. 1961. *Daily life of the Aztecs: On the eve of the Spanish conquest.* Stanford: Stanford University Press. Trans. from French. Original: Paris. Hachette, 1955.

Sprenger, J. 1987. *Trail guide to the Las Vegas area.* Privately published.

Steiner, S. 1976. *The vanishing white man.* New York: Harper & Row.

_____. 1968. *The new Indians.* New York: Harper & Row.

Stevens, D. & Agogino, G. N.d. *Sandia Cave: A study in controversy.* ENMU Contributions in Anthropology, 71. Portales: Eastern New Mexico University Press.

Swartley, R. 1993. *Touring the pueblos.* Albuquerque: Frontier Image Press.

Tainter, J & Levine, F. 1987. *Cultural resources overview: Central New Mexico.* Albuquerque: U.S. Department of Agriculture Forest Service.

Ulibarrí, S. 1977. *Mi abuela fumaba puros: My grandmother smoked cigars.* Berkeley, CA: Quinto Sol Publications.

Ungnade, H. 1965. *Guide to New Mexico mountains.* Albuquerque: University of New Mexico Press.

Utley, R. 1987. *High noon in Lincoln: Violence on the Western frontier.* Albuquerque. University of New Mexico Press.

Vigil, A. Ed. 1993. *Day trip discoveries.* Santa Fe: New Mexico Magazine.

Wallace, E. & Hoebel, E. 1952. *The Comanches: Lords of the south plains.* Norman: University of Oklahoma Press.

Watson, D. 1960. *The Pinos Altos story.* Privately published.

Weigle, M. & White, P. 1988. *The lore of New Mexico.* Albuquerque: University of New Mexico Press.

Weigle, M. Ed. 1987. *Two Guadalupes: Hispanic legends and magic tales from northern New Mexico.* Santa Fe: Ancient City Press .

_____. 1976. *Brothers of light, brothers of blood.* Albuquerque: University of New Mexico Press.

Wenger, G. 1980. *The story of Mesa Verde National Park. Mesa Verde National Park, CO.* Mesa Verde Museum Association.

Wilson, J. 1987. *Merchants, guns and money: The story of Lincoln County and its wars.* Santa Fe: Museum of New Mexico Press.

Winter, J. 1988. *Stone circles, ancient forts and other antiquities of the Dry Cimarrón Valley.* Santa Fe: New Mexico Historic Preservation Division.

Wozniak, F. 1985. *Across the Caprock: A cultural resources survey on the Llano Estacado and in the Canadian River Valley of East Central New Mexico for the Bravo CO2 pipeline.* Albuquerque: University of New Mexico Office of Contract Archaeology for AMOCO Production and Bravo Pipeline companies.

Index

Index